I saw
myself

JOURNEYS
WITH
SHAH ABDUL LATIF BHITAI

Shabnam Virmani & Vipul Rikhi

PENGUIN
ANANDA

An imprint of Penguin Random House

PENGUIN ANANDA

USA | Canada | UK | Ireland | Australia
New Zealand | India | South Africa | China | Singapore

Penguin Ananda is part of the Penguin Random House group of companies
whose addresses can be found at global.penguinrandomhouse.com

Published by Penguin Random House India Pvt. Ltd
4th Floor, Capital Tower 1, MG Road,
Gurugram 122 002, Haryana, India

Penguin
Random House
India

First published in Penguin Ananda by Penguin Random House India 2019

10 9 8 7 6 5 4 3 2

ISBN 9780670091669

Typeset in Sabon by Manipal Digital Systems, Manipal
Printed at Replika Press Pvt. Ltd, India

www.penguin.co.in

MIX
Paper from
responsible sources
FSC® C016779

This is a legitimate digitally printed version of the book and therefore might not
have certain extra finishing on the cover.

Contents

Authors' Note

Translating the poetry of Shah Latif has been a daunting and an exhilarating experience at the same time. Daunting because neither of us is a native Sindhi speaker, nor do we read the Arabic script of the Sindhi language. Hence many hours and days were spent with Abdullah bhai, Umar kaka, Kaladhar bhai, and others, in grasping the Sindhi words, their grammar, syntax and meanings. However, a more primal and vivid access to the *feeling* behind the words came to us through an immersion in the songs, stories, recitations and conversations amidst a community of lovers of Shah Latif's poetry in Kutch. The flavours of this orality, for us, have been a vital part of interpreting and re-rendering the text, and it is this perhaps that became the exhilarating part of this enterprise, apart from engaging with the intensity of Latif's poetry itself.

The border between India and Pakistan partitioned a vibrant and immense cultural and poetic legacy of Shah Latif. As seekers of mystic philosophy, we started exploring the land of Kutch on this side of the border in a quest for Latif in the year 2009, seeking from time to time to breach that invisible line that kept us deprived of a fuller immersion in his much vaster oral tradition just across the border in Pakistan. But political hostilities held sway and repeated denials of visas kept us thirsty for that experience. This book shares, then, our unique and particular slice of experience through explorations on 'our' side of the border.

As with any mystic worth his salt, Latif has a thriving oral tradition, where poems get added on to his oeuvre, enlarging and often enriching it. We have included several such evocative poems, which we did not find reflected in any textual compilation. Rather than dismiss these poems as 'inauthentic', we include them here as a tribute to the growing republic of poetry which follows the departure of a great mystic poet. These poems are indicated in the poetry section of this book with the acronym for 'oral traditions' (OT).

Many of the poems we heard in the field, however, were also found in published editions of the Risalo, references for which are given as follows: Yakoob Agha (YA), Christopher Shackle (CS) and Manishankar Dwivedi (MD) (see bibliography for full references).

Some of the poems we discovered only in books rather than in the field, and for some of them our translations have relied entirely on translations (in Hindi and English) by other authors, recreated here with our own feeling for Latif acquired through an immersion in his oral tradition.

We urge our readers, too, to encounter this orality by listening to some of the poems and stories featured in this book as songs and interviews on our web archive, www.ajabshahar.org, part of our wider work on mystic poets since 2002 at the Kabir Project at the Srishti Institute of Art, Design & Technology in Bangalore.

These journeys with Latif opened many new doors for us. We glimpsed a whole new world, startlingly fresh, sometimes even disorienting. But we also touched a world beyond linguistic and cultural boundaries, which felt poignantly familiar.

Our limited insight into the language or actual Sufi practice notwithstanding, we hope to have shared with our readers in these pages something of both these worlds.

Shabnam and Vipul
May 2019

1

One Palace, One Million Doors

Journey into Kutch

Let's go, my sweet
to the land of the beloved

Where nothing arises
and nothing subsides
Let's go!

I awoke
in this palace of dreams
and I wept
Let's go!

– Kabir

A poet's voice calls out across the centuries—tender, artful, persuasive—asking us to wake up. Get moving. Leave the 'palace of dreams' in which we hold ourselves captive, and set out in search of a hidden country, the land of the Beloved. In response to the call, we're on the move and we follow the voice all the way to the western corner of India—the land of the white desert—Kutch.

The landscape blurs through the car window as the hot wind hits our eyes. Poems shimmer like mirages, beckoning us with elusive secrets. A paradox unfolds. Journeying outwards on the trail of mystic songs, it seems we are being led within. Constantly on the move, driving from village to village, there is a sense that we are being led to a space that's utterly still.

We've been on the heels of Kabir for a while now, tracking the poet's words, which have flowed like a river across space and time. Kabir lived in Varanasi in north India over 500 years ago, but his poems have flowed long after his time in multiple streams, pouring themselves into new metaphors and languages, ceaselessly adapting to new contexts and cultures.[1]

When we venture into Kutch—a border district of Gujarat in western India—we find Kabir mingling in this stark saline land with many other resonant voices. His dohas flow seamlessly with Mekan Dada's Kutchi *duhadaas*[2] and Shah Latif's Sindhi *beyts*,[3] and this easy intermingling of voices gently reminds us of the pointlessness of most human divisions. The choice of stepping out of boundaries is always profoundly available.

Kabir says the well is one
Water bearers many
Their pots are of different shapes
But the water in them is one

– Kabir

I thought the path was one
But there were a thousand million
Whoever took whichever one
Made it across the ocean

– Mekan Dada

One palace, one million doors
Countless windows in between
From wherever I look
The Beloved is before me

– Shah Latif

This pithy, two-line verse form was once described to us by a *paanwallah* in Varanasi as '*gaagar mein saagar*', or 'an ocean in a pot'. The poem is small but its import can encompass the world.

A 'dead poets' society' seems to stir to life here in Kutch in the all-night village satsangs, where the songs of Kabir, Ravidas, Kheem Saheb, Meera Bai, Trikam Saheb, Brahmanand, Mekan Dada and Shah Latif, among others, jostle good-naturedly with each other. After all, this is no religious or academic debate where differences in philosophy are teased out with toothcombs that divide. This is a satsang, a musical gathering where the dividing lines between religious and linguistic traditions fade, as a generously shared truth surfaces.

We were in one such late-night satsang in the village of Hodka. The moon had climbed right over our heads and it seemed as if the collective *surta* (awareness) of the gathering, too, was on a steady climb into the sky.

Long after the city concert has ended its short run of a modest one or two hours, and audiences are getting into their cars to go home, the village satsang begins to deepen and gather speed. One can sense this moment, this mood shift, when the spaces between singer and song, between singer and listener begins to melt. Some listeners pick up the extra pair of *manjiras* lying around and merge their bodies into the collective sound. Some get up and dance with no one in particular looking on. Some just clap or shout out an encouragement from time to time.

A song ends, the gathering echoes its salutations to the saint–poets with a lusty, collective *jai ho!* and a hush falls.

An upward arrow shot through the sky
There dwells a body
In this body, the Unseen resides
My awareness is locked there, seekers
Come watch the Lord's play!

– Kabir

The mystic's call to come to the hidden country is in the same breath a call to enter the body. In song after song these poets invite us to enter this unknown space, the self. A place we think we know quite well, since we carry it around with us all the time, but a place that might be more like an *ajab shahar*, a 'wondrous city', more mysterious and unfamiliar to us than we imagine.

We tend to read the invitation to 'enter the self' figuratively, as a metaphor for more *mental* activity. But what if we're being asked to read it more literally, as a call to enter and experience the *physical* body? To feel the interplay between mind and matter, to alight on an experience of the universe within.

What if the poet has actually seen things that we cannot imagine? At the level of ordinary human scale, spaces and times make sense to us. We understand that there are continents and oceans and cities, days and nights and hours. But at a more galactic scale, things begin to lose their meaning and become incomprehensible (to us). We don't really grasp the idea of vast distances between galaxies, or the 'time' (billions of light years) that light takes to travel to us from distant stars. Similarly, if we could experience our bodies so deeply, almost at a cellular scale, it may reveal wondrous things that our minds cannot grasp right now. The radical thought proposed by this poetry, which insists so much on the inner journey, is that all this can be *known* or *seen*. That this knowledge lies within our reach. Indeed, the self is the only place to find it.

Your body is the mosque
Your heart the inner chamber
For contemplation

Don't just fast ritually
Behold the invisible within
At all moments

Know yourself
From the inside out

Allah stands before you
Present in every person

And so this is how we meet the eighteenth-century Sufi, Shah Abdul Latif Bhitai, in the land of Kutch. The cadence and rhythms of his Sindhi beyts, the piercing strains of his *kaafis* and *waais* and, most of all, a searing passion bristling in his poems, begin to call out to us. And over several ensuing years of travel in Kutch, as our inquiry into Shah Latif deepens and unfolds, we find his voice always intertwined with the voices of Kabir and other Bhakti poets.

Walking into the universe of Latif takes us into unexpected places within our body-selves . . . and we find ourselves trudging across a lonely harsh desert with Sasui, tackling the surging river waters with Sohini, wandering the forests with Ramkali and trapped in a dark fortress with Marui.

~

(Abd = servant of; Abd—Allah = servant of God)

It is not long before we meet Abdullah Hussain Turk of Dhrab village in Kutch, a man steeped in Sufi thought and song. We had met him once many years ago, much before any stirrings of Sufism had entered our hearts. On that day we were at a studio in Bhuj, recording with local singers and he was helping us with translations. He was sitting on the smooth carpet of the studio with his eyes closed, listening to the Sindhi verses of Shah Latif being recorded, and all of a sudden he began to weep soundlessly. It became palpable in that moment that we were on the outside of a deeply interior experience. We were witnessing the power of poem to cause inner and outer meltdowns.

Later we asked him what had made him cry. He said it was a poem. Sasui—the heroine of an iconic folk legend—has spent a lifetime wandering in the desert in search of her beloved Punhu. One day comes this:

Deluded, I forgot
I myself am Punhu

I wasted all this time
Searching for him

No knowledge
Is worth anything
Without a glimpse
Of the beloved within

Years later here we are with him again, on the road, meeting with singers and other people whose lives are entangled with Shah Latif in deep ways. There is the soft-spoken and regally graceful Umar Haji Suleiman of the cattle-herding Fakirani Jat community of Asari Vaandh village, who utterly savours the delights of storytelling. He is one among many other village elders who are self-taught scholars of 'Shah' or 'Shah Sayeen', as he is affectionately and respectfully called within the tradition. Shah's poems seem to have seeped into the very fibres of their being over decades and even lifetimes of immersion. Then there are the younger seekers and singers, such as Mazharuddin who works at a tourist hotel in Dhordo, and Ataullah Jat who runs a tea shop in Bhuj. Also there is Mavji Jagariya, who plays the *daak* and *dhol* and sings bhajans to wake up the Goddess in the temple of Mata Na Madh village, but whose heart is given over to singing the kaafis of Shah Sayeen. But the deepest spring and fount of knowledge on Shah Latif in the region, undoubtedly, is the late Abdullah bhai with whom we had the rare privilege to travel over several years.

Chai and beedis notwithstanding, Shah's poems seem to be Abdullah bhai's true nourishment. Always ready to share the inner import of these poems, their *ishaara,* and always close to tears when he does so, it was Abdullah bhai who opened the doors of Shah Latif for us.

~

Shah Abdul Latif lived from 1689 to 1752 CE, writing most of his poetry in the first half of the eighteenth century. Soon after his birth, the Mughal empire in Delhi began to collapse and a Sindhi religious sect from Balochistan—the Kalhoras—gained ascendancy, ruling Sindh during much of Shah Latif's later life, a time of relative political stability in Sindh.

Latif is widely held to be the greatest poet of the Sindhi language. Most of his poetry was collected into a single work now referred to as *Shah Jo Risalo*. ('Risalo' means 'treatise' or in a looser sense 'message'.) It is said that when the Risalo was first compiled, Latif threw it into the Kirar lake near Bhit because he thought his verses ran the danger of being misunderstood. Later, on the persuasion of his disciples, he allowed another compilation of the Risalo to be made.

Most of what we know of Latif's life comes to us in the form of anecdotes and legends from the oral traditions. Latif was born in a village called Hala Haveli in Sindh in a prominent Sayyad family (held to be descendants of Prophet Muhammad himself). Though born in a 'high' family, he is always described as being gentle and compassionate in manner, and restrained and austere in his habits. Latif is reputed to have been well-versed in the Qur'an and the Hadiths, and was also deeply attached to the poetry of Rumi as well as his great grandfather, Shah Abdul Karim Bulri, who was already locally revered as a Sufi poet and saint. Latif was also probably a man of languages, being proficient in Arabic, Persian, Saraiki and Urdu, besides his mother tongue, Sindhi.

As a young man, Latif fell in love with a wealthy landlord's daughter, in the town of Kotri. The girl's father did not approve of the match. Disappointed in love, Latif is said to have left home and wandered for three years with Nath Panthi yogis in parts of Gujarat and Rajasthan and the entire breadth of Sindh. Part of their travels revolved around a pilgrimage to the temple of the Goddess in Hinglaj, Balochistan. Later, in 1713, he was able to marry the woman he loved, once her father had passed away. However, his wife also died early in the marriage and they did not have children. His life was spent mostly in contemplation and music, and because of his poetry, Latif acquired a certain following as a saint.

Shah Latif's literary and spiritual influences are diverse. He always carried copies of the Qur'an and Rumi's *Mathnawi* with him. At a young age his travels with the Nath Panthi yogis gave him intimate knowledge of an iconoclastic stream of Hinduism. His poems have references to *aayats* from the Qur'an as well as to yogic vocabulary and practices.

Literary scholars favouring Islam lean towards interpreting his poetry entirely as a call to Islam. On the other hand, many Hindu–Sindhi and other scholars tend to stress the influences of Vedantic thought in his writings. Latif himself was not bothered with narrow sectarian concerns. According to a story, he was once asked by a disciple whether he was Shia or Sunni. He replied that he was in between the two.

The follower said, 'But Sayeen, there is nothing between the two!'

'Precisely,' replied Shah Latif, 'I am nothing.'[4]

~

Shah Latif's popularity amongst the laity is quite extraordinary. As the staggering breadth and depth of the poetry of the Risalo begins to reveal itself to us, we begin to understand why. For the Risalo is a poignantly intimate chronicle of *Sindhiyat* and its multi-layered topographies—literary, socio-political, cultural, emotional, physical and metaphysical.

Shah Latif was proficient in many languages and yet he made a striking departure from his predecessors in composing his poetry *entirely* in the spoken lingo of lay people—Sindhi—ignoring both Arabic, the language of the Qur'an, and Persian which was the courtly language of his times.[5]

Many of the thirty 'Surs' (poetic chapters or musical modes) of the Risalo are based—explicitly or implicitly—on well-known folk stories, fables and love legends of the region. Some even take off from smaller historical personalities and events. For instance, when the cotton industry of the Hyderabad region boomed in Shah Latif's times, fuelling the livelihoods of thousands of artisans and almost every rural household began to sport a spinning wheel, in the poet's imagination the 'spinner' became the figure of a 'seeker', her industriousness symbolic of her spiritual practice—and Sur Kapaiti was born.

When a tributary of the Indus changed course and its canals dried up, turning large swathes of riverine land into barren tracts of destitution, this became an image for impermanence and the undependability of the world—and Sur Dahar was born.

Shah Latif had a finger on the pulse of his audiences and he clearly assumes and builds upon their *familiarity* with historical events and folk tales of the region. Unlike Rumi, who recounts entire stories in his poems, Shah Latif almost never narrates full tales. He only signals and references. Culling out iconic moments or images or moods from these stories, he then builds them into powerful motifs, imbued with allegorical meanings.

Many of his poems are akin to strokes of a paintbrush, which build one upon another, coming together to create a vast field of experience, an emotionally pulsating canvas of a particular rasa, a particular raag, a particular story, a particular quest. For listeners just one brush stroke or beyt can signal and summon the mood of the entire painting, just as the typical movement (*pakad*) between a few musical notes can evoke the spirit of an entire raag. Similarly, in the reception of these poems, each one works like a *pakad*, a totem that signals the particular landscape (of the entire Sur) that is about to unfold.

In the oral traditions of Shah Latif, as with many other mystic poets, what listeners celebrate is an aesthetics of *recognition* and not just originality. Listeners delight in *recognizing* an already familiar feeling, moment or story, tasting the rasa of revisiting it, while also delighting in a new turn of phrase or insight that *this* particular rendition or poem brings to it. Through *repetition*, the *return* to a familiar trope, story or meaning, a *remembrance,* through song or poem lovingly sung and resung, quoted and recited, the old is thus cast into a new vessel. What is ancient is thus renewed, like the wellsprings of an old body of water.

Several Surs of the Risalo are based on everyday occupations—farming, spinning, seafaring—and the lives of ordinary people—weavers, blacksmiths, potters, fishermen. Many words and terms that have since fallen into disuse or are rare can be found in Latif's poems—intricate names and forgotten terms for embroideries, farming methods, certain kind of clouds and desert winds, grasses and shrubs. Umar kaka tells us that he was in the fishing business for twenty years and was astonished to discover in one long beyt a range of names for different ropes and boat parts, many of which he was himself unfamiliar with!

Shah Latif was hardly far removed from the lives of his listeners. He was very much a people's poet, not a remote 'literary figure'. He had himself walked, breathed, sweated, delighted in, and known the lives of the ordinary people of Sindh, making him not just a great Sufi poet but also a great *folk* poet.

~

Seeking a quiet life, Latif decided to spend his later years in a secluded spot. With hard physical labour, he and his followers built a small village around a mound which was simply known as 'Bhit' (literally 'sand hill'). From here Latif earned the honorific 'Bhitai' (one of the Bhit, also spelt Bhittai). The present-day town of Bhit Shah has emerged from this small village and is especially identified with Latif as its patron saint. The town houses a splendid dargah built for Shah Latif by the Sindhi ruler Ghulam Shah Kalhora and to this day his urs (death anniversary) is celebrated here each year, a three-day musical and spiritual carnival that welcomes all alike—men and women, rural and urban, Shia, Sunni and Hindu—and from dusk to dawn his poetry is brought to life and offered anew to the earth and the sky in the cool night air.[6]

It is held in legend that three weeks before his death, Latif confined himself to a cave-like underground room and spent the entire time in fasting and prayers. When he came out, he asked his disciples to play music. After three days of continuous music, his followers discovered that the motionless Latif had already breathed his last, to the accompaniment of some unknown note in the melody which had struck a chord in his heart.

~

They say about the aboriginal peoples of Australia that through their songs they *sing* into existence a 'dream universe', where lakes are the teardrops of dragons and cracked mountains the broken hearts of gods. Every piece of landscape begins to speak a story through the song. When the song ends, the spell is broken. The universe dissolves. We wake up.

Such was the feeling inspired by our encounters with Abdullah bhai and other singers and seekers of Shah Latif in Kutch. The songs and conversations conjured a dream universe of Shah Latif stretching luminously across the contours of Sindh, a land partitioned in two by the border between India and Pakistan. We began to roam inside this universe. And before we knew it, we were in conversation with the land itself, through the poems of 'Shah Sayeen'.

O mountain
Why don't you speak?
Tell me if my beloved
Passed this way yesterday

~

O cloud
If you learnt your job from my eyes
You'd never run dry!

~

Trees, stop growing!
Mountains, don't be tall!

Eyes, stop weeping
So I can follow the footprints
Of my beloved

Latif speaks in the voices of Sasui, Moomal, Ramkali, Sohini, Noori, Leela, Marui—legendary women of this region who loved and lost, and later grew through folklore into mythic poetic figures. As we wander, the feelings of pain and longing expressed in these women's voices stir dimly to life in the uncharted corners of our own souls. Each woman assumes a life and begins to speak to us. All of them are yearning for the beloved, but the texture and fabric of each one's context, struggle and personality are unique.

I—me, you, everybody—am a latter-day seeker on the same trail. I begin to feel all these women reside in me. Somehow I recognize myself in each of them. Sometimes I am Sasui, walking alone in a desert of desolation. A landscape of emptiness and loss separates me from my beloved.

> The mountain burst into flames
> When it brushed against my pain
>
> Oh friend
> The earth was scorched

Sometimes I am Ramkali, who has quit the pleasure palace of her father king, and wanders in search of her gurus, the Nath Panthi yogis, those true ascetics who once gave her the intoxicating taste of detachment.

> Forget what is past
> Begin right away
> Die today, yogi
> Tomorrow's too late

Sometimes, when I feel trapped inside the walls of my small mind, I am Marui, a village girl abducted and held prisoner by a powerful king in his fortress.

I see a dream, King
I am going home
Plucking fruit with my people
Among the sand dunes

I still have a hope, King
Of returning to my land

And when transgression beckons, I am Sohini, poised on the brink of a tumultuous river. On this side are respectability and husband, and on the other shore, my beloved.

Do I take the plunge?

Dark night, frail pot, no way to swim
Yet she flung herself in!
She did not wait, nor hesitate

The stormy river turned around
Love turned it into higher ground[7]

2

At Midnight She Leapt

The Legend of Sohini

The time may have been the fifteenth century or earlier. The river may have been the Chenab, by the banks of a village called Gujrat in the Punjab of present-day Pakistan. In any case, our story begins here and now. Sohini has plunged into this river in spate, which has no end and no beginning.

On one side stands her husband Dam, twirling a rosary between his fingers. On the other shore, waiting amidst a herd of buffaloes, is her lover Mehar, playing softly on his reed pipe.[8]

Dam is symbolic of the day, of convention, of social respectability. He is safe—the contained and containing. He is the mosque, the temple, the office, the prison, the mall. He is the institution, the establishment. He is also Sohini's own fearful, limited self.[9]

Mehar is symbolic of the night, of one who has gone across, who does not live on the banks of respectability any more. In his darkness, Sohini senses the possibility of expansion. He is ecstasy, madness, desire. He is love, fulfilment, death. His song penetrates and bewilders her. It's the mystic sign, the unstruck call, which, once heard, will not be denied.

> The jingling of his flock's bells
> Stirs me deeply
> How can I sleep?
> Ten times a day I pine for him

I'll wear the chains of his love
Till death

Where does this story begin? In a village, by this river, lives a potter called Tulla. He sculpts vessels of clay and his daughter Sohini adorns them with beautiful floral patterns. One day, with a passing caravan on its way to Delhi from Bokhara, arrives Izzat Baig, a wealthy merchant. He stops by Tulla's shop. Struck by Sohini's beauty, he loses all fancy for the pots and falls in love with her.

In order to be close to her, Izzat keeps returning to the shop to buy more and more pots, selling them off at cheaper prices. He abandons the idea of profit. He is no longer a wealthy trader; he is a lover. His only care is Sohini, his only calling, love. Eventually he gives up being a merchant altogether, and takes up a job as buffalo-herder with Tulla himself. From 'Izzat' Baig, the object of conventional esteem, he becomes Mehar or Mahiwal, the 'keeper of cows'.

Mehar and Sohini begin to have secret trysts. When Tulla finds out, he is enraged by a liaison that defies caste and community. He abruptly marries Sohini off to another potter from the Kumhar community—Dam. Mehar in turn becomes a fakir, and goes off to live on an island across the river.

So long since I saw him
I wonder how my sweetheart is
Eyes overflow with love
They burst into rivers and seas

~

So long since I saw him
I wonder how my sweetheart is
The pain of his love
Entwines me like a creeper

~

So long since I saw him
I wonder how my sweetheart is
A thousand suns have set
Lying in wait for him

He, whose absence
Was intolerable even for a second
Has not been seen for years

Their secret trysts continue. Initially Mehar comes to Sohini, on
this side of the river. But when he takes ill and is unable to swim,
crossing the river becomes Sohini's calling.[10]

To long for that shore
To plunge into water
Is the lot of besotted ones

Ten times a day
Dam admonishes me
But reason, judgement, shame
Have all been gutted
In the fire of love

~

Dark night, frail pot, pools of blackness
No sign of moon, river in tumult
For his sake Sohini steps out
In the middle of the night

This must be God's will
Or who would jump
Into this manic maelstrom?

Sohini makes her way down to the riverbank. Her husband sleeps
the deep sleep of unconsciousness. From across the river come the

sounds of tinkling bells, wafting lightly on the night wind. Her murshid Chhutto puffs quietly on his chillum, watchful. The river flows on, indifferent.

> Standing at the edge
> They cry out, 'My love!'
> But they love only their lives
>
> Some claim, 'I'm all yours'
> But wet only their big toe
>
> He comes to those
> Who plunge in with a smile

Sohini's song is to *take the plunge*, not stand on this shore wondering what it feels like to be on the other side.[11] Her hymn is one of immersion. She takes on the swirling waters with only a baked clay pot, a *matka*, as her float.

Night after night, Sohini swims across the river. Legend has it that when she got married, her murshid Chhutto made her promise that she would stop meeting Mehar. Late one night, Chhutto is in the midst of his prayers when he spies Sohini stealing across to the river. He challenges her: 'Will you break your promise to your guru?' Sohini replies:

> Those who hear the bells
> Of Mehar's buffaloes
> Why talk of guru
> They would break a promise
> To God himself!'[12]

The poetry of Shah Latif resists any kind of sanitizing of the story as a flat metaphor of the 'soul's search for union with God'. This dance between spiritual and earthly love is what makes this poetry edgy and powerful. Sohini seems to refute a God found within the boundaries and frameworks of legalistic religion, in favour of one that she experiences outside such fetters.

But Sohini's radicalism fades in the light of dawn, and she returns to keep up the pretence. In this perhaps lies her failure, our failure. We do not heed the call in its entirety, we return. We are afraid to fully cross over. We want to inhabit both worlds, sail in two boats, ride two horses, have our cake and eat it too. Latif speaks of the conflict in Sohini's heart, and he speaks *to* her, expressing both empathy and advice, pointing out the way ahead.

> Neither here, nor there
> Poor girl's in the thick of it
>
> He waits on the other bank
> Swirls of water engulf her
>
> Dive deeper, don't think!
> He's kind to those who drown
>
> ~
>
> Don't leave the house, Sohini
> Or don't return!
> Smash duality
> Take hold of oneness
>
> ~
>
> Perish close to Mehar, Sohini
> Don't think of return!
> Don't reveal to Dam
> The radiance of your sweetheart

For her indiscretions, Sohini is punished. The upholders of the day will not be denied their revenge for their own lack of love. Those who have abandoned their own Mehars for their respectable Dams cannot abide a Sohini. Sohini's sister-in-law, Dam's sister, creeps into the bushes one day to replace Sohini's baked pitcher with an unbaked one. When Sohini leaps into the river that night, the pot crumbles.

It's a blessing the pot cracked[13]
It was a barrier, a block
My breath resounds
To infinite sound
My being becomes a drum

Everything I had is laid
At the feet of the beloved
Union is the prize

~

The pot shattered
No prop remained
Lovestruck Sohini died

This is when she began to hear
The sound of Mehar

The pot, made of the five elements and baked in a womb-like furnace, is a symbol of our body and, in a larger sense, the very notion of self. Taking *earth* and *water* the Potter kneads vessels into shape. Stoked with *air* and baked in *fire* they turn out beautiful like our body-selves, occasionally holding but often losing an awareness of the fifth element—*space* or emptiness. And this self, this body with an ego, is our vehicle to negotiate the waters of life. A fragile float that keeps us fearful, keeps us from riding the waves. But curiously, if it could break, not just in physical death but before that, in the living death of the ego-self, all the fears that hold us back would go with it. The final ecstasy is not to meet with Mehar, but to merge with the swirling waters of the river itself.

> Beloved, Sohini, river
> All three are one
> The water itself is me
> This is the mystery of mysteries[14]

Sohini drowned in the river that night, and Mehar, when he heard her cries, jumped in as well and joined in her fate. It is said that their bodies were recovered from the river and now lie buried in the city of Shahdadpur in Pakistan.

And so the memory of Sohini becomes a powerful archetype, trickling deep into the collective psyche of the people of Punjab and Sindh, gathering force like a whirlpool, erupting subsequently in songs, stories, paintings, frescoes, films and even curiously a musical raag called 'Sohini', which may or may not have come before her, sung in the late-night or pre-dawn hours, purportedly to evoke a mood of 'sensuous longing'. Several poets sing in the voice of Sohini. They sing of the pot, to the pot, and in some songs the pot even responds, telling Sohini, admiringly, that it has not been fully baked in the fire of love as she has![15]

> Those who plunge, emerge
> That's how it's always been
> Submit to the rampant river
> And meet with Mehar

3

Call Him a Sufi

Sur Kalyan and Sur Yaman Kalyan

Stuffed with desire
Yet you call yourself a Sufi

To be a Sufi
Is no bed of roses

Take off your 'Sufi' headdress
And put it in the fire

Shah Latif is known as a Sufi poet. The term 'Sufi' is used so loosely in popular contemporary culture (you might soon find Sufi soap bars to buy in the market) that it requires some explanation. Briefly, Sufism is a particular set of practices, beliefs and/or schools, located broadly within Islam. It developed soon after the advent of Islam and has been described as Islamic mysticism or the inner dimension of Islam, perhaps somewhat like Kabbalah to orthodox Judaism.

There have been a number of scholars, theologians, saints or poets who have been described as 'Sufi', by themselves or their peers, one of the most famous among them being Jalalludin Rumi. Sufism arrived in India along with Islam, and soon took root. Among the prominent Sufi saints were Moinuddin Chishti of Ajmer at the turn of the thirteenth century and Nizamuddin Aulia of Delhi at the turn of the fourteenth century. The most famous Sufi poet was Amir Khusro, who was a disciple of Nizamuddin Aulia.

By the time of Latif, the influence of Sufism was already well-entrenched in the subcontinent (even impacting and interacting with Bhakti poets like Kabir). Particularly in the area of Sindh and Punjab, there had already appeared some well-known Sufi saint–poets, including Shah Hussain and Sultan Bahu, and Bulle Shah in Punjab was a contemporary of Shah Latif. Lal Shahbaz Qalandar (thirteenth century) was a huge cultural influence as an iconic Sufi saint who had settled and died in Sindh.

So Sufism was very much in the air by the time Latif grew up in Sindh. His own ancestor, Shah Abdul Karim Bulri, was a Sufi poet. Latif was not initiated into any particular Sufi order, doctrine or practice, and is considered to have been an Uwaisi Sufi, one whose connection is directly with the divine.[16] He was widely recognized as a saint, both during and after his lifetime. This is a critical aspect of being a 'Sufi' poet. One does not set out to 'become' a 'Sufi poet', but rather one is a Sufi practitioner and seeker who may happen to express himself or herself in poetry.

When Latif refers to Sufism it is not in any structured or doctrinal way. More than being an 'identity', to be a Sufi meant to be part of a particular way or stream of thought and practice. In a sense, to be a Sufi meant to be a practitioner, or something like a 'devotee' in the Hindu sense (a Bhakta), someone committed to finding out the truth about oneself, life and God, within a mystical framework.

By 'mystical' is meant the simple understanding that the fundamental truths of human existence cannot be grasped within a framework of ordinary logic and rationality. This is a basic starting point. The Sufi has already understood that spiritual truths do not lie within the realm of the mind or of discourse, and this distinguishes him or her sharply from the theologian.

The set of practices that have come to be associated with Sufism, such as whirling or *dhikr/zikr* (meditational chanting), are designed to lead consciousness out of the realm of logic and into another dimension.

It is with this basic background in place that we can begin to understand some of Latif's startling use of imagery and metaphor, often quite shocking, to expound his understanding of the way.

The Risalo begins with the Surs Kalyan and Yaman Kalyan. In a sense, these two Surs can be said to embody the core of Latif's philosophy, if it can be called that. ('Philosophy' and 'thought', or even 'worldview', do not adequately capture what is meant here.)

Sur Kalyan begins with an invocation to Allah, as the Ancient, the First, the All-Knowing, the Most Powerful and the Highest. It goes on to praise Muhammad as his special emissary. Having set this foundation for his poetry within the basic framework of Islam, Latif begins to expound one of the most fundamental Sufi tenets, the Oneness of God or Existence or Creation (*Vahdat-ul-vujood*). In beyt after beyt, Latif describes Allah as *'vahad-hu-lashareek'* (One without a peer, who stands alone).

> He is This and he is That
> He is death and he is life
>
> He is the beloved's body
> And its breath
>
> He is enemy and well-wisher
> Both here and there
> Also hiding in the heart
>
> He is the one looking at himself
> In his own light
>
> ~
>
> He himself is the great, the glorious
> Himself is the graceful
>
> He is the face of the beloved
> And its incredible beauty
>
> He is the teacher
> And the student is he

He himself is his thought
Manifested

This whole reality and truth
Can be grasped
Only from within

~

Don't call him lover, you fool
Nor call him beloved
Call him neither Creator nor creation

But this can be understood
Only by those
Whose faith is unflinching

What is the inner meaning of this 'oneness of God'? In the outer sense, it is what is usually called 'monotheism'—there is no God but God, or there is no God except Allah. You may not bow down to any other gods, all of whom are false gods. In the inner sense, though, it quite simply means that there *is* nothing except God. God and the world are not two. Everything is not just a reflection of God. It literally *is* God.

This is the basis of the famous statement of Mansur Al-Hallaj, which led to his execution on grounds of heresy. Mansur became an iconic figure in Sufism because of his execution. Many subsequent Sufi poets, including Latif, refer to Mansur and his statement in their poetry.

Mansur proclaimed, 'Ana al-Haq', that is 'I am Truth' or 'I am God'.

A fatwa was issued against him for heresy and he was subsequently executed after he refused to recant. This is a landmark event in Sufi history. Rumi says in one place that every particle of creation is as guilty as Mansur, because constantly it proclaims, 'I am God!' When a tree says so, no one seems to mind. Why is it a crime when a good man says so, asks Rumi.[17]

It is not that Mansur meant that *he* was God. He meant that there *is* only God. Just like the trees, the leaves, the animals, the stones, and every particle of creation is God. There is no separate 'I', which is 'not God'. This is the essence of Oneness, or 'vahdat'.

Latif has referred to this beautifully in Sur Sohini.

> On land and in water
> Every living thing, every creature
> The flowers and the trees
> Cry out in concert
> We are God
> We are the light of God
>
> They should all be hanged
> According to the Shariah!
> They are allies of Mansur
> How many will you execute?

The confusion between appearance and inner truth is not easy to overcome for the literal-minded, whether they are dry religious jurists issuing fatwas or modern-day atheists given over entirely to the evidence of the senses. For this category of people, there is only the appearance, nothing 'behind' or 'within'. For those that can see, there is only the inner truth, nothing 'in front'.

> The many came from the one
> Both of these
> Belong to the same truth
>
> There is only the One
> Nothing beyond or outside
>
> ~
>
> I swear upon Allah
> That only Allah exists

And all the sound and fury of the world
Which appears not to be him
Is also him

To realize this 'oneness' is no mean task. All the evidence of the
senses and the mind rebels against it. We see ourselves as separate
from others. We see others as separate from us. Even two people
in love are unable to fuse into one and remain keenly, and often
bitterly, aware of their differences.

Latif's solution to this problem is a drastic one. 'You' must be
murdered, butchered, annihilated. Better still, you must *want* to be
killed.

I'm in love with one
Who carries daggers!

I press ahead
In the field of love

My head's on the chopping-block
Now slaughter me, beloved

~

I look for the head and can't see the torso
I look for the torso and can't see the head

Hands, wrists and fingers chopped
And dropped
Who knows where

When oneness is the bride
The groom is cut to pieces

~

'Slaughter' and 'Search'
Begin with the same letter
Both belong to the road![18]

Set out
Experience them
They bring good health

Latif seems to revel in the violence of the imagery. The startling symbolism consists of the gallows, the chopping-block, knives, axes, blades, acts of butchering and scattered pieces of flesh. In some poems Latif even names internal organs and how they must be carved out and boiled in cauldrons. Strangely, for Latif, this violence to the self is fundamentally fused with the experience of *love*.

This can throw us initially, since this is not necessarily a conception of love that we are used to from popular culture. There are no roses and lilies here, only the chopping-block, the scaffold, the gibbet and the gallows. What kind of love is this? In an iconic couplet, Kabir speaks of the 'house of love'. One may enter this house only if one can cut off the head and leave it outside the entrance, much like one's slippers. Similarly, in Latif, love and the 'head' do not go together.

The gallows call out, friends
Who'll walk with me to their end?

Only those may come
Who chant the name of love

~

The gallows call out to lovers
Don't hold back

> If love truly fires your loins
> Cut off your head
> Then dare speak
> The name of love

Rumi describes it thus: The corpse floats in the river, while the living man sinks to its depths. To float in the river of life, one must be like the corpse.[19]

Oneness, slaughter, love. How do they all hang together? In Urdu poetry the word 'bismil' is used to describe both a slaughtered animal and an afflicted lover, suggesting that the two states are not very far from each other. The state of love is a state of being slaughtered, cut to pieces, blown to bits. It's a state of 'no-self'. It is a drastic situation.

'No-self' is a hard place to get to (provided one even wants to get there!). In Sur Sorath, Latif says that real existence lies in non-existence, and that to be *fanaa* (annihilated) is to be *baqaa* (immortal), that is, effacement is eternal life. This is from Yaman Kalyan.

> One cup, two drinkers
> Love doesn't work like this!

> Those who fall prey
> To the game of numbers
> How will they taste love?

> Existence arranges it so
> That they remain deprived
> Of the experience of union

'Love', that enchanting, alluring thing, lies in that direction, the one of annihilation, according to the Sufis. The well-known metaphor of 'intoxication', very widely used in Sufi poetry points to a state of 'bekhudi', which means both drunkenness and 'no-self'.

In a stroke of genius, Latif combines the two metaphors of 'slaughter' and 'intoxication'.[20] If you want a sip of this drink (of love, of 'bekhudi', of exhilaration, of knowledge—and all these things are not separate from each other), you must pay for it with your head.

> If you crave one sip
> Go to the wine-maker's distillery
>
> Cutting, chopping, tearing into shreds
> Chunks and bits of bone and flesh
> All this is done by him
>
> If at the end you get
> Even a small portion of his wine
> It's still very cheap, says Latif
>
> ~
>
> Some in the front
> Some in the rear
> Many heads lie here
> Near the chopping block
>
> If you can offer your head
> You, too, will be accepted
> Don't think it's a small thing
>
> Can't you see on the ground
> All these heads lying around?
> This distillery uses
> Heads as fuel!

Intoxication is a special state. It is simultaneously a state of ecstasy (of a 'high' or 'masti') and of knowledge, a special kind of knowing (which is not from the locus of the mind). It's a cup of poison, or poisonous wine, because it can literally be fatal. In a series of rhythmic beyts that create a taut, poetic medley through progressively subtle variations, Latif urges the seeker to offer her head for just one *cup* of the wine, for just one *teaspoon* of the wine, for just one *sip* of the wine, for just a *drop*, a mere *taste* and finally to hear just a *whisper* about this wine! Even *yearning* for it requires a sacrifice of the head.

Latif uses the local folk legend of a woman wine-maker called Mokhi. The folk tale (which may refer to a historical incident) recounts how one day, while Mokhi was making her wine, a venomous snake fell into her pot without her knowledge. When that particular batch of wine was served to her customers, all of them, one by one, fell sick and died. Latif picks up this figure of Mokhi, the wine-maker, typically a low-caste person, and transforms her into the murshid or the guru, the spiritual guide who serves out this special drink, this cup of poison, which is fatal to the separate self.

> This Mokhi is a suspect character!
> She belongs to a lowly caste
> She hands out cupfuls of poison
> And kills many a healthy man!
>
> ~
>
> All the healthy men are dead
> Mokhi, may you never die!
> But, tell me, how is it
> That you live without your customers?
>
> ~
>
> All the healthy men have died
> Mokhi, may you die too!
> Who will drink your outrageous potion
> Now that all the drunks are dead?

The head, or the mind, with its argumentations and objections, its logics and lines of thought, must literally be kept aside. The mind

and the sense of 'I' are not very far from each other. Putting aside
the mind means also putting aside the sense of self.

This sense of self, this 'I', is like a sorcerer's spell, putting us
all to sleep, and distorting our perception of the world. This is a
common conclusion reached by spiritual and esoteric traditions
across time and geographical location, from Vedanta to the Buddha
to Bhakti and Sufi poetry to the modern teachings of G.I. Gurdjieff,
to name just a few. To step into a world of real magic, one must
break the spell of this false enchantment.

> The world is full of 'I', 'I', 'I'
> It's hard to comprehend
> This spell of self-enchantment
> Cast by the magician

The murshid and the 'beloved' merge into one as the figure who
can remove this spell of enchantment. In Surs Kalyan and Yaman
Kalyan, many metaphors unfurl to describe this relationship. The
beloved is the ironsmith who moulds the iron into shape in fire. He
is the horseman, trampling the seeker under his horse's hoofs. He
is Cain, the killer, out to get you. Or then, he is the physician, and
you, the seeker, are the diseased.

Lack of love is the real malady in this world. The beloved as
physician brings the cure. He is distinguished from the usual doctors
(perhaps Mullahs and Qazis and jurists) who cannot even correctly
diagnose the disease. Several beyts berate false physicians, calling
them blind as bats who hang upside-down, and only serve to make
your malady worse.

To be 'healthy' in the worldly sense, says Latif in several verses,
is to be far removed from the state of love. True health, on the other
hand, is fatal in the worldly sense. No one in sound mind and body
can approach the station of love, proclaims Latif.

> You flinch if a thorn pricks you
> How will you bear being stabbed

In the face by love?
Why do you even aspire to love?

One must recognize one's own lack of love as the disease. Only then
the treatment can begin.

You are the beloved
You the physician
You are the pain and you the remedy

Oh master, this suffering
You give it and you take it away

Medicines are effective
Only if you want them to be

~

You are the beloved
You the physician
To call out to you my sole remedy

Only you can assuage
The pain in my heart

~

You are the beloved
You the physician
You are the hot iron rod!
You are both guide and lord

I'm amazed why
So many 'doctors' exist
To boss over us

~

> While the doctor tries to treat my pain
> The beloved strikes
>
> He cuts further into the wound
> And brings it all to naught

To be wounded is a privileged state. It has the danger of being misdiagnosed by run-of-the-mill doctors. But it also has the potential to draw the attention of the physician who can bring healing. The irony is that the one who wounds is the one who saves. And perhaps to be wounded is to be saved.

In a strange twist, Latif says that misfortune is real fortune. To be struck by illness can be the biggest blessing.

> Understand well, oh seeker
> Whatever is given by him
> Is given in all mercy
>
> Never consider it an unkindness
> If he wants to kill you
> Consider it a special favour
>
> He unites his favourites to him
> In this manner

His will and his mercy ('*razaa*' and 'rehmat') are one and the same. There is mercy hidden behind every act of his will. The human mind cannot always fathom this, but what it can do is to cultivate acceptance ('razaa') and patience or forbearance ('*sabr*'). To go against or to chafe against what is given reinforces the sense of a separate self, at war with the world. Latif stresses on patience and humility endlessly.

One begins to think of health only when one acknowledges the disease. Those who have been struck are the ones who have knowledge. Latif says that you must spend time with the wounded ones.

You must get infected yourself. You must develop this unease, this longing for real health and relief. You must be cut. You must bleed.

> The slaughterers are the saviours
> The saviours are slaughterers
> He is the one who slaughters me
> And he is the balm for my soul

> ~

> Those struck with iron arrows
> Groan piteously
> Their wounds ooze blood

> Those who have been coloured red
> In the field of love
> They writhe and moan

> They bandage themselves
> Treat their own wounds

> At least one night must be spent
> With such wounded ones

Be wounded. Be sick to the soul. Be cut through and through. Be intoxicated. Be out of your senses. Be annihilated. Burn.

> Go ask the moth
> What it means to burn

> They hurl themselves into fire
> With no concern for their lives

> Their innards are pierced
> With spears of love

It can be hard to understand this insistence on losing yourself. An acrobat knows that she cannot let go of one rope without having another rope to grasp on to. What is the other rope here, once you let go of what you know? What might you hold on to?

Nothing that is visible.

This requires trust. The other rope is not visible. You are not even sure (with your mind or senses) that it exists. This requires guidance from the murshid, who reassures you that it is not only all right but essential and beneficial to let go of what you know. Latif uses the figure of the 'moth' to explain this. But before that, a story.

It is said that once all the flies of the world got together and went to the King of Moths. Moths are held in greater esteem than flies, and so the flies developed a desire for upward mobility! They buzzed about and presented their requisition to the King of Moths that they should be given the status of 'moths' and admitted to their club. After all, they cried, we too have wings and fly around like moths do!

The King of Moths replied, 'Sure. The job of a moth is to search for the light. Go and seek the light. And if you can find it, I will declare you all moths.'

The flies buzzed off immediately, keen to bring back news of the light before the moths. They flitted across towns and villages and streets, finding a bonfire somewhere, a smouldering pyre elsewhere, or a row of lamps and candles in another place. They sped back to the King in double-quick time and recounted their discoveries to him.

'Now you must deliver your verdict,' the flies demanded of the King.

'What verdict?' asked the King.

'Let your moths come back. Then we will know whether we won or they did, whether we found more light or they did,' the flies cried out.

'Oh, that verdict has already been delivered, my friends!' exclaimed the King.

'How so?' asked the flies, bewildered.

'You fools! Those who have found the light, what need would they have to come back?'

Latif says:

> If you want to be called a moth
> Come, extinguish the fire!
>
> This fire has roasted many
> You must roast the fire
>
> Seek the truth
> Extinguish the flame
> But never spell out
> Your inner secret to others

The inner secret could refer to the mysteries of the esoteric path. Sufism is classically described as having four stages. These are Shariat, Tariqat, Maarfat and Haqiqat. We could describe them in somewhat simplified terms.

Shariat is the stage of outer observation, which includes the usual obligations of prayer, fasting, charity, holy pilgrimage, etc. It is the realm of outer or prescribed law. Latif does not oppose Shariat for the sake of opposing it, but he urges the seeker to use the observances of Shariat to move further into the stages of Tariqat, Maarfat and Haqiqat. Latif also hints at a difference between outer Islam (appearing outwardly to be a devout Muslim) versus inner Islam (a true believer and practitioner). He says that the mystical realm is above the categories of heaven and hell, or Islam and Kufr (belief and unbelief).

Tariqat is literally the way, or the path, to inner mysteries. This could be one of the Tariqas or Sufi orders, or it could be an individual practice or set of practices. Two well-known practices are dhikr or zikr (chanting or remembrance of Allah's name) and *tasavvur* (contemplation or visualization of Allah's or the murshid's qualities). These relate to two of the essential qualities or faculties of mind: verbalization and visualization. The attempt is to use these faculties consciously and towards a specific end, rather than be used by them, as tends to happen in ordinary life. Tariqat is the realm of Practice.

Maarfat is the experience of inner mysteries or revelations through the practices which the seeker undertakes under the guidance of his or her murshid. It is the realm of Knowing. This knowing is related to Ism-e-Aazam (the Highest Name or the Great Name) or the Kalma (traditionally the Muslim confession of faith but, in a more abstract sense, the Word). Experiences of sound and light, which are the twin qualities of this dimension, bring one closer to God. These experiences are very similar to those described in the poetry of the Bhakti poets such as Kabir.

The Mughal prince Dara Shikoh, son of Shah Jahan and brother of Aurangzeb, who was extremely interested in the Sufi path and took Sarmad as his murshid, and also translated the Upanishads into Persian, writes thus:

> [The] practice of hearing the Voice of the Silence is the path of the Fakirs, the Sultan-ul-azkar or the king of all practices.
>
> This sound existed even before the creation of the worlds, and exists even now and will continue to exist even when the worlds enter into non-existence. This sound is called the infinite and absolute sound. There is no practice higher than of hearing this sound.
>
> From many authentic traditions, collected in the six authentic Hadith volumes, we learn that our Prophet (may the blessing and peace of God be on him) was devoted to this practice, both before and after his attaining the rank of the prophethood.[21]

Finally, Haqiqat is the stage of arriving at a definite knowledge of the truth. This is the realm of Truth. Mansur's statement of 'Ana al-Haq' relates to this stage.

Latif does not directly expound on the meaning of these stages, but he does reference them non-doctrinally, from time to time, as the stages on the path, in various Surs. He does give a fuller description, though, of who is a Sufi or what it takes to be a Sufi.

The proponents and practice of charlatanism must have been then as they are now. Easy to call yourself or claim to be something exalted; harder to practise it. Latif describes the requirements of being a Sufi.

> The Sufi is not sectarian
> He is beloved of no one
>
> He is always at war within
> But shows nothing on the outside
>
> Those who wish ill to him
> He is their greatest well-wisher
>
> ~
>
> Give something to a Sufi
> And he is unhappy
>
> Give nothing
> And he is thrilled
>
> Call him a Sufi
> Who keeps nothing
> For himself

The headdress or woollen garment or flowing robe or the whirling do not a Sufi make. These are mere outer symbols of what is essentially an inner quality. But captivated as we are by the senses and external reality, the outer often substitutes for the inner. Doctrines take the place of inner truths. Book knowledge becomes more important than heart knowing.

This is the quandary of the upholders of 'law', the mullahs or qazis who presume to interpret the word of God and lay down laws for their fellow men and women. They read books and presume to 'know'. But 'Alif', the first letter of the Arabic alphabet, which represents Allah, is the only letter worth reading, says Latif. To know Alif is to know everything. Alif again refers equally to the Word of God, and God and the Word are not two, but one.

As for those who presume to enforce the letter of the law according to their own light, Latif has no kind words for such people. Like any number of other Sufi poets, Latif takes a hard-hitting look at the role of scholars, preachers, rule-keepers and lawgivers.

> Wretch, how did you become a Qazi
> By a mere study of letters?

> You guess and you speculate
> Dole out opinions and beliefs
> But truth is nothing like this!

> Go ask Satan
> About the taste of this drink

In another verse, Latif describes Satan or Azazil as the perfect lover, before pride and self-importance got the better of him. One who was so high fell thus to the lowest depths. Kaladhar Mutwa, a Sindhi writer based in Kutch, recounts to us an Islamic legend about Satan. It is said that subsequent to being banished from paradise, Satan still goes up sometimes and listens to snatches of conversations between God and the angels, where the former might be explaining some mystery of existence to the latter. Satan manages to hear only some bits of it, before he's discovered by the angels who chase him away by throwing stars at him. (This is one explanation for the phenomenon of shooting stars!) So Satan receives some parts of knowledge, adds his own bits to it ('guesses and speculates'), and comes down to earth to mislead and misguide mankind. In this sense, the qazi who guesses and speculates and is led by a mere study of letters is like Satan.

Latif has nothing but scorn for people like these.

> With all their surface talk
> These mullahs mislead people
>
> All this blabbering
> Takes them further away from God
>
> The beloved is closer than the breath
> Yet they don't look for him
>
> They don't understand
> The secret of breath
>
> They scream and cry
> Like ghosts devoid of flesh
>
> ~
>
> They read endlessly
> Nothing enters their heart
> The more they read
> The deeper they sink
>
> ~
>
> Oh mother, that mullah is a mess
> Like bile bursts in the stomach!
> He senses the truth of Allah and yet
> He wallows in the sludge

To be a mullah, or to be even a 'Sufi', confers upon one an identity. The gist of the Sufi quest, on the contrary, is to lose this sense of fixed identity, to experience free space, what the Buddhists or the Bhakti poets would call 'Shoonyata', emptiness or nothingness.

One of Latif's dearest inspirations was Rumi. In a series of beyts, he spells out Rumi's teachings as he received them within himself. This is what he says:

> The Many are in search of the One
> The way to it is beauty
> This is the teaching of Rumi

> First, lose yourself
> Then, lay eyes on the beloved

The *Diwan-e-Shams-e-Tabrizi* of Rumi (also called the *Diwan-e-Kabir* or the Great Collection) tells the story of the lover who would enter his beloved's house. He knocks at the door.

'Who is there?' is the question from within.

'It is I,' says the lover.

'Go away. There is no place for you here.'

The lover goes away dejected. But he returns after a year. He knocks again at the door.

'Who is there?' is the question from within.

'It is you who are within, and you who are at the door,' replies the lover.

'Then, enter,' comes the voice from within.

Echoing Kabir from an earlier time,[22] Latif ends, as he begins, with the anthem of oneness.

> How will a single heart
> House both Self and God?
> There isn't space for two swords
> In a single sheath

4

The Mountain Burst Into Flames

The Legend of Sasui

Oh grief
I long to grow in you
I would trade a million joys
And my head besides
In exchange for your caress

Deeply programmed as we are, to always and only seek happiness (and often desperately), this comes as a strange cry. We tend to perceive grief as an aberration ('Why me?'), as a roadblock to some normative notion of happiness we feel entitled to. How then are we to understand Sasui when she speaks of sorrow in this way?

Most have a handful of sorrows
I have many rooms full
Before I could spread my wares
Buyers left the marketplace

~

Don't take the name of love
Love's feet run somewhere else

Hang in with sorrow
Trade in longing and separation

Who is Sasui? What is her sorrow?

Born in a Brahmin family, Sasui is abandoned when her horoscope predicts that she will grow up to marry a Muslim. In an all-too-familiar folk-legend moment, she is set adrift as a baby on a river in a box, to be discovered downstream by a childless washerman, Muhammad, in the city of Bhambhor. He names her Sasui, or 'moon', and raises her as his own daughter.

When she grows into a young woman, news of her beauty reaches Prince Punhu, son of Ari Jaam, king of Kech in Balochistan. Punhu arrives in Bhambhor disguised as a vendor of musk and perfumes. Sasui and Punhu soon fall in love and decide to marry. Ari Jaam, upholder of convention, is opposed to the 'unequal' marriage. He sends Punhu's brothers to abduct him. They arrive on their camels for the wedding. After the celebrations, while Sasui sleeps, they get Punhu drunk, bundle him on to their camels and depart before dawn. When Sasui wakes up she finds that Punhu is gone. Brushing off her family's fears and concerns, Sasui sets off into the desert alone, in search of her beloved, following the tracks of the retreating camels.

The night of unconsciousness, followed by Sasui's epic search through the desert, becomes a spiritual allegory for Latif, and he unleashes a powerful surge of poetry, exploring the fabric of loss, search, endurance and arrival. One Sur was not enough to contain her story. Latif dedicates five whole Surs to it—Kohiyari, Aabri, Hussaini, Desi and Mazuri. Perhaps Sasui was closest to Latif's heart.

To be unconscious, as Sasui and Punhu were—one drunk, the other asleep—is to suffer a vital loss. Yet most of us don't feel any real sense of loss. We don't even have an inkling that we may be asleep. This is *khwaab-e-ghaflat* or Sleep of Heedlessness or Negligence (as it is termed in Sufi thought) in which we constantly forget to be alert about our thoughts and actions.[23] Kabir too urges us constantly to 'wake up!' We may sometimes hear this call through our intellect in tepid ways. But to feel it in our very guts, in every single fibre of our being—that in our ordinary lives we are *asleep,* that our life and habits are riddled with unconscious ways of being—this is an experience of a different order. It is a blow, a shock that eludes most of us; or perhaps it is an experience that we carefully avoid. Sasui receives the full impact of this shock when she wakes up. It's only *then* that she becomes aware of what she is missing, of what she has lost.

> I slept in love, but now love
> Doesn't let me sleep
>
> I wasn't awake when he came
> The one for whom
> I stayed awake through my sleep
>
> Friends, how could I forget
> That sleep and love
> Don't go together?

When 'morning' arrives, Sasui awakens and her search begins. Across the ages, in many a legend, wandering through the desert has symbolized the soul's journey in this world. Jesus spends forty days in the desert besieged by the devil's temptations, before he arrives in Jerusalem as Christ. Latif himself had the experience of wandering in the great desert stretches of Gujarat and Sindh. So, too, wanders Sasui.

If Marui is trapped in a tower, Sasui is on the move, in a vast, unending desert. She represents the eternal seeker in quest of a retreating beloved.

> The destination is not clear
> And I've carried no water
> The mountain path is cruel
> The desert sun harsh

Beloved, come to me here
Where I'm most alone
With my grief

~

He's not found by sitting on your ass
He's not found on a soft, warm bed
He's found by those
Who walk the path and weep for him

The immense, lonely desert becomes her field of attention and awakening. Everything here begins to signal the simultaneous presence and absence of the divine. She begins to converse with the elements . . . the floating clouds, the desert shrubs, the scorching wind, the unforgiving rocks, the ceaselessly rising and setting sun, and most of all the implacable mountain . . . She upbraids them and chides them. She hurls pleas and entreaties at them. They all become implicated in her story, they become characters—sympathetic or adversarial—in the unfolding theatre of her union with the divine.

I haven't met my beloved
And you are setting, sun

Take this message to my love
Go tell them in Kech
Wretched thing
She died on the path

~

Trees, stop growing!
Mountains, don't be tall!

Eyes, stop weeping
So I can see the footprints
Of my beloved

~

A blistering wind arose
Scorching the whole world

The sky rained sighs
Birds cried out
Fluttering on Punhu's trail

Cattle were aghast
Shepherds saddened
Animals went into mourning
Giving up their breath

The whole desert grieves
For Punhu

In an impassioned soliloquy directed by Sasui to the mountain called Pab, a poignant drama unfolds, one that straddles the entire Sur Kohiyari.

Between me and him
A mountain
Rough and steep

Those who cling to life
Are daunted, dismayed

I invite death as escort
And cross over

~

O harsh mountain
You splice my body
Like a woodcutter saws a tree
My fate is tangled with you
Why else would I be here?

~

The mountain burst into flames
When it brushed against my pain
Oh friend, the earth was scorched

There is no more hope
Of joy in my mind

~

The mountain and the girl
Sat together and wept
Sobbing, silent
Not speaking of their love

There is a sudden and gut-wrenching realization that Sasui means something else, too, by the 'mountain'! The mountain is companion and enemy, implacable and yet it weeps. This mountain is within. It stands in the way. Death is the way to cross this mountain.

Sasui steps boldly into the desert, leaving all notions of security and permanence behind. She could have stayed behind and pined for her beloved to return to her. But she follows her calling to set out on a possibly fatal search.

The desert heat, a scorching sun beating down on Sasui, images of fire and burning . . . This is *tap*, literally 'heat', an ancient Indian word for serious spiritual practice. It is not an intellectual exercise or a fanciful flirtation with spirituality. Life itself is at stake. Everything is to be lost, everything is to be found.

You caught fire
Now don't stop burning

Fan the flames
Till they singe the sky

Forget all things
Raze your world to
Nothing

~

Die, and then live
And you will bask in his radiance
Follow this advice
And you will find him

~

Don't wail without a true cry
Don't walk without a true gait
Don't burn without true fire
Don't weep without true tears

~

Burn as long as you live, Sasui!
There is no rest without burning
In heat and cold, keep walking
This is no time for loitering

The desert is an apt setting for the kind of quest Sasui has undertaken. It is a place where all non-essentials are stripped away. This is a pure search for what can only be found in emptiness. Sasui takes nothing with her when she steps into the desert. She seems to signal to us that the more we 'have', the more we are hampered.

Leaving all your clothes behind
Set out stark naked
Those who walk with nothing
Reach farthest

~

Those who bedeck themselves
Remain forsaken
Those who set out with nothing
Find union

Walking in the fields of grief and pain, in the desert of her loneliness, near her death, Sasui realizes at last that the search has led her in an opposite direction—Punhu is not 'out there', but 'in here'.

> O foolish girl
> The man you seek
> Is not in the mountains
>
> The oasis you seek
> Is in your heart
>
> You ask strangers
> For the way to him?
> Why not ask yourself

At the very end of the journey, one discovers perhaps, as Sasui does, that one needn't have walked so far or suffered so much. And yet, how can one discover this truly, without having walked so far or suffered this much?

Sasui loses her self. This is the price for gaining Punhu. Her discovery on this path is that this 'death' is imperative, that death is alive, that death is far more vital than what we know as life.

> I myself am Punhu
> Sasui has no more charm
>
> The trees are full of this song:
> The world is an image of God
>
> This mad one has etched him
> On her heart
>
> ~
>
> Diving into myself
> I spoke with my soul

There were no more mountains then
Nor lack of Punhu
I became him

So long as I was Sasui
Life was full of grief

Sasui understood a difficult secret—that happiness can lead us astray, but pain is the path itself. Grief was her beacon.

Towards the end of her journey, legend says that Sasui was accosted by a goatherd who tried to molest her. When she prayed for deliverance from her situation, the earth itself split open, swallowing her whole, leaving just the hem of her skirt revealed above the land.

When Punhu 'wakes up' from his intoxication, he comes running back towards Bhambhor to look for his Sasui. He finds the lamenting goatherd in the desert, who describes Sasui's fate to him. Punhu asks the earth to swallow him up as well, so that he may lie next to his beloved. A shrine marking their memory nestles in the Pab mountains a few miles to the west of present-day Karachi.

It is said that while travelling through the desert, Shah Latif once came across a solitary hermit wandering in the hot sands of the desert, feverishly repeating the line of a poem—*Alone, alone, wending towards Punhu!* Shah Latif instantly recognized the poem as his own. As he reached out to the hermit, the old man collapsed in the poet's arms, continuing to chant this solitary line from a forgotten beyt—*Alone, alone, wending towards Punhu! Alone, alone, wending towards Punhu!*

With great compassion and in a soft voice, Latif whispered to the old man, the remaining words—*The hills are tough, but they are a boon. Gather your aches, you will reach him soon.* Hearing the beyt completed, the hermit breathed his last. A deeply moved Shah Latif dug a grave for the man, burying him there with his own hands.[24] Perhaps this story signals to us the extent to which the figure of

Sasui inhabits the innermost worlds of the people of Sindh, how intimately her epic and solitary walk through the desert falls in step with the journeys of ordinary men and women through their lives, searching for meaning, searching for their Punhu.

In present-day Pakistan, near the highway to Kech, standing alone in the middle of the desert is a stone formation, which has a shape uncannily reminiscent of a woman. It is solitary and stark, almost as though sorrow itself had immobilized and got etched into the land. It has been dubbed Sasui by the local population.

A cry rang out in the void
Like the chord of a violin
Or was it a woman?
It was the call of love

~

A cry rang out in the void
Was it a koel?
Reverberating through the land
It was the call of love

5

My Breath Resounds to Infinite Sound!

Singing the Waai

It is said that once, angered by Latif's devotion to music, his popularity and his unorthodox Sufi views, the maulvis of his time banned his poetry and song, citing the Shariah to claim that music was heretical in Islam. Latif got annoyed and locked up his musical instruments, the *damboors*, in a small room. The story goes that on the night before jumma, which was the designated time for playing and singing, the five-stringed damboors began to play music of their own accord in the locked room. The clerics backed off in alarm and withdrew their ban.

In a curious echo of this tale in present times, Abdullah bhai tells us about a music festival he recently organized in a Kutch village, inviting many local singers and seekers to share their interpretations of Latif's poems. A local cleric issued a fatwa against the gathering, pronouncing it anti-Islam. Tensions mounted and volunteers for the event were frightened and discouraged. However, on the day of the festival, the number of people who turned up to participate surged into several thousands. The maulvi backed off and the festival proceeded as planned.

> I put away the Qur'an,
> And took up the damboor—
> Behold, such secrets got revealed!
>
> In the mirror of my eyes,
> I had a glimpse of Muhammad

How can I abandon this damboor, O Bulleya
Which showed me
The way of ecstasy?

– Bulle Shah

Shah Latif's profound reverence for music is evinced in the fact that the Risalo is a collection not so much of poetry meant for reading, as much as it is a collection of musical verses meant for singing. The extent and amount of alliteration in the original poetry, so hard to translate, is breathtaking, and lends a peculiar musicality to all the verses. The Surs into which the Risalo is divided are chapters clustering poetry around a specific theme, but more literally they are 'musical modes' based on specific Indian raags, intended for a musical experience. Shah Latif was clearly among those Sufis who recognize the power of sound in spiritual practice.

So many Surs themselves are replete with references to the power of music. In Sur Pirbhati the fiddle-playing musician is cast by Shah Latif as the 'seeker' and in the story of Sur Sorath the musician and his music have the power to demolish the ego of the seeker, and in that sense the musician is the guru or murshid himself. In Sur Sohini the sound of the cattle bells across the river creates unbearable restlessness and longing, compelling her to take the plunge. In Sur Ramkali, Shah Latif's deep longing for the music of the yogis unfolds in several beyts.

Their music hides a secret
With the power to destroy me

More exquisite than the pipes
That camel riders play
Or even their flutes

Sweeter than
The cattle bells
That drove Sohini crazy

More agonizing
Than the strings of the fiddle
That sliced off the king's head

Nothing like it has been heard
In Hind or Sindh

Those who hear its melody
Know how rapturous it is
They step into ecstasy
Dissolving their selves

A peerless music
That God himself applauds
What can I say?

Bells may enchant goats and sheep
But this pierces the human heart

Says Abdul Latif
This music brings back to life
Even the dead

Popular wisdom credits Latif with innovating the five-stringed instrument called the damboor to which his poems have been sung for centuries in a musical form called the waai. Some say the waai form of singing was created by Maulana Rumi himself and later popularized to a great extent by Latif's ancestor Shah Karim. This was a time when Sufi philosophy and songs may have become more popular than the reading of the Qur'an itself.

Body, the rosary
Breaths, the beads
Their hearts, damboors

Their veins vibrate
To the chant of oneness

Awake when asleep
Even their slumber
Is worship

(Sur Aasa)

Shah Latif's commitment to music as his path was resolute, and one that repeatedly ran afoul of the religious leaders of his time. It is recorded that he was deeply influenced by the Pir of Luwari, and approached him to become his disciple. However, when the Pir asked him to relinquish his musical instruments and practice, he refused and the matter stalled there. He was blessed nevertheless by the Pir with a 'chaadar', which according to Shah Latif's wishes was draped on his tomb after he passed away.

Given Shah Latif's persona and views, it is not surprising that his spiritual and poetic legacy was embraced by all communities, and the oral tradition that keeps his poems alive in Kutch flows in both Hindu and Muslim communities. His songs are sung in the *kaafi* style, to the accompaniment of a *tambura*, by Hindu Dalit communities. The kaafi is a generic form of poetry and music in the Sufi tradition, and uses a refrain to structure a full song centred around one theme, similar to bhajans in the Bhakti tradition. Famous among the earlier Sindhi singers in this tradition are the well-loved Bhagat Kanwar Ram and Mohan Bhagat, and it is this idiom that has flourished amongst the contemporary Dalit singers and mingles with the songs of Kabir and other Bhakti poets in the satsang traditions of the region.

In another musical variant, the kaafi form of Shah Latif's verses is also sung by Muslim communities to the accompaniment of harmonium and banjo. However, in a style considered most authentic to the tradition started by Latif himself, his poems are sung in the form of the waai by the cattle-herding Muslim Jat communities, preceded by a series of beyts to the accompaniment of damboors. This is a less accessible form of singing (and listening) than the kaafi form, as it involves a more specialized learning process and, for many, a more cultivated taste of listening.

Each Sur in the Shah Jo Risalo is divided into *daastaans* (literally, stories, but loosely used in the sense of chapters). Each daastaan or chapter consists of a series of beyts and ends in one or more waais. Each singer picks up the thread of the previous singer's beyt, and sings another evoking the same theme, creating a complex musical and poetic ambience. The waai is a longer verse form, in the genre of a song, comprising a refrain, sung to a beat accompanied by a rhythmic playing of the damboor. Traditionally beyts and waais are sung by groups of male singers, sometimes as many as ten or twelve, with multiple damboors creating an intensely powerful musical experience.

Sumar Kadu Jat and Mitha Khan Jat are cousins who belong to a small village called Bhagadia in Kutch and seem to be the last exponents of the waai form in India, along with the older Jaan Muhammad. They have been training a few new recruits over the last few years to ensure that the form does not disappear entirely from India. They themselves learnt this form of singing from their uncle who lives across the border in Pakistan, but have since then lost touch with the living tradition of waai, which continues to flourish in the Sindh region of Pakistan. They can only be vicariously present (through Whatsapp and mobile forwards) among the waai singers who gather to sing at Latif's dargah in Bhit Shah. It is a tradition that Sumar Kadu and Mitha Khan are now cut off from and thirst to reconnect with.

We visit them in the village of Bhagadia one evening and settle down late at night to listen to them sing.

~

The waai hits you in the gut.

If one were to imagine a form that might best capture a conversation between seeker and God, between lover and elusive beloved, this might be it. No weary preliminaries, no pretty embellishments, no polite barriers, no delicate overtures, no middlemen to broker this conversation. The waai is a kind of a visceral cry, a weeping, a lament, a communion, a trance.

The vibrations from their damboors overpower our bodies as we listen. Waai singing uses two kinds of voices—the thick (*gauro*) and the thin (*sanho*). The 'thick' is the normal male pitch of singing, but nothing prepares us for the 'thin'. A startling, high-pitched cry of longing for the beloved. It is this falsetto sanho that strikes the chord of separation—for it is a kind of wail, or a *loolaat* as Abdullah bhai terms it—a baby's howl for its mother. Full-grown men weeping in the voice of a child . . .

They seem to enter another dimension as they sing, accessing some altered state of reality, clearly far removed from the world of show and tell, of stage and singer, of technique and acclaim.

There is a trembling within me when I sing Shah's waais, says Sumar Kaka. They're not poems, they are daggers. They can cut you up and cleave you into two, he says. But then, you wonder: why should he return, again and again, to imperil himself on this blade?

The answer arises, beautifully, in a Latif poem:

> The beloved's knife
> Cut right to the bone
>
> For Allah
> Lovers gladly
> Chop themselves
> To pieces

> (Sur Kalyan)

6

How Can I Forget?

The Legend of Marui

Destiny captivated me
Why else would I be here?
Fate brought me to this place
But heart, body, breath
Belong to them

Oh King, let Marui return
To her people!

What might be the deeper significance of yearning for one's home and one's people, trapped in a fortress in an alien land, subject to the attentions of a cruel king?

Once upon a time in a small village called Maleer in the Thar desert, among the community of the shepherd nomads called Rabaris, lived a girl called Marui (*maah-rui* or 'moon-face'). The Rajput king of a neighbouring kingdom, Umar Soomro, hearing the fame of her beauty, came to the Rabari camp one day, riding a horse. He approached Marui, asking her for water. Being a herder, renowned for their generous hospitality, Marui unhesitatingly held up her pot to him. Seizing the moment, Umar abducted Marui, whisking her away with him to the city of Umarkot, his capital.

Umar asks Marui to marry him, promising her his kingdom, its riches and the honour of being his chief queen. When Marui refuses,

Umar is enraged and imprisons her in a fort. He deploys both fear and temptation to persuade her but she stands her ground. Years of hardship and solitary confinement do not weaken Marui's resolve. She longs for her land, Maleer, and her kinsfolk, the Maroo. She refuses to eat, drink, sleep, bathe or even comb her hair. Close to death, she asks the king to let her be buried in Maleer. Moved by her unflinching integrity, the king relents and lets her return to her village. In a moment reminiscent of Sita's travails when she returns to Ayodhya, Marui is made to undergo a test of 'chastity' by her village folk, before she is reaccepted.

There are several ways to read this tale. Many read it as a paean to 'patriotism' (Marui's unwavering love for her land). Marui becomes a particularly emotive icon for the Sindhi diaspora, many of whom were separated from their homeland due to political conflict or reasons of trade or the Partition between India and Pakistan in 1947. Not surprisingly, our patriarchal culture also glorifies Marui as an exemplar of a 'good' (chaste) woman, as she resists the advances of a kidnapper king.

But Shah Latif's evocation of this tale tugs powerfully in a different direction. He celebrates Marui's chastity not because he's enamoured of the notion of female chastity in itself, or else he would hardly celebrate the deeply transgressive, extramarital love of Sohini for Mehar. Rather, Marui's 'chastity' becomes a metaphor for remaining 'untouched' by the temptations of this world.[25] Marui's resolve is not so much about preserving her 'female honour' (a patriarchal notion, in the first place), but about not giving into the temptations of wealth and power, staying true to a way of life and being (that of the herders), which represents purity.

> They are joyful with little
> And live content
>
> And yet they are physically
> Strong and resilient

They wrap their bodies
With rough blankets
And move without
Heaviness of ego

In Maleer you can feel
The power of the herds-folk

In the poetic imagination of Latif, the image of Marui imprisoned in a fort becomes a metaphor for the soul enmeshed in the body. The king, who would seize upon Marui's beauty and consume it if he were allowed, becomes a symbol of the *nafs*, the ego or the mind, which wants to lure the soul into worldly gratification. Maleer becomes a figure for the soul's place of origin, and its people—the Maroo—the true company that the soul kept there. As long as Marui resists the advances of her own grasping mind, her 'Umar', she keeps an unbroken connection with the place she came from.

These are ever festering wounds
I yearn for union
Separation has destroyed me

King, my memory dwells on them
Who dwell in the desert
My eyes thirst for
The sight of my people

More than the idea of 'chastity', it is the idea of 'simplicity' or 'frugality' that is being invoked. Invoking the powerful image of the desert nomads—the Rabaris (the Maroo)—their capacity for living lightly, their virtues of non-possession and simplicity, Shah Latif asserts through the voice of Marui the power of spiritual austerity. Marui's gaze views the luxuries and gratifications of the palace as mere inanities, not worth the corner of the hem of a herdswoman's rough garment, which is hued with the fabric of truth.

Herdswomen don't wear silk
Rough gowns please them more
Than fancy shawls or brocade

O Soomra, I choose the wool blanket
Over your gilded offerings

Let me die of shame if I abandon
The legacy of my ancestors

~

Desert women
Wear black bangles
Gold for them
Is a harbinger of woe

With my people
Penury is a privilege
And hunger, happiness

~

Happy those born in their homelands
Who have the desert as their shelter!

The Golra creeper and the Gugryan bush
Offer them protection
My people roam in such jungles

It's as if the wilderness itself
Was made into my bridal bed

The idea of remaining 'untouched' by that which is unnatural or
alien gets another metaphor in the figure of the oyster. According to
local belief, though the oyster is surrounded by seawater, it remains

steadfast in its vigil for a single drop of rain, for only that water can slake its being and also form the pearl.

> The oyster is born at sea
> And yet it craves the rain
>
> This two-layered creature
> Refuses the bitter seawater
> As well as the sweet river
>
> The pearl is formed when
> You can stay thirsty in deep water
>
> ~
>
> Learn steadfastness
> From the oyster, friends
> It refuses all kinds of water
> And lives in hope of rain

Unlike Sohini who plunges into the river each night and Sasui who takes off into the desert, Marui is trapped, unable to move. Through her voice Latif explores the agony of feeling 'stuck', the feeling of being hijacked and held hostage by one's own mind, caught in the confines of its often futile, self-destructive patterns. But in the frustration and 'stuck-ness' of that space and moment, Latif also evokes (and invokes) the power of *remembrance*.

The importance of remembering comes up in several spiritual traditions. Well known is *simran* in the Bhakti and Sikh traditions, and zikr in the Sufi and Islamic traditions, both of which translate as 'remembrance'. Remembrance as meditating on the mystic Name, or the ninety-nine Names of Allah; remembrance as chanting (internally or externally) certain mantras or Qur'anic phrases. In the Christian tradition, too, the Holy Communion is enjoined as: 'Do this in remembrance of me.'

How can I forget?
The goodness of my people
The joy of their companionship

Friends, says Latif
It's raining in the land of my kin
How can I forget?

~

I remember him
Since the day of the promise
To love him, and him alone

That memory is immutable
He's called 'neither born,
Nor birthing'[26]

What can Marui do?
Sooner or later she will die
With that vow
Etched in her heart

What is the 'vow etched in Marui's heart'? What is the 'promise' she cannot forget?

Abdullah bhai recounts to us a creation myth in Islam. When God set about creating the universe he placed into it the sun, moon, stars, earth, sky, trees . . . Then with the four elements of fire, water, wind and earth, he fashioned the body of the human being. The fifth element was the *rooh* or spirit. When the rooh was sent to earth to live in the body of a human being, she was not pleased with this dark, unwelcoming place, and returned, unwilling to make it her home. God then decided to lure the soul back into the human body by placing in it a *noor ka tukda*, one small fragment of his own eternal light. The trick worked, and the spirit consented to make the body her home. When all souls were sent to earth, God asked them to make a promise, to take a pledge, never to forget that only He was their true Beloved.[27]

> Am I not your truest love?
> Hearing those words
> I answered, yes!

> In that instant
> My heart was pledged
> To him

> ~

> No call to 'Be' had rung out then
> No ether, no flesh
> No Adam, no form
> It was then, in that moment
> That I met with you
> My lord

> ~

> No call to 'Be' had rung out then
> No moon, no sun
> No virtue, no sin
> Just one
> Only one

> It was then, says Latif
> That Allah unfurled the riddle
> I grasped the mystery
> I saw, I felt
> His presence

Now it so happens that most souls—most of *us*—forget this contract with God, and once we begin to live in the body and the world, we take on many other lovers.[28] When Azraeel (Death) comes to take us away, we cling to the body, slaves to our unfulfilled desires and aspirations.

We are faced here with the all-too-familiar human dilemma, to be in this world yet not to cling to it. Latif quarrels with his Beloved, asking why he set all of us such an impossible challenge?

> The beloved tied me up
> And flung me into the sea
> Standing on the shore, he said
> Watch out, don't get wet!

> (Sur Aasa)

Marui struggles and chafes in her (indeed *our*) existential paradox.

> King, I've lost my beauty
> That enviable splendour
> A smoke rose up in the heart
> My face has become black!

Marui's lost 'beauty' evokes the idea of a radiance that is lost in the company of Umar (mind/ego/nafs), a light within that has been dimmed, in our forgetful engagements with the world.

> Their faces are full of light
> Who live in Maleer

> Some lucky ones have returned
> Their crimes forgiven

> I'm a cursed one
> My beauty destroyed

All through her struggle, what Marui seems to hang on to, unwaveringly, almost as a survival tactic, is the act of *remembering*.

The practice of awareness brings release, a reclaiming of the *noor ka tukda*, the spark of radiance, with which we have all been bestowed.

With this steadfast practice of remembrance, she weaves with a fine needle the thread that connects her to her homeland. A thread which, through all her travails, she keeps unbroken.

Such a fine needle
Knits my heart to my Maroo
An unbreakable bond!

My brittle body and bones
Are with you, king
But my heart's in the desert

~

I thank those beautiful days in jail
Trapped in my tower I wept
Endlessly, out of longing

Tears of remembrance
Washed away
My earthly desires

Love released me
From the illusory
Shackles of captivity

7

Every Day These Eyes Laugh and Weep

Sur Aasa

Every day these eyes
Laugh and weep
Eager to get a glimpse

They've found him
A thousand times
Yet they crave the joy of search

Even when fulfilled
Eyes thirst
To gaze upon the beloved

One evening the conversation turned to eyes. We mulled over the mystery of the longstanding affair that poets have had with eyes. There may be a million love poems on the beloved's eyes, or eyes that have seen the beloved; eyes that are beautiful, or eyes that are drunk on beauty. We were gathered in the house of Ismail Jat in a remote village of the Banni grasslands in Kutch that evening. The day was darkening as we spoke, and the night was waking up.

The poems of Shah Sayeen were being recited, as well as those of Kabir and other poets. In the mad swirl of his love, Latif was speaking of eyes, and speaking *to* eyes. Closed and open eyes, loving and wandering eyes, in-turned and gouged-out eyes. Eyes that seem to have a will of their own, eyes that go and fall in love in the wrong place, eyes that get us into deep waters!

> They didn't confer with me
> These eyes
> Before falling in love

> They entangled themselves
> Where there are no entreaties
> Or remedies

> My wrecked heart longs
> And waits
> And melts into nothing

One has heard of the idea of a 'witnessing self'—a higher self which observes and watches the egoic self—but here curiously we are witness to eyes themselves.

> They didn't take my consent
> These eyes
> Before falling in love

> They've strayed into
> A dangerous market
> Where no one haggles
> And the price is steep

> You offer your life
> To close the deal

> ~

> Eyes get angry at eyes
> They suffer miseries

They've learnt how to love
Now their tongue's got sharp

Eyes laugh, cry, get upset
And then again
Are mollified

Sur Aasa contains stunningly layered and delicately nuanced poems about eyes and the nature of seeing in the deepest philosophical sense. Latif speaks of sight into insight, of gaze—blinking, unblinking. He asks us to notice the *nature* of our gaze, the *direction* of our glance, what it means to see and what we are really seeing.

Reverse your gaze
Go against the grain

People plunge downwards
But you should soar to the sky

Look only inward
To reach for the beloved

The Sufi makes us aware of two ways of looking, two types of readings, two kinds of meanings—the *zaahir*, or the obvious; the *baatin*, or the hidden. Zaahir is that which is outer, evident, manifest. Baatin is the secret pearl, the concealed truth. These stories—of Sohini, Sasui, Marui and others—reveal two different worlds, two different truths about life through their zaahir and their baatin, but only if we become receptive to the visible *and* the unseen, the sensory *and* the veiled.

Don't look with the eye
Of worldly love

Those who seek open-eyed
Find him missing

Only they behold him
Who close their eyes[29]

Those of us who rely on the resources of our limited, sensual gaze
are like blind men misunderstanding the nature of the thing that is
the elephant.

Blind men quarrel
Over a dead elephant
Groping and prodding
Unable to understand
Unable to see

Those with real sight
See the shape of the beast
With the light of insight
They illuminate us

In this poem Shah Latif is referring to an ancient parable which
has inspired diverse philosophies—Hindu, Jain, Buddhist as well
as Sufi—and perhaps he encountered this story in a poem by Rumi
which has made this fable famous. The tale is well-known. Four or
five blind men touch different parts of an elephant, and describe it
variously as a snake, a pillar, a fan, a broom or a spear, depending
on the part that they touch. Each of them pathetically confident
about his specific delusion, they begin to quarrel.

Rumi says, 'The sensual eye is like the palm of the hand. The
palm has not the means of covering the whole beast.' The human
gaze is hopelessly one-sided. In order to perceive a holistic truth
(that captures all sides and facets of a situation or object) or an
inner truth (the baatin which is not evident to the physical eye) we
must close our (outer) eyes and open an inner eye. Kabir says, *Antar*

ke pat khol, toke piya milenge. Open your inner eye, and behold the beloved.

> Don't befriend
> These physical eyes
> Don't scatter your glances
> Here and there
>
> Look intently, inquiringly
> On the road to reality

In *looking* for the beloved, trying to *see* the true nature of reality, we find it beyond the grasp of these everyday eyes, beyond mere sensory apprehension.

> I look for a limit
> But you are out of the box
> Your beauty beyond speech
>
> Length or breadth
> Cannot capture you!

Generally 'blind faith' is counterposed against the light of reason and intellect. However, in a reversal that is characteristic of Sufis, Latif calls *reason* blind, for its resources are woefully inadequate. It offers a partial gaze.

> Reason is stunned
> You are beyond its grasp
>
> How would the blind
> Bear witness
> To a beauty such as yours?

~

Reason is astounded
And shatters to pieces

How can the blind spot
Your signals of love?

~

Reason is baffled
And skulks in shame

Staggered by your immensity
It's no longer cocky

It cannot bear
The sight of you

This might be a startling idea for us. Reason is blind! How does our reason cope with this assertion? Does it rebel and try to reassert its primacy? Or does it learn to surrender, to a vaster, inner, more integral way of seeing and understanding?

The self-obsessed man bears a partial gaze, whether he is 'logical' and 'rational' or not. This obsession with the self is, for the Sufi, the deepest irrationality.

If in your eyes
You still see your self
There is no surrender

Lose the self
Then chant, Allah-u-Akbar!

~

To hell with duality
Save me from that fate

Strip me of this 'I'
So that you may find yourself

~

'I', 'You', 'Us', 'Them'
Free your heart of these four!
The flames of suffering
Won't touch you then

~

The self is a veil
Obscuring you from yourself
Watch out, be vigilant
'You' are in the way
Of union

Our eyes must seek out nothing else. A glimpse of the beloved doesn't come at a cheap price. We must lay them down—our wandering, straying, distracted eyes, our restless ways of seeing—giving up *all* our attention to the beloved alone.

If with the first light of day
The beloved is not beheld
Pluck out these eyes
Feed them to the crows

~

Love with deep love
This love is not so simple

Hide even your hiding
So distraction
May not see you

Sight consumes most of our waking attention—perhaps more than all the other senses combined. Therefore, to pay attention to the nature of our attention means to a great extent to look after our looking.

In my individual consciousness, my world arises. Consciousness is the light by which I see. This light, when it 'goes out', falls upon objects—I perceive people, things, ideas. When I become too strongly identified with any object, in a sense I become that. Becoming identified successively with different things, I become fragmented. I lose the wholeness of my consciousness. In a sense, I lose my radiance. *'The light of the body is the eye; if therefore thine eye be single, thy whole body shall be full of light,'* said the Christ.

To recollect oneself—to be of single mind or purpose—is therefore also to be whole. Once the beloved is glimpsed, the story changes.

> Neither being, nor non-being
> These are mere turns of thought
> The beloved's brilliance
> Has gone beyond seeing

Perhaps eyes are a code for consciousness or attention. In this sense, our attention is the only true jewel we have.

> The beloved approaches
> How may I welcome him?
> On a tray full of pearls
> I lay down my eyes

> – Poet unknown

We could string our attention into a single, beautiful necklace, or then again our eyes may flit and our pearls scatter. These very eyes lead us astray and these very eyes lead us to a glimpse of the beloved. How well we focus our seeing, how consciously and towards what we direct our attention, might well determine in the end the value of our gaze.

> In that marketplace of eyes
> Will mine fetch a good price,
> Beloved?

Night was upon us. The inscrutable sky, studded with stars, pulsed strangely in the distance. A hush fell, as each of us pondered the impossible question:

Will they?

8

Let's Go To Kak!

The Legend of Moomal

The story begins dramatically. Hamir Soomro, king of Umarkot, and his three ministers, including Rana (or Rano), are out on a hunt when they are accosted by the strange figure of a yogi.

> Yesterday the Yogi was met
> A beggar-like fellow
>
> A shawl on his head
> Lovely rosary round his neck
>
> The fakir showed us a vision
> And wounded our hearts
>
> ~
>
> Yesterday the Yogi was met
> Glowing like the moon
>
> An abundance of longing
> Was awakened in our hearts
> By the fakir

In the next few verses, it becomes clear what is transpiring. What is the vision that has caused a wound in their hearts? Who is this longing for?

Yesterday the Yogi was met
In the early morning hour

His beauty was radiant
But he wept tears of blood

One who gets entangled, he said
With one named Moomal
There's no escape for him

~

Yesterday the Yogi was met
An ash-smeared beggar

A glowing green shawl
Slung over his shoulders

Tell us, oh fakir, they cried
The truth about this Moomal!

The yogi is speaking of a woman named Moomal. It is evident that the men are fascinated. The yogi's demeanour, the light on his face, the glint in his eye, the tremor in his voice when he talks of Moomal, all cast a spell on the four men. They cannot help but long to know more!

In a strange way, this yogi predates another famous old man of poetic legend, the 'ancient mariner' of Samuel Taylor Coleridge, he of the glittering eye, who appears in literature in another continent some fifty-odd years later. Like Latif's yogi, he too accosts some men, three guests on their way to a wedding, casting a strange spell on one of them, compelling him to listen to his story.

It is an ancient Mariner,
And he stoppeth one of three.

'By thy long grey beard and glittering eye,
　　Now wherefore stopp'st thou me?

The Bridegroom's doors are opened wide,
　　And I am next of kin;
The guests are met, the feast is set:
　　May'st hear the merry din.'

He holds him with his skinny hand,
　　'There was a ship,' quoth he.
'Hold off! unhand me, grey-beard loon!'
　　Eftsoons his hand dropt he.

He holds him with his glittering eye—
　　The Wedding Guest stood still,
And listens like a three years' child:
　　The Mariner hath his will.

Latif's yogi is as compelling as the ancient mariner. He is also one who has returned, almost dead-alive, from an indescribable voyage, an incredible journey. The yogi narrates to the four men the wonders and beauty of Kak Mahal, the palace where Moomal resides, located in Ludano in the midst of the desert. The river Kak flows nearby, which gives the palace its name. The yogi is overcome with emotion with each mention of the place. Speaking about Kak opens up his old wounds. The men cannot help but wonder, what place could this be, which had such an effect on him.

It is hard to decipher whether the impact of Moomal and Kak on the fakir is a good one or a bad one. On the one hand, the fakir looks utterly stripped and devastated and beside himself. On the other, his face glows like the sun. In fact, his face shines so brightly that the four men are unable to gaze steadily at him.

The sheen on the yogi's face
Emanates from the glaze of love

He was born like a moth
Now he burns like the sun!

He has returned from Kak
The maidens there
Have made him bloom like this

The yogi is clearly in some kind of a state. His eyes are red. He has
induced a similar state in his four listeners.

The first daastaan of Sur Moomal–Rano ends with a waai
which poses this evocative question as the refrain: *Kak halbo
kadhe? When will you head to Kak?* How much more time before
you go there? None who goes there ever returns. So, tell me, when
will you go there? It is a call from Karim, the almighty power. When
will you heed this call?

This is the dramatic and compelling set-up, the first act, of the
legend of Moomal and Rano. Latif has shaped it almost like a play.
Readers (or listeners) are drawn into the mystery of Moomal (and
the yogi), as is Rano, who is one of the four men listening with rapt
attention to the yogi.

The second daastaan begins with the four men urging the yogi
to give them a fuller description of Moomal, Kak and Ludano. Why
does he weep tears of blood like this? The yogi responds to the
seekers' curiosity.

Moomal's eyes are fierce tongs
In a single glance
They capture all men

Would-be lovers arrive . . .
Whoever comes is cut down!

Moomal is revealed as a killer who has slain millions of men. Kak
Mahal is a veritable minefield of deathly traps. The banks of Kak
River are littered with graves, says the yogi. All kinds of 'high and

mighty' people have been struck down. But Moomal is democratic
in her destruction. Moomal's victims include princes, hunters,
scholars, saints, ascetics, nobles and plebeians, all. She spares
nobody.

> Kings, warriors, noblemen
> All are called to Kak
>
> Everyone goes
> None has ever returned
>
> All of them rode
> With great enthusiasm
> To their doom

Thus the yogi creates a peculiar dilemma for his eager listeners. On
the one hand, the incredible beauty of Moomal (which in turn has
imbued *him* with such beauty, in spite of all his protestations of
being wrecked). On the other, the near-certainty of death.

> The yogi roused them
> And created a deathly difficulty
>
> The banks of Kak, he said
> Overflow with passion
>
> If you were to go there, seekers
> You would behold
> Mighty rivers of love

What should the men do? Should they step back and save themselves
and pretend that they never met this strange yogi? Just carry on
with their lives as before? Or should they answer his question which
keeps pounding in their ears insistently?
When will you head to Kak? How much more time?

Latif presents a dramatic resolution to this dilemma. It is abrupt, clear and decisive. There was never really any choice.

> Let's go, let's go
> Let's go to Kak!
>
> Where love overflows
> And consumes all else
>
> All can behold
> The beloved
>
> ~
>
> Let's go, let's go
> Let's go to Kak!
>
> Where love flourishes and grows
> There is neither day nor night
>
> All can behold
> The beloved
>
> ~
>
> Let's go, let's go
> Let's go to Kak!
>
> Where the big cauldron
> Has been set on boil
>
> That colour has dyed millions
> Like the red of the betel leaf

Once one has heard of Kak, one cannot resist going there. The decision is already made. One must plunge headlong, knowingly, to one's death. The four friends have their camels ready for the journey.

Latif now draws our attention to the camel who must make this journey. The camel is enticed to travel to Kak by the prospect of all kinds of fruits and flowers that it can feast on once it gets there, as well as sandalwood leaves. Ludano is a land full of delights. It may begin to become clear (as also in Sur Khambat) what Latif means by the 'camel'.

> Oh camel, you've been raised
> To make the journey

> Step carefully, says Latif
> On the slippery slopes of Ludano

> Your tussle is with Moomal
> Morning and evening
> Night and day

> Heed the advice of your master
> And you'll be able to pick
> The lotuses of Kak

The second daastaan ends with Rano alone making it to Kak, through the process of overcoming obstacles, determined to behold the beauty of Moomal.

The third act (or daastaan) begins with descriptions of the beauty of Moomal and her attendants (or sisters). The special quality of Moomal's beauty, according to Latif's description, is that it sets aflame the heart of whoever sets eyes on it. Moomal's lovers come from far and wide in search of her beauty.

It quickly becomes clear, however, that no ordinary lovers are meant here. By inference, Moomal's beauty too appears to stand for something more than just the beauty of a woman which entices a man. Latif calls these lovers *kaapdis*, that is, ascetics or yogis.

Those ascetics who blossomed
In the colours of Kak
That hue never leaves them

It's a bitter drink
Of joy and intoxication
Drunk by those mad ones

Those who seek Ludano
Fulfilment is experienced
Only by them

The colour of Kak holds fast. Latif is hinting at something other than earthly beauty. He then goes further and says that these ascetics cannot be detained even by Kak, that they go beyond and further in their quest, that what they seek is the ultimate knowledge and experience.

Kak could not hold the ascetics
Wealth meant nothing to them

Even princesses were left behind
Such was their state

The girls tried hard to woo them
But they migrated to another land

We forget for a moment that it is the story of Rano's quest for Moomal that we were in the middle of until, suddenly, Latif returns to it, turning the tables completely. Rano's quest is already complete. It is now Moomal who has been wounded by the arrow of Rano's love, and is in the throes of the pains of separation from him. There are descriptions of Rano's beauty now (instead of Moomal's) and how he is the best and finest among men. And, for the first time, Latif begins to speak in the voice of Moomal.

To understand this twist in the tale, we should now summarize
the folk legend of Moomal and Rano, which Latif has picked up
and evoked so dramatically. The legend comes down in several
versions, with slight variations in the different tellings.

Once there was a king called Nand (or Nind) Gujjar in Mirpur
Mathelo, Sindh. He had nine daughters, the eldest of whom was
Moomal, and the second eldest was Soomal. Moomal was renowned
for her beauty and Soomal was known for her cleverness. King
Nand had pleased a yogi with great powers, who told him about a
magical deer (or pig), one of whose teeth had the power to create a
path through water.

Nand hunts the deer down and finds the tooth. Pleased with his
new instrument, Nand thinks about hiding his royal treasure where
no one would look for it. He brings his entire treasure to the ocean,
parts the water with the power of the deer's tooth, and buries his
treasure there. Then he comes back to his palace, and gives the
tooth to his eldest daughter Moomal for safekeeping, thinking of
her as the most innocent among his daughters.

Meanwhile, there was another yogi who had spied on Nand
and who now knew where the royal treasure was hidden. One
day, when Nand was not around, this yogi approaches Moomal
pretending to be a sick man, and asks her for a cure. Moomal
promises him any help that is in her power and offers to call the
royal physician or to give him money. But the yogi insists that there
is only one cure for his illness, and that is the animal tooth that she
wears around her neck as a pendant. Moomal willingly takes off her
necklace and gives the yogi the tooth. The yogi quickly proceeds to
retrieve Nand's treasure from the sea.

Some time later, desiring to lay eyes on his treasure again, Nand
asks Moomal for the tooth. Moomal informs him of the yogi's
complaint and tells her father that she has given the tooth away.
Nand is infuriated at losing his treasure! He's almost about to kill
Moomal, when Soomal intervenes. She says that she has a plan to
recover all of Nand's lost wealth and asks her father to give her
some time. Nand agrees.

Moomal, Soomal and their seven sisters arrive in Ludano, Jaisalmer, in the Thar desert, on the banks of the river Kak. Soomal has a great palace constructed there, which comes to be called 'Kak Mahal' or Kak Palace.

Since fame of Moomal's beauty had spread far and wide, Soomal decides to leverage this to their end. She has it announced that whoever can penetrate the mysteries of Kak Mahal and reach the inner chamber of Moomal would be rewarded with her hand in marriage.

This palace is a honey trap for all potential suitors of Moomal. It has high walls and within them lovely, enchanting gardens, which draw the visitors in. There are labyrinths wherein it is possible to wander forever. There are many streams which appear to be deep, unsurpassable rivers. There are bridges over some of these streams which are flimsy and give way easily. There are ferocious tigers guarding the entrance to the palace and some suitors faint from the sight, though the tigers are not real. Inside the palace, if one is able to reach that far, there are divans in the entrance hall with false bottoms (all except one), so that one plunges into the jaws of a deep well as soon as one sits on a divan.

Many suitors come, laden with wealth, in order to pursue Moomal. They lose everything they come with, unable to penetrate to the inner chamber of Moomal, and sometimes they lose even their lives. Soomal is thus able to recover all of Nand's wealth that Moomal had inadvertently lost.

In another version, the simple explanation for the treachery of the Kak Mahal is that Moomal has it built because she wishes to find a worthy match, and wants to weed out all the fools, cowards and inepts. This version accords Moomal more agency.

At the same time, in Umarkot, there is a king called Hamir Soomro. He has three trusted ministers, one of whom is Rana Mendhro (or Mahendro), also known as Rano. In some versions, Rano is also Hamir Soomro's brother-in-law, by virtue of being married to his sister. Soomro and his three ministers hear of the beauty of Moomal and the challenge of Kak. All four of them set out to take up the challenge. Soomro and his two ministers, who try first, fail to reach the entrance of the palace and return without success. Then Rana makes his attempt.

In one famous incident, when confronted with a ferocious and seemingly impassable body of water, Rano does the betel-nut test. He takes a piece of betel nut and throws it over the illusory ocean. The nut simply bounces a few times and comes to a rest. Rano understands that this is merely glass and simply walks across what seemed impassable.

> The four friends came to Kak
> Rano alone threw the betel nut
>
> He entered Kak
> Where Moomal dwelt
>
> He passed Kak's lotuses
> And marched ahead

Rano forces one of Moomal's sisters or a maid, called Naatar, to help him navigate the labyrinths of the gardens. When Rano penetrates into the entrance hall, he refuses to sit on any of the divans that Moomal offers him. Instead, he persuades (or coerces) her to sit first. Moomal knows the single divan which is without a false bottom and sits on it. Rano then joins her and sits next to her.

In another version, the test for Rano is to pick out Moomal from among an array of nine beautiful women. He sees a bee buzzing over the head of Moomal and is able to identify her, having been informed by Naatar that Moomal bathes in the fragrant pools of Kak every day.

In short, Rano is able to pass every test and he becomes the worthy conqueror of Kak. He spends the night with Moomal, who accepts him as her partner. In the morning, Rano returns to Umarkot and to his companions.

Thereafter, every night, Rano makes the long journey between Umarkot and Ludano on his camel, arriving at Kak Mahal by night, spending the night with Moomal, and returning in the morning.

There are differing accounts as to how and why this happens. One version is that Hamir Soomro does not like his brother-in-law, Rano, consorting with another woman far away. So he imprisons him and keeps him at Umarkot. Rano manages to befriend and bribe his prison guards. And so he's able to slip away each night on his camel to meet Moomal, and returns before dawn to his prison.

In another version, Soomro asks to meet Rano's new bride, Moomal, but Rano is reluctant to have Moomal meet the king, fearing that she will be swayed by Soomro's position and his greater beauty (Rano is said to be cockeyed in this version). So Rano scares Soomro by saying that Moomal is a killer of kings, and that he must not meet her in the guise of a king. He brings Soomro to Ludano disguised as his servant but Moomal realizes that this is not a servant and Soomro's identity is revealed. Moomal is upset with Rano for not trusting her. And Soomro is furious with Rano for lying to him about Moomal. So Rano is imprisoned by Soomro when they return to Umarkot.

In either case, Rano has to make this long journey between Umarkot and Ludano each night to meet Moomal. The twist to the story comes here.

One night, Rano is delayed in getting to Kak Mahal. In one version, this is because Soomro sees the red soil of Kak on Rano's camel's feet and smells the fragrance of sandalwood leaves, which are found only in Kak, which the camel has been eating. And so Soomro has iron nails driven into the feet of the camel.

Whatever the reason, Rano is late in getting to Kak. Moomal is annoyed with him or perhaps simply lonely. She asks Soomal, her sister, to dress like a man, particularly like Rano, and to lie with her in bed. Soomal does so. The two sisters fall asleep in each other's arms while waiting for Rano. When Rano finally arrives, he sees Moomal lying in the arms of another 'man'. He is furious and draws his sword to kill the lovers, but then thinks the better of it.

He forgets, or deliberately leaves, his riding cane behind and rides back to Umarkot.

When Moomal wakes up in the morning, she sees Rano's riding cane and realizes her mistake. At once she sends an emissary to Rano in Umarkot explaining the entire situation. Rano refuses to believe her. He refuses to relent.

Some time later, Moomal comes to Umarkot, disguised as a merchant. She befriends Rano as a man and the two spend a lot of time together playing chess. One day the sleeve on her arm lifts inadvertently and Rano sees a mole on it which he recognizes as Moomal's. He exposes her and asks her to leave, ignoring her pleas to be forgiven and accepted.

Distraught, Moomal builds a pyre in front of Rano's palace, sets fire to it and jumps in. When Rano realizes what has happened, he regrets his harshness with Moomal, and he too jumps into the pyre, to be set aflame along with his beloved. And thus the two lovers are united in death, as in several other love legends.

The first thing to note here is that there is no outside agency which is the apparent cause of the lovers' separation (as in Punhu's brothers abducting him on his wedding night or Sohini's father forcibly marrying her off to Dam). The cause lies within. This trope is repeated in the Leela–Chanesar story. In an overt sense, Moomal is responsible for her own fate. And so, when the story flips, and Moomal longs for Rano, rather than Rano pressing on towards Moomal as in the first half of the story, a lot of the sentiment expressed by Latif is about recognizing one's own folly. It's also the more familiar ground for Latif of speaking in the woman's voice, voicing the pangs of longing (akin to Sasui, Sohini and all the other 'heroines').

Moomal was unable to wait. She was not patient enough. She used a substitute in asking Soomal to stand in for Rano (in Leela's case, the substitute is not even a human one). It speaks to how we are willing to make do with distractions and amusements and make-believe in the absence of the real thing. But the false cannot substitute for the real. When this is realized, the pain of one's own mistakes and errors hits home. This situation becomes an opportunity for Latif to reaffirm faith in and commitment to the truth (Rano), in the voice of Moomal.

> Don't be so distant, Rana
> Don't be upset
> Enough upsetness already!
>
> Relieve me of my flaws
> Do justice to my heart
>
> There is no parallel, says Latif
> To the beauty of the beloved
>
> Cover up my darkness
> And fill me with delight

What is interesting is that Latif keeps shifting the symbolism that he infuses into the story. Especially in the first part, it appears that Rano is the seeker (who is captivated by an account of Moomal's beauty) while Moomal is the sought-after beloved. We have seen in Kalyan and Yaman Kalyan (this is also the case in Sur Sorath), how the beloved is often described by Latif in terms of one who butchers, who takes lives, who demands heads. Moomal, here, is no different. She is described as having been the end of many a valiant seeker. She has swallowed up entire armies of men. The lure of Moomal is irresistible. No one who has pursued her has ever survived.

In a sense, then, Moomal represents the spiritual quest. While a 'person' undertakes this quest, there is no person left who can actually 'return'. ('When oneness is the bride, the groom is cut to pieces.') To pursue the path of oneness (or love or spirituality) is by definition to lose the very basis of 'personhood'. Will any 'seeker' actually return (and from where?), with a medal or degree certifying the completion of his or her quest?

While there is a brief reversal here of the trope that is much more common with Latif (the woman longing for her far-off beloved), yet, when he shows the man as the seeker and the woman as the beloved, there is a marked difference in the tone. Rano's quest is a very manly one—based on strength, skill and penetration. It is not the utter giving of oneself which Latif usually expresses in the voice of his women protagonists. Rano's is almost a conquest. And so, Latif manages to almost sidestep Rano and his mission and, instead, describes much more the yogis or fakirs who have annihilated themselves in their quest for Moomal.

There is no description of Rano melting with any mention or notion of surrender or love. This is an interesting and curious dichotomy. The yogis are able to be 'feminine' in the sense of being able to 'annihilate themselves'. Rano is never feminine in this way. He is in quest of Moomal. He attains her. There is no suggestion anywhere, even in Latif, that he is *in love with* Moomal.

Are there both 'male' and 'female' aspects to the spiritual quest? If so, why is Latif persistently and obsessively drawn to the 'female' one much more? Why does Latif seem much more at home expressing the spiritual quest in this voice, the woman's voice? Sohini's, Sasui's, Marui's, Leela's or Moomal's voice?

Sure enough, Latif turns to Moomal's voice very soon. Moomal *is* in love with Rano. And so this aspect of the legend, Moomal longing for Rano, takes up much more of the Sur than the other way round.

What the brief reversal does—the male seeker in quest of the divine represented by a female figure—for the oral folk traditions, sometimes steeped in orthodoxy, is also very interesting. In the field in Kutch, among all the oral scholars and lovers of Latif, we found a strange and curious insistence that Moomal represents *kabr*, or the grave. While—as we have already mentioned—in other Surs the figure of the butcher very much represents the guru or God, it is not allowed to be admitted at all here that Moomal may actually represent God.

Moomal's proclivity for destruction is read as the workings of death. The beyt in the Sur about the banks of Kak being littered with graves is read (specifically by Abdullah bhai) as referring to Moomal herself as the grave. There is also an apocryphal beyt attributed to Latif on his deathbed (referred to later in this chapter), where he speaks of encountering Moomal, and this is read as going to the grave (though it is also possible to read it as merging with the divine).

Moomal cannot be Allah because Allah is very much a male figure. Mehar can be Allah, Rano can represent the Beloved, Punhu can stand for the divine, but it is uncomfortable that Moomal represents the One. She is better off being cast as death (woman has typically been held by patriarchy to be destructive for man anyway, ready to swallow him up or unhinge him, from the time of the Vedas when seductive apsaras were being sent regularly to disturb the meditations of sages). It doesn't help of course that Latif switches metaphors quickly and with ease, without bothering about difficulty of interpretations for others. So Latif also uses Moomal and her sisters to represent lures which the yogis transcend. Besides, the latter part of the Sur has Moomal as very much the seeker and Rano as the beloved.

But it is possible to read Moomal in the early part of the Sur as the fierce aspect of God. Only a valiant one like Rano can reach her. It is not a station meant for cowards or half-hearted ones. Descriptions of Kak, laden with walnuts and grapes and gardens and sandalwood trees, are also reminiscent of Paradise. The yogi is a figure who has been wounded by God. That's why there is radiance on his face and he is able to captivate the four men. The yogi represents the guru or the murshid who points to the experience of the divine. Moomal is the Unattainable One, who demands lives as the price to reach her. To see Moomal is the lot of a true Rajput prince. All this speaks resonantly of the seeker as a warrior and the sought as the awe-inspiring divinity.

However, as soon as Moomal herself appears (from the third daastaan onwards), she loses this faraway quality (even though her beauty is described) and she becomes quite human, or at most a houri of Paradise whom the yogis are able to ignore on their way to God. Now Kak itself becomes the potent symbol of divinity, one which colours the yogis irretrievably. As the Sur proceeds, Rano morphs into the beloved, and Moomal into the seeker.

> Moomal had shot many
> With her arrows
>
> Now she herself is struck
> In the head
> With the arrow of Rano's love

Moomal acknowledges Rana as her true beloved, the only one who could show her the truth. When Rano finds Moomal in the arms of another, he does not utter a word. He leaves in silence. But his riding cane, left behind, becomes a potent symbol of her error for Moomal.

> I heard your reproach
> And lost myself
>
> Millions came to Kak
> With their treasures and wares
> Only Rana removed my doubts
>
> Kak has no meaning for me
> Come back quickly, my love!

Kak, the symbol of pleasure, allurements and enticements, is metaphorically laid to waste. All the fragrances, fruits, flowers and perfumes of Kak, all its wealth, is no longer meaningful for Moomal. Kak is now a trap for the one who made it as a trap for others. Kak becomes a figure for the world and all its blandishments, which lose flavour at some point..

> Kak is scorched, trees are burnt
> All manner of pleasure
> Is reduced to cinders

Since you left, oh beloved
My heart is rocked by wave
After wave of longing

Come quickly now
To fulfil all the promises
You made to me

In typically strong words and images, Latif describes the experience of feeling wrecked when once you have had a taste of the divine, but you lose that contact through your own naïveté or folly.

Friends, Rana has laid waste
To my heart
He has made it a desert

My insides have been blown
To bits

I feel my heart is no longer
Inside my chest

~

Friends, Rana has laid waste
To my heart
My life is a ruin

He has hacked and chopped
My mind into pieces
My whole body trembles

I feel my heart is no longer
Inside my chest

For the seeker, who has been shaken out of her stupor, things are no longer how they were. Everything is changed. Former satisfactions become meaningless. It is not as if Moomal cannot once again ask Soomal to dress as a man and lie next to her. Or that she cannot get another man. But that is no longer enough. Now only Rano will do.

In a moment typical of Latif, the longing itself becomes the fulfilment. Slowly, but surely, Moomal begins to feel the presence of Rano inside her. Clouds of grace begin to appear in Moomal's barren heart.

> I was stark naked
> The Beloved covered me up
>
> He clad me with his name
> And transformed me into a cloud
> Of blessing over Kak

The Beloved is Sattar (one of the names of Allah), which means One who veils all sins. To cover or to veil all one's mistakes or sins is in effect to efface them. No error is etched in stone. Allah is held to be All-Forgiving, Infinitely Merciful. With enough realization, penance and purification, Allah himself undertakes to efface one's mistakes.

We remember now the camel that Rano had prepared to set off in his quest for Moomal. That camel is now with Moomal, since she has become the seeker. Moomal prepares her camel, ready to set out for Rano. But when she discovers Rano within, in which direction can she go?

> Which way should I turn my camel?
> There is radiance on all sides!
>
> Within lie the gardens of Kak
> Within lies Ludano
>
> There is Rano
> Just Rano
> Nothing else

But let us return to and celebrate equally the idea of Moomal as the divine. Moomal as the one who pulls true seekers in and presents them with the ultimate reward, which is personal death. In a beyt from the oral traditions, attributed to Latif as he lay on his deathbed, Moomal represents the ultimate station, which Latif, the seeker, has sought, known and tasted. (In local lore, it is claimed that the last two lines of this verse were spoken by Latif from beyond the grave . . .)

I've packed up my bed,
says Latif

I've set it down
By the banks of Kak

I've left everything behind
And merged into Moomal

I've solved the riddle
And now am at ease

9

If You Want To Be a Yogi

Sur Ramkali

Forget what is past
Begin right away
Die today, yogi
Tomorrow's too late

Although Ramkali is not one of the so-called seven heroines of Shah Latif's verse, the details of her legend come to us through Abdullah bhai, and his fluency in oral wisdom and its traditions. Ramkali was a Sindhi princess, who as a young girl wanted to learn *tilism*—magic. Her father, the king, summoned his courtiers. They informed him that the only people who could teach the princess magic were the yogis who belonged to the Nath Panth. The Nath Panthis worship Shiva and belong to the spiritual lineage of Gorakh Nath and his guru Matsyendra Nath.

The yogis were invited to the king's palace and asked to teach the young princess magic. They pitched camp on the palace grounds, lighting up their *dhoonis* or logfires, symbolic of a fire they keep burning within. The young princess eagerly ran to them each morning to learn their secret arts. However, she got a lot more than she bargained for, and so eventually did the king. More than magic tricks, the yogis gave Ramkali a powerful glimpse into their spiritual practice and philosophy.

They fill their warehouses
With hunger

The yogis care not for food
They guzzle down thirst

~

Where there is no sky, nor earth
No light of moon, nor trace of sun
There the yogis congregate in hordes

Duality cast aside
They meet the lord in nothingness

~

No cloak, nor loincloth
Their huts abandoned
And empty
They encounter the lord

Ramkali was struck, enraptured. She couldn't get enough of being with the yogis. However, one day the princess woke up to find that the yogis had disappeared from the palace grounds, their smouldering dhoonis the only sign left of them. She was devastated. But didn't Ramkali know that these yogis are wandering seekers who never make any place their fixed abode?

They've merged the part
With the whole
They've built their abode
Beyond time and space
I can't live without them

A desolation spreads over the princess's heart. She longs to be with the yogis who showed her the vision of another world. And yet, she cannot do so while remaining a princess.

Their camp is forlorn
No music fills the dawn
Grief grips my heart
While they've moved on
I can't live without them

~

Tie me up in ropes
And take me along!
Their singis spilt out secrets
Plunging daggers in my heart
I can't live without them

Latif enters into the heart of Ramkali's dilemma: being in the throes of attachment towards those who have given up all attachment. She wants to cling to those who have let go of everything. He passionately urges Ramkali (and perhaps himself and all of us) to stop looking for yogis outside and to become herself that which she seeks.

If you want to be a yogi
Let go of all thirst
Become the slave of a slave

With the sword of patience
Your own identity slay
Then call yourself a yogi!

~

If you want to be a yogi
Kill your brother
Leave your wife
Make love to your mother

Rise up from your slumber
Then call yourself a seeker!

~

If you want to be a yogi
Cut off all ties

Hitch your heart to them
Who are unborn
And never will be born

Then, seeker, you will step
Into the field of love

Ramkali left her high palace and stepped into the field of love, reminiscent of another princess in another time who did the same thing—Meera Bai. She became a yogin and set out. Searching and wandering for many long years through forests and far countries for her true gurus, the yogis, Ramkali eventually died in the forest. Abdullah bhai says that this could have been her only destiny. She was wounded. The arrow of love had pierced her.

Ramkali's love wasn't the love of a specific person—like Sasui's for Punhu, or Sohini's for Mehar. More like Marui's love for her land and people, Ramkali's love was beyond the individual. She was in love with the yogis' way of being, with what they had shown her, with what she had learnt by being with them. This was the separation she was unable to bear.

They seek no one's company
Nor let anyone seek theirs
This is the way of the yogis
I can't live without them

~

> They played their singis
> And effaced themselves
> This is the way of the yogis
> I can't live without them

The ascetics don't have much, but what they do have is their music. They sing and they play the singi, a kind of wind instrument made out of shells. Latif, as we know, had a deep and powerful connection with music. For him, the yogis' singis are like the bells that draw Sohini to the other bank, the surando that inspires Rai Diach to give up his head, the pipes and flutes that the camel riders play—only, more powerful! He claims in a verse (quoted in Chapter 5) that even the dead awaken on listening to this music, that it can make corpses jump out of their graves. Perhaps the metaphoric indication here is that even those who are deeply unconscious can begin to become conscious on hearing this music.

> Their music rips off
> The shroud over my heart
> Their singis snared me
> I am disconsolate
> I can't live without them

But this requires a special kind of listening. We need to begin to move to a different tune from what we do now.

> Be the one who praises
> Don't seek to be praised
> It's a big disease
> To garner praises for oneself

> Those who flee the world
> Avoid all flattery
> And walk inconspicuously

~

If we fretted as much for God
As we do for food, money or fame
The path would be clear
All worries would disappear

Tuning into his inner ear, a very young Latif had also left his home in
a state of *vairaag* (non-attachment) and wandered with the yogis for
several years, travelling with them to many places including Narayansar,
Dwarka, Ganja, Lakhpat, Haro, Lamakan, Kabul and Hinglaj. Latif
imbibed their ways, followed their practices and spoke their language.
He ate what they ate and lived as they lived. And then, it is said, for
some unexplained reason, one day he was abruptly abandoned by the
yogis.[30] They left him sleeping. Latif's own life mirrors Ramkali's tale.

So when Latif yearns for the yogis' company in his poetry,
and longs for their way of being, it is an intense and personally
felt experience, not a theoretical idea. When he speaks about the
characteristics of a true yogi, it comes from the real experience of
having seen all kinds of them—true ones and fake ones, those still
far from the path and those who have arrived.

Their heads gather dust
Their hair turns grey
They've smoked their selves away

The yogis unite
With the guru within
They don't need to put on
Outer shows any more

~

Any old fool
Can get their ears pierced
You need to cut off your head!

Latif says, associate
With true yogis and seekers

'Allah brings light
To whomsoever he favours'

This path is for those
Who can renounce both worlds

~

Fine clothes on the outside
And rags within
They search like an ass

Finery within
And rags on the skin
Their search leads to God

Sur Ramkali, one of the longest chapters of the Risalo, is astounding for the ease with which it mixes its gods and religions. One destination for the wandering yogis was Hinglaj, a famous pilgrimage site in Balochistan, about 250 kilometres north of Karachi, which houses the deity called Hingula Devi, revered by Hindus as well as local Muslims who call her 'Nani' (grandmother). Not surprisingly, in Sur Ramkali, Latif freely fuses terminology and themes—Hindu and Muslim, yogic and Sufi. The supreme reality is referred to flowingly and interchangeably as Raam, Allah, Haq and Hari. These yogis are also *lahootis* and the guru is also the murshid (parallel terms from the Sufi vocabulary).

The yogis have wonderful ways
Neither afraid of hell
Nor hankering for heaven
Neither infidels, nor Muslims
A single prayer on their lips
'Make me your slave!'

~

The naked seekers of Shiva
Take delight in Dwarka

And head off to Hinglaj
To see the Goddess
Hazrat Ali leads them on!
I can't live without them

Orthodox Muslim critics tend to be defensive, almost apologetic, about Latif's passionate tributes to the yogis, and even try to explain away this phase of his life as 'youthful recklessness' before age and sobriety brought him firmly back into the fold of Islam. However, it seems to us that Latif slips spontaneously and deliberately between these vocabularies with the evident conviction that what looks like two is not two. The true yogi or Sufi (and the two are one) has gone beyond these divisions.

The yogis roasted their selves
Demolished identity

No sin, no virtue
Only tears of blood

And you stand there asking
Their caste?

~

The beloved's face
Is the mihrab[31]
All of creation a mosque

No Qur'an
No right, no wrong

They've claimed a knowledge
That staggers the intellect

Say, to which direction
Should they bow and pray?

I'll Set Fire to the Pearls!

The Legend of Leela

I'll set fire to the pearls
Hurl the necklace into a pit!

Oh Leela, you beauty, says Latif,
How did you fall into complacency?

You know the King is proud
A powerful monarch

His majesty extends
As far as the eye can see

That master, the apple of your eye
You traded him for some pearls!

Leela's tale comes to us from the late thirteenth century. Leela is the wife and chief queen of Soomro Chanesar Dasra, king of Thatta district in Sindh. Chanesar is a man renowned for his strength and beauty. Kunru, the princess of Lakhpat, a neighbouring kingdom, desires Chanesar as her husband. She sends a plea of marriage through one of Chanesar's ministers, Jakhro. However, Chanesar is in love with Leela and rejects Kunru's plea. Kunru then vows to attain Chanesar as her husband and, along with her mother, hatches a new plan.

Kunru and her mother disguise themselves as servants and enter into the service of Leela as maids in waiting. Soon, Kunru becomes Leela's favourite attendant. Kunru figures out that Leela is a beautiful woman with a good heart, but that she also has a great weakness for jewellery. One day, when Chanesar is away, Kunru displays to Leela a dazzling necklace of priceless pearls, and reveals her own identity. Leela is infatuated with the necklace and wants to possess it. Kunru says that she can have it, provided she can pay the price. She asks to spend just one night with Chanesar in return for the necklace. Lured by the necklace, suppressing any misgivings, Leela agrees.

One night, Chanesar comes to his bed in an intoxicated state. Seizing the opportunity, Leela sends Kunru to her bed to lie with Chanesar. Kunru spends the night with Chanesar, who does not realize that he's making love to another woman. When he discovers Kunru in bed with him in the morning instead of Leela, he's flabbergasted. Kunru explains the bargain to him. Chanesar is disgusted with Leela and banishes her from the kingdom. He takes Kunru instead as his chief queen.

Leela's entreaties, her regret and repentance have no effect on Chanesar. She is publicly humiliated and forced to leave the kingdom. Leela returns to her parents' home and starts living there.

Some time later, Jakhro, the king's minister, who is betrothed to a girl from Leela's village, is refused the girl in marriage. The girl happens to be Leela's cousin. The family pressures Jakhro to do something to redress Leela's situation. Jakhro undertakes to bring Chanesar to the village and effect a reconciliation between him and Leela.

As part of his wedding ceremonies, Jakhro invites Chanesar to the village. The king watches a row of women dancing in celebration. He is particularly struck by one woman. He asks her to remove her veil. When the veil is removed, he sees that it is his erstwhile beloved wife. Shocked, he collapses and dies on the spot. Leela rushes to his side, and she too dies upon realizing that Chanesar is dead. The lovers are reunited, as always, in death.

It is interesting to note that the women are the active agents in this tale. Kunru is the one who plots to snatch Chanesar as her husband. Leela is the one who barters him away. The tale is intriguing also because it involves this fantastic bargain—a pearl necklace for the husband's bed (for a night). This bargain reminds us of Faust who bartered his soul for worldly power, success and wealth.

This necklace becomes the pivot around which most of Latif's poetry turns in the Sur.

> The sorcery of the pearls
> Consumed me completely
>
> I thought they'd be mine
> Forever
> Kunru outwitted me

The necklace becomes a symbol for the lures of the world. Latif keeps switching between speaking in Leela's voice, regretting her action, and speaking in his own voice, addressing Leela in the second person, pointing out her error to her.

> Those pearls were not real, Leela!
> The necklace was a trap
>
> Real gems lie further
> These ones are all fake!
>
> This falseness has misled many
> And caused them
> Estrangement
>
> ~
>
> What you thought was a string of pearls
> Turned out to be a noose of sorrows

> Chanesar has cast you out
> Embraced the servant girl instead

> Oh, how can one bear such discord
> With the beloved?

Soon it becomes clear that, in Latif's reading, Leela's primary error is pride. She was sure of her hold on Chanesar. She believed she was too clever and beautiful for anything adverse to happen to her. She did not even conceive that she could be abandoned.

> The glamour of the gem
> Gave rise to arrogance

> You quibbled with Chanesar
> And caused this rift

> The page has been turned
> Estrangement
> Your punishment

> ~

> The glamour of the gem
> Made you arrogant

> This ass called arrogance
> Has ruined millions

> Chanesar has turned away
> Estrangement
> Your punishment

The necklace comes to stand for all the attractions of the world, for which we keep bartering away our soul, a Faustian bargain which is perhaps made every moment. The German folk legend of

Faust, or Faustus, is haunting in its evocations here. Faust makes a famous deal with the devil—to barter his soul in return for all the knowledge, power and gratifications of the world. This legend is invoked each time we compromise integrity for the sake of gaining power or gratification.

Leela is Everyman and Everywoman, in that sense, the quintessential human who is misled by her self-confidence, who throws away what is real and valuable for the charms of the world. Chanesar is the ultimate beloved, the one who knows the inner truth of every person, behind the outer appearance.

> You were so intelligent!
> But you misjudged your husband
>
> Did you think a necklace
> Would make you more alluring?
>
> Put on a thousand ornamentations
> Yet the Friend despises falseness
>
> He tests the worth of your heart
> Like a jeweller examines diamonds

It is clear that the necklace represents outer beauty, outer show, which is meant for others. Leela realizes this herself. It is brought home to her, very painfully, that the beloved does not appreciate false beauty, that he can see through it. It is possible to fool the world with appearances. But the beloved has other requirements.

Latif communicates this simple truth beautifully.

> No adornment on the arms
> No necklace round the neck
> No doing up of hair

No lining of the eyes
No making up of cheeks
No reddening of lips

When I was as plain as plain can be
The beloved accepted me completely

~

Gold bangles and bracelets
Shining red necklace
Oiled and perfumed hair

Ah, the cruel irony
Now he pays no attention to me

This truth, of course, is simple. But it is very hard to follow as long as one is invested in the world's values, which place emphasis on the facade. Leela realizes that her position as 'chief queen', as the favourite 'wife', as an incredibly beautiful and intelligent woman, all contributed to her downfall.

Why are some wives
Abandoned by their husbands?

Pride alienates the Partner

~

Let me not be 'Wife'
Since it creates vanity

Better rejection and estrangement
Which will make him remember me

The story involves a neat reversal. The one who was servant becomes queen. The one who was queen loses everything. It is instructive that as the woman who was a princess but who consented to be a 'servant', Kunru gains the ultimate prize. Latif, both in his own voice, and in Leela's, keeps referring to Kunru as the 'servant' or 'maid', in spite of the fact that she is actually princess of Lakhpat and later becomes Chanesar's queen.

> I thought sharing his bed
> Was enough to please him

> He works differently
> A servant is more dear to him

Even while making all the points that Latif wishes to make through the tale, he respects the story's structure and also its humanness. Many poems pick up on Leela's particular situation, her leaving the palace in despair, or her womanly jealousy at another woman sharing her man's bed.

> My bed is now hers
> She sleeps with you
> Wrapped up in our sheets
> In the palace where we lived

> Chanesar, I did not expect
> Such harshness from you!

Latif, both in Leela's voice and in his own, cautions against pride and cleverness as the primary error. Because, in the end, only one who can be 'servant' will be close to him. One who indulges in individual pride will lose.[32]

> Smarter than all my friends
> Renowned for my cleverness
> Now I can't even
> Raise my head

~

Lord, let me not be clever!
Cleverness brings grief!
He was kind to me
Only in my simplicity

In front of Chanesar, one cannot argue for one's own virtues and minimize or justify one's errors. This is the Friend who sees into the heart. What then can be hidden from him? To the world it is possible to present a made-up front, acceptable and passing muster, all the cracks papered over and invisible. In the eyes of the world, one can be a 'good' or an admirable person. But in the eyes of one who already knows all our secrets?

Humility is the only way. Again and again, on the spiritual path, humility comes up as one of the primary qualities. Ownership is one of the ways in which we lose touch with this quality. The pride of possession. Leela wants to possess everything—both Chanesar and the necklace. She wants them to adorn her, rather than the other way round. In the end, she is deprived of both.

Don't argue with him, Leela
Don't show yourself off

The Friend belongs to no one
Neither to me nor to you

I have seen many favourites
Left weeping at his door

~

If you wish to please the beloved
Please him with your tears
Leela, let entreaties flow
This is the path of humility

The Friend is to be wooed with tears and entreaties rather than necklaces. Tears can appear like weakness. But, as Latif

says in another place, spirituality runs contrary to the world's
ways.

> All are married women
> All wear necklaces

> To meet the beloved
> They dress themselves up

> But he attends to those
> Who come to him with humility

Having come to a full realization of her folly, Leela becomes aware
of what a bad bargain she made. Instead of gaining both, she lost
both. The necklace symbolizes that which leads us to lose our
perspective of what is really valuable and true. The necklace that
she so desired becomes a hateful thing.

> There is a blot on my heart
> Strangling me slowly

> For Allah's sake, don't go!
> I'll burn that necklace in the fire
> In your very presence

There is a parallel with the case of Moomal. Both Moomal and
Leela exchange or replace the real thing (Rano or Chanesar)
with a substitute (Soomal or the necklace). Both are rejected and
abandoned by their beloveds. Only then do they 'wake up' to a
sense of their own folly. While Moomal's downfall was perhaps due
to impatience and compromise, Leela's is due to vanity and conceit.

As in the case of Moomal, we found a strange dissonance in the
way the Leela–Chanesar legend, as poetically rendered by Latif, is
sometimes interpreted in contemporary oral folk traditions. There
is an insistence on seeing Leela as Azazil or Satan. The basis for this

is the error of pride, which is also Satan's primary error. So Leela is conflated with Satan in a somewhat inelegant and distorted way. The poetry does not seem to support this reading at all. Latif is unfailingly sympathetic towards Leela. (Unlike some members of the oral tradition who seemed to come from a place of patriarchy, and very much reading Leela as a faithless woman, akin to a serpent!) Even when Latif berates Leela it is with more than a touch of wistfulness over her choice.

If anything, it is more reasonable to read Leela as Adam, as Yakoob Agha does in his *Ganj-e-Latif,* and Kunru as Satan. There are a few verses which are intriguing in this respect.

> Chanesar already knew
> The story and its end
> The necklace was just an excuse
> For what then happened

The 'fall' of Adam was already ordained and the 'apple' became an excuse. Latif says in another verse that Chanesar was already 'annoyed' with Leela, and he uses the necklace as a pretext to replace her with Kunru. All this can be mapped on to the story of Adam or of Satan. It is possible to zealously read the poetry in terms other than itself.

However, our impression is that Latif is not so fixed. He may imply something in one verse and then move on to another shade of meaning by the next (while scholars and readers lag behind). As we said before, the story is also just the story. Maybe Latif is simply saying that Chanesar was already aware of Leela's pride, just as God is said to know what is in our hearts (not the front that we put up for ourselves and the world).

As the Sur concludes, there arrives a whiff of redemption in the desert of desolation. Just as Chanesar comes to Leela's village in the legend, so also does the poetry evoke the spirit of reconciliation. In spite of a thousand errors in the past, the beloved still comes, every single day, to see if our houses have become a little clean.

All past actions, all karma, can be swept up and offered to the fire,
as sacrifice. We remember now the passion with which Leela hurls
the necklace into the fire.

> I'll set fire to the pearls
> Hurl the necklace into a pit!
>
> If you consent to relent
> I will consent to everything
>
> Only merging with you again
> Will relieve me of my taint

After all the cries of anguish, the Sur ends on a healing note of
atonement.

> Leela, rise up!
> Sweep your courtyard
> Be stricken not with grief
>
> Offer yourself and your ancestors
> In sacrifice to the beloved
>
> ~
>
> Leela, be stricken not with grief
> Get up and clean the house
> The beloved is at your doorstep!
>
> He has returned to the one
> Who is low
>
> He stands just outside
> Your courtyard

11

A Cawing Clamour Fills the World

Sur Karayal

Marui has vanished from Maleer
Nor is she in Umar's fort

There's no trace of Punhu in Kech
Nor any seeker left in Sindh

The magic palace is bereft of Moomal
No yogi meditates on Ganjo hill

Sohini leaves no chafing husband
To find her Mehar within

No saint is met, these days
In mausoleums or burial grounds

There are no murshids or wise men left
In the smoking charnel grounds

(Sur Marui)

~

The knowers of gems are gone
Says Latif

Where once master craftsmen
Carved and sparkled jewels
Today they hammer iron

(Sur Sri Raag)

~

Crows descend
A cawing clamour
Fills the world

Sensing the changing wind
They left

The swans flew away
To distant lands

(Sur Karayal)

Driving across the salty desert of Kutch, we stray into the region between Chhaari and Fulay villages and come upon a large shallow lake spreading across 80 square kilometers called the 'Chhaari Dhand' (salty wetland). During a good monsoon the place gets inundated with water which lasts throughout the year, becoming a haven to thousands of water-fowl.

Gazing upon this teeming aviary we see crows, owls, peacocks, cranes, herons and swans—feeding, nesting, squawking and chattering. Shah Latif must have gazed upon this very sight a few centuries ago and seen 'samsara', an overcrowded world of swarming humans, in the grip of their sorrows and ecstasies, unaware of their mortality or life purpose. What's more, he saw that the birds that bring grace and beauty to the pond, have long since flown.

This yearning nostalgia for a time gone by, for a whole generation of seekers that have gone, erupts in the voice of Latif in many Surs. But in Sur Karayal perhaps it finds its fullest expression.

Using the rich metaphors of birds in this short Sur, he weaves a poignant, wistful aura, of a deep sense of loss for a vanished era, a time when there were people to be found who had a stellar depth of seeking—the peacocks and the swans.

> No peacock survives
> No swan
>
> Owls flutter about
> Crowding their nests
>
> My world is overtaken
> By lying, thieving herons

These poems by Shah Latif, written at the beginning of the eighteenth century, curiously echo a contemporary angst, a sense of living in degraded times. Hearing them we wryly recognize the owls, crows and herons that overcrowd our shallow ponds. In Shah's world the herons symbolize an unconscious life, an indiscriminate consumptiveness, for they gobble up whatever comes in front of them—whether insect, frog or fish.

> To wallow in the shallow
> Is the way of herons
>
> In the perilous deep
> You will find the swan
>
> ~
>
> Her gaze piercing
> The swirling sea waters
> She stands still
>
> Scouring the depths
> She finds pearls to thrive on

The swans, on the other hand, don't grab at the shallow offerings of this world. Their awareness is watchful, alert, seeking another kind of nourishment—the pearls. And pearls can be found only by 'standing still' in the waters. This is a hint towards meditation, a quieting of the binary mind.[33] One cannot see one's own face in murky waters.

> Clear waters are now murky
> Muddied by the herons
> Swans stay away
> Embarrassed

> ~

> Fly back, O beauteous swan
> You are remembered
> Wistfully on this side

> Steer clear of hunters
> Rapaciously
> Plotting your end

Here Latif strikes an ominous tone, signalling the presence of hunters. Those beautiful swans that remain in our world are a threatened species, their presence precarious in our midst.

> In the lake, one swan
> Fifty hunters lurk on its banks

> The solitary one
> Rides the waves
> O Allah, with your grace

Who are these hunters that Shah Latif warns us about? In speculating on the answers to that question, let us go back to Shah's own historical time. And this time, for a change we shall not narrate a fable, a legend or a tale, but a well-recorded event from the political history of Sindh.[34]

~

The year was 1718 and Shah Latif was a young man of twenty-eight. By now he had already travelled far and wide with a broken heart, in the company of yogis and dervishes. The Mughal emperor ruling from Delhi at that time was Farrukhsiyar, a weak and irresolute king. The medieval capital of southern Sindh was Thatta, where the Kalhora Sindhi kings ruling from the north would have liked to extend their influence. It was a time of feudal oppression, in which landless peasants got sucked into a cruel vortex of debt, making them bonded labour for generation after generation.

Shah Latif had many mentors and friends whom he visited frequently and had a deep connection with—one of whom was Shah Inayat of Jhok.[35] At this time Shah Inayat had returned to his village of Miranpur near Jhok, after long years of seeking and travelling. He had been initiated by his murshid Abdul Malik Burhanpuri of Bijapur in the Deccan region of India into the Qadiri Sufi order.

But Shah Inayat didn't retreat into an inner world, unmindful of the desperation and harsh reality of peasants' lives around him. Rather, a century before the birth of Marx, here was a Sufi who began to invite the farmers to his lands for an experiment in collective farming.[36] Imagine a Sufi commune in the eighteenth century in southern Sindh, where along with a radical social philosophy, the seeds of mystic philosophy were sown in the hearts of the farmers, who started becoming fakirs and initiates. Shah Inayat was a vocal critic of landlords as well as the orthodox maulvis of the region. A confrontation began to escalate, between this revolutionary Sufi and his band of 'harees' (landless peasants) on the one hand and the feudal landlords and maulvis on the other. Shah Inayat coined the famous slogan, *Jo khede so khaaye! (Let the one who tills be the one who eats!)*, and farmers started flocking to him in thousands, relieved to be free of the clutches of their feudal landlords.

Unhinged by the growing influence and popularity of Shah Inayat's social experiment, clerics and landlords sent complaints to Delhi, and in a typically ill-advised move, Farrukhsiyar, the Mughal emperor, instructed the ruler of Sindh at that time—Yaar Mohammad Kalhora—to crush the uprising.

> The world's undependable
> A bogus game, a bitter taste
>
> Birds bustle on trees
> Chirping and chattering
>
> Don't they hear it coming
> The lash of the falcon?

Apart from the socio-political tensions underlying this conflict, there were clearly religious ones. Schimmel tells us that by now the lines were getting drawn in Sindh between Sufi fraternities with affinities to Hindu mysticism and the more orthodox Islamic orders gathering their ranks under the Naqshbandi restoration.[37] Needless to say, Shah Inayat was a potent symbol of the Sufi fraternities and he had disturbed the socio-political and religious status quo of the region.

An army gathered. Behind it was the clout of the Kalhora rulers, the governor of Thatta and the local landlords. They laid siege to the village of Jhok for several months. Bands of fakirs fought back valiantly, roaring with the cry of 'Allah!' as they were put to the sword. Finding it difficult to dislodge Shah Inayat from Jhok, the rulers invited him for peace talks to Thatta. To avoid further bloodshed, he agreed to go for a parley with the powers that be.

> Beware of the bird-catchers
> They swarm the shores

The decoy tricked you
You alighted
Where you shouldn't have

Even though his safe passage was personally vouchsafed by Yaar Mohammad Kalhora on a copy of the Qur'an, Shah Inayat was betrayed. He was declared a heretic and arrested.

Courtesy will vanish from this world
Close on its heels, decency
Dignity will disappear
And with it, humility
Trust between men will dissolve

The day swans sit in conference
With crows, says Sayyad
Nothing will remain

A few days later, on 7 January 1718, Shah Inayat was executed. Before being executed, he was cross-examined by the governor, and it is recorded that he responded to every question with a poem by Hafez Shirazi, the well-loved Persian mystic. In his last moments, Shah Inayat blessed his executioners with these words: *You have saved me from the fetters of being / May God grant you rewards in both worlds!*[38]

He soared into the sky
Crying, Allah is One!

Hurtling into the hurricane
Which tests all birds
The swan emerged
Unscathed

Apparently, when Shah Inayat was executed, several of his disciples sacrificed their lives alongside him, shouting 'La ilaaha illa'llah!'

This so rattled the rulers that immediately after Inayat's execution, they issued orders prohibiting the shouting of the name of 'Allah' and despatched a herald all over Thatta town crying out a warning to that effect.

Censorship however never fared well with poems, stories or songs. Repressed outrage and emotions flow through the fault lines of the collective unconscious, erupting in fables and lore, which lovingly grieve and dignify those who have passed—remarkably imaginative in the manner in which they capture the spirit of those whom they seek to commemorate.

According to one flamboyant and poignant legend, when Shah Inayat's severed head was sent to Delhi, it recited a stream of mystical verses all through the journey, till it arrived in the court of Farrukhsiyar. This poetry collection is titled 'Besar Nama', Ballad of the Headless.

A head cut off
And laid at the feet of the Friend
Is just as well
A heavy burden has been shed
And that's just as well

– Shah Inayat

This poem has survived as an iconic memory of Shah Inayat. Many years later, Shah Latif wove the first line of this famous poem into a beyt in Sur Sohini.

Watchful of the currents
Sohini grips her pot
And plunges in

'A head sacrificed
At the feet of the Friend
Is just as well'

This is the test of love
Union, the prize

Allah, may you take them across
Who keep trysts
In the dead of night

Many other Sufis of the land also wrote tributes to Shah Inayat. While the conservatives of Sindh rejoiced in his execution and reviled his memory, Shah Inayat passed into the hearts of millions of Sindhis as Shah Inayat Shaheed (martyr). The town of Jhok was destroyed. According to oral tales told in the regions of Sindh, about 25,000 fakirs were murdered in this devastating event and lie buried on Makli Hill, 250 kilometres north of Karachi.[39] Yaar Muhammad Kalhora was given several villages as a reward, and he consolidated his hold over southern Sindh. And thus ended a truly extraordinary experiment that brought together the spiritual and the political in amazing, unprecedented ways.

No doubt this event sent Shah Latif into deep mourning.

I searched the lake
I peered in vain
For my beloved Karayal

That flamboyant bird
Of swaying step
Did not return

So dear to my heart he was
The bird that has flown

Perhaps the 'Karayal' in this poem (Karayal means 'peacock') refers to the martyred Sufi? Many writers agree that Shah Latif composed several beyts as a covert tribute to Shah Inayat in Sur Ramkali,[40] but

it seems entirely plausible that many beyts of Sur Karayal too carry
a flavour of that pathos.

> An age ago, the lake turned dry
> Yet footprints glisten
> Of the swan who walked this way
>
> Can herons hope to emulate
> The gait of a swan?

~

From the oral traditions of Kutch we hear another tale, one that
resonates in elusive ways with this Sur and the story of Shah
Inayat . . .

Many centuries ago, in the regions surrounding the famous Kala
Dungar (Black Mountain) and later the hill of Chitraanu, roamed
a notorious bandit called Karayal. He was a large-hearted outlaw
who, along with his band of thieves, looted from the rich and shared
with the poor, a well-loved man who died a tragic death in a failed
heist. Trying to loot the treasure of the king of Dharagadh, Karayal
got stuck in a trap of quicksand skirting the king's fortress.

With his body mired in the quicksand, the bandit Karayal said
to his son, 'Cut off my head and run away! Take my head home and
hide it. The king's men shouldn't recognize my body, else they will
not let you or your mother live in peace.'

So the son brings home the head of his father, and giving it to
his mother Kapuri, he tells her not to utter a single cry, not even a
sigh of grief. The king's guards are out and about, looking for signs
of mourning in the village homes, to catch the culprit of the failed
robbery attempt. For many months, Kapuri bites her lip, unable to
mourn her beloved.

But then the rains arrive, and the clouds begin to thunder in
the sky and peacocks—the 'karayals'—begin to clamour, and that's
when Kapuri cannot hold back her tears. Neighbours ask her, why
do you weep, and she responds in the veiled words of poems . . .

I searched the lake
I peered in vain
For my beloved Karayal

That flamboyant bird
Of swaying step
Did not return

Perhaps Sur Karayal expresses the repressed grief of a woman, Kapuri, couching her tears in metaphors of birds, even as it echoes the repressed grief of the people and the Sufis of Sindh in a time of brutal political repression, mourning in guarded expressions the passing of a martyr, a stellar seeker, a swan who flew into the blue.

Perhaps this tale was a true story that happened during Shah Latif's time. It is also entirely possible that the tale itself could have been spun in the popular imagination, derived from the story of the martyred Shah Inayat Shaheed. For the parallels are unmistakeable. The Robin Hood–like spirit and compassion of the bandit and the Sufi; the traps laid by the Dharagadh and Kalhora kings; the severed heads, both carried away albeit to different destinations; the unexpressed anguish . . . Perhaps the Sufi revolutionary is the bandit Karayal is the 'peacock/swan' of Sur Karayal—metaphor for a valiant seeker who is no more.

Was it the flagrant political backlash faced by Shah Inayat that led to Shah Latif never being an outspoken critic of political regimes?[41] He was a 'simmering cauldron' by his own admission, and it would be in the voice of later Sufis such as Sachal Sarmast that the 'lid would be blown off'. These are Shah Latif's own words, when he met an eight-year-old Sachal, and had a prescient feeling about the explosive verse that the little boy would grow up to write.[42] Whether it was political caution or a deliberate ideological choice of restraint, Shah Latif speaks out in thinly veiled ways. In Sur Karayal he warns us about the need for vigilance, about the vulnerability of true seekers, the ever-present threat of bird-catchers and hunters. And what's more, he tells us how to make ourselves invulnerable to them.

> Why tarry on the shore?
> Why walk the path of hordes?
>
> Come into the garden of Oneness
> Dive into the soul of Shariat
> Walk the way of Haqiqat
> In the company of swans
>
> With the murshid's words as your guide
> Cleanse your heart
> Let go of the self
>
> When 'you' disappear
> Who will the hunter grasp?[43]

In a Sur suffused with outward lamentation of changing times, hunters and bird-catchers, there come some intimations for searching within. As a true Sufi whose gaze is cast fiercely outwards *and* inwards, Shah ends with a beyt that gives us pause, that turns the definition of the hunter on its head.

> The bird and the cage are one
> One, the lake and the swan
>
> When I looked within
> I saw the one who causes pain
>
> That bird-catcher hunter
> Who roams
> My own being

12

The Moon in My Lap

The Legend of Noori

Water below
Flowering branches above
My beloved close to me

All my desires were met
Not a single one unfulfilled

~

Water below
Flowering branches above
Profusion all round

In the swirl of water
A hint of Tamachi

The northern wind blows gently
Water rocks the boat
The lake has become a cradle

The story of Noori is unique among the 'seven heroines' of Latif in that it does not end in a (seeming) tragedy. The lovers do not die together to be reunited in death. There is no tearing away of the beloved from the lover, and the subsequent throes of longing and pining.

Rather, this is a story of union, fulfilment, bliss and togetherness. It is curious, and not a little delightful, to come upon such a scenario in Latif, who is otherwise so given over to pangs of sorrow, grief and pain! It is instructive that the one virtue that enables all this, in Latif's words, is humility.

Humility is not the most fashionable trait going around these days. We are taught to compete, be forward and aggressive, claim what is rightfully ours, proclaim and display our strengths, and project ourselves endlessly in order to gain success in the world. And success is held to be the greatest virtue in the world, especially at a time when the means don't matter anymore.

Latif's attention is hardly on success in the world. But even in the non-worldly domain, these values can tend to replicate themselves. So-called 'spiritual people' can be quite full of themselves! Latif, on the other hand, is eager to sing the virtues of modesty and humility.

The Sufis often recommend abasement, self-effacement and even humiliation as tools on the spiritual path, as ways of making sure that one does not get ahead of oneself, or too full of oneself. In this context, humiliation and humility are often intimately related. Leela's story is an illustration of this. Such an emphasis on 'lowness' is not always easy to understand for the modern mind, but then Sufis have always run contrary to the ways of the world.[44]

A tale from the life of an early Sufi sheikh called Ibrahim Bin Adham can be offered as an illustration. Bin Adham was a king who renounced his kingdom and became a wandering ascetic. Once, after several years of meditation in the desert, he was on his way with his small retinue to Mecca. The Meccan elders all came out to welcome the well-known sheikh, of whom they had heard. Not liking any kind of publicity, Bin Adham went ahead of his retinue. Usually the servants would go ahead of the caravan. Bin Adham was dressed as a commoner. The elders asked this man, whom they did not recognize and presumed to be a servant, news of the sheikh. This man started raining curses upon Bin Adham, abusing him in every possible way. This enraged the Meccan elders who started beating him for abusing a Sufi sheikh, until Bin Adham's retinue arrived and informed them that they were beating the very man whom they had come out to welcome! This was Bin Adham's way of abasing himself, not believing in the 'honour' being accorded to him.

The story of Noori and Tamachi comes in great and colourful detail from the folk oral traditions, as we heard it from Abdullah bhai and Umar kaka. Noori is the daughter of a fisherman and woman who live in the region near Kinjhar lake in Sindh. The area was populated by 'low-caste' Mohani fisherfolk who earned their living by fishing in the lake.

In other versions, she is said to be an illegitimate royal child who was abandoned near Kinjhar lake. In this version, Noori is found and adopted by a fisher couple. When she grows up, she alone is 'fair' among all the 'dark' fisherwomen of the Mohanis. Popular tellings can tend to privilege such accounts, where the protagonists of folklore are always of royal or Brahminical descent, with fair skin or esoteric knowledge embedded in their genes! Even a low-caste Muslim weaver like Kabir has not managed to escape this fate!

As a young woman, Noori is struck by leprosy. Noori's father cannot get any man from the village to marry Noori in this condition. In despair, the father goes to a Sufi dervish and starts serving him. When the dervish is pleased with his service, he asks the fisherman what he wants. Noori's father narrates his difficulty with regard to his daughter's malady. The dervish advises him to fill water from a nearby pond and give it to Noori to drink. The fisherman does as he's told. This water has an incredible effect in that not only is Noori's leprosy cured, but her face begins to emanate such an incredible radiance that it becomes impossible for anyone to behold her steadily. (Noori comes from the word 'noor', which means radiance.)

The fame of Noori's newfound resplendence spreads rapidly through the village. Soon all the fishermen who had refused marriage with Noori earlier, ask for her hand in marriage. Noori's father rejects all the proposals, citing the suitors' earlier refusals.

Jam Tamachi Samo is a king in a part of Sindh in the fourteenth century, with his capital at Thatta city, close to Kinjhar lake.

News of Noori's beauty soon reaches Thatta, and Tamachi's ears. Tamachi becomes keen to set eyes on Noori. He organizes a hunting expedition as a pretext to head into the area around Kinjhar lake.

When the hunting party arrives at Kinjhar, Tamachi is unable to find a single woman who could be described as beautiful. Where is Noori? He's informed by the locals that Noori doesn't step out of her hut at all during the day. Her parents are old and infirm, so she catches fish from the lake herself, but only at night, when the entire village is asleep. Tamachi and his courtiers decide to pitch camp for the night near the lake.

As night deepens, Tamachi is unable to go to sleep. At a certain hour after midnight, he suddenly espies a brilliant explosion of light over the lake. Tamachi immediately calls his courtiers and local advisers and asks them for an explanation. They inform him that this is the brilliance of Noori. A whiff of wind must have blown away the veil from her face!

The oral traditions quote a beautiful beyt describing this moment.

Kinjhar looks aflame!

Where is this light coming from
At this hour of the night?

There is neither cloud, nor lightning
Nor the blaze of the sun

It was the veil lifting
Just a little from her face

The fisherwoman has climbed aboard
Her boat

Tamachi is now impatient to get a good look at Noori. He asks his ministers to arrange it by any means. In the morning, the king's ministers go into the village and command all the villagers to come and pay personal tributes to the king. The villagers begin to stream in one by one. All of them bring a gift, big or small, for the king.

Noori arrives, with a veil over her face. She brings a *pabodo*, a small lotus fruit, for the king. She lays it down near the king's feet and steps back humbly. Something in her demeanour strikes the king as different from everybody else.

'What is your name?' he asks her.

'Noori,' she responds.

The king later sends a message to Noori's father, asking for her hand in marriage. The proposal is accepted. Noori and Tamachi are married at the lake itself.

Tamachi prepares to take Noori back to Thatta with him. Noori protests. She says that she's a simple fisherwoman, not fit for a grand palace in a big city like Thatta. She says that the king has several queens, who are 'high-born' and belong to 'nobility', and that she would be an object of mockery for them. The king appreciates her dilemma. He says that since he could be there without any such difficulty, he would stay with her in Kinjhar for as long as she liked, until she was ready to go to Thatta with him.

Tamachi sets up court at Kinjhar and runs his administration from there! (In Latif's poetry, he's even found fishing among the fisherfolk.) When Tamachi's queens get to know that he has married a fisherwoman and set up house in Kinjhar, they are outraged. They arrive in a group to lodge a protest with the king or to win him back.

> All the queens dressed up nicely
> To woo Tamachi
>
> But behold their surprise
> He moves among fisherfolk
> With a net in his hands!

When Tamachi is confronted with his queens' protests, and the general murmur of disapproval from the aristocracy of Thatta, he sets up a public test for his queens. He announces that he will take one of his queens for a special ride in the royal carriage the next day. He asks all his queens to appear in front of him, and he would choose one from among them. All the queens embellish themselves with make-up, jewellery and fine clothing, and line up looking resplendent and elegant. Noori appears in the costume of a fisherwoman and stands humbly at the end of the line.

The king passes along the row of queens, looking at all the sophisticated and fashionable women, appreciating their beauty. But only when he arrives at Noori does he come to a stop. She presents him with a lotus fruit. He asks her to climb aboard the royal vehicle. Noori is thus the chosen one. (In Abdullah bhai's version, this 'test' takes place in Kinjhar, and only subsequently does Noori move to the palace in Thatta, once she has been officially chosen. In other versions, this trial takes place in Thatta itself.)

When they are on their ride together, the king asks Noori why she did not dress up for the occasion. Noori says that she did not want to forget who she was, where she came from, and the fact that she had been made queen in spite of being nothing.

This is the core feeling of Noori's story. In spite of becoming 'queen', she never loses her simplicity. This, for Latif, becomes the emotional core around which he builds his poetic narrative.

No trace of pride
Or vanity in her heart

Her eyes her only ornament
Yet she captured his heart

They all stood in front of the king
Her art alone was successful
In attracting him

~

Noori picked out a fresh lotus fruit
And presented it to Tamachi
In front of all the queens

Samo returned the gift with love
And raised her above
Everyone else

The baatin of this story, in Latif's universe, is not hard to decipher. The 'foul-smelling' ('Gandhari') fisherfolk represent the entire human race. They are described as low, wretched and repulsive. But there is one among them (Noori) who shines bright, and who 'redeems' the rest of her 'low' community with her own light. And the quality, paradoxically, which allows her to redeem the rest of her people, is her own essential humility, her powerful sense of her own 'lowness'.

The story of Noori and Tamachi is told in Sur Kamod in the Risalo. Latif describes in some detail the ways of the fisherfolk, their work and their instruments, bringing an intimacy of knowledge and a feeling of sympathy to their vocation. But he also insists on their smelliness and the filth in which they live. Attributing 'foulness' to the fisherfolk is a double-edged sword. The metaphor of the 'low-caste woman' and the 'high-born king', too, is problematic in its social and gender implications. It is easy to lose sight of the metaphor, and perhaps it is problematic enough to use it in the first place. Latif uses a gendered metaphor for the spiritual quest practically throughout his poetry (see the chapter on 'The Woman's Voice'). What is new here is the use of caste or social standing. This insistence of 'lowness', and on the humble woman seeker, can be jarring to our modern sensibilities.

There are enough beyts in this Sur, and in the Risalo as a whole, refuting the importance of caste in the spiritual quest ('high birth' can in fact be a hurdle).

Noori's humility is unparalleled
Samo fell in love with that

All those who were queens
Were left behind

But it requires a kind of 'double mind' to see Latif's use of current
social reality as metaphor, and at the same time his undercutting of
that social reality. Several beyts point out clearly that Latif is not
talking about fisherfolk at all, but about us—you, me and everybody
else. When he describes the fisherfolk and their work, he seems to
speak more literally. When he describes them as 'low' or 'foul', he
moves into metaphor and seems to refer to the human species itself.
And he can do this seamlessly, from one beyt to the next.

How is the whole human race 'foul smelling', how is everyone a
'Gandhari'? Abdullah bhai explains this entertainingly in this way.
He says that in Islamic mythology it is said that Allah has specially
deputed a particular angel for one specific job: When a man sits
down to crap, the angel whispers in his mind to look down.

The man squats on the ground to shit. Now the man knows what
has come out of his backside, still he looks at it! Why? So that he can
be reminded—look what you ate and look what has come out from
the other end. Anything of the world that a man consumes turns in
the end to shit. Abdullah bhai says that, literally and metaphorically,
there is always some shit and piss inside the human body.

Latif begins the Sur with the following verses. As usual, he
speaks in the woman's voice, addressing her beloved (Noori is
speaking to Tamachi).

You a great King, I a fisherwoman
The site of all imperfection

Your high queens
Look so elegant

Seeing them do not forget
This low smelly one

~

You a great King, I a fisherwoman
Full of grievous defects

Fish stains and scum
Stick fast to my dress

Seeing this do not neglect
This low smelly one

~

You a great King, I a fisherwoman
Full of a million flaws!

You know quite well
The state of my being

Seeing this do not forsake
This low smelly one

It might be easy to admire or like a Sohini or a Sasui, given their fiery and defiant natures. However, it is useful to recognize that humility is also agency. It is also a choice, a way of being, an act of will, perhaps the highest one in the spiritual sense.

Noori sees herself clearly. She does not pretend to be something she's not. She's aware of her own flaws. This prevents her from developing arrogance. The remarkable thing is that she does not become arrogant even after she's elevated to the station of a queen. This very humility is her strength. She does not rely on anything outside of herself.

Because Noori remains so keenly aware of her own shortcomings, she does not undergo a fate similar to Moomal or Leela, who have to suffer a 'fall' in order to see better sense. Noori's humility is contrasted with the pride of the 'noble queens' of Tamachi's court who are offended that a 'low-caste' one could be raised above them. Those who are low spiritually may think of themselves as 'high and mighty', based on birth or worldly position. This is probably a kind of veiled criticism of social hierarchies which emerge in religious or spiritual orders, such as descendants of the Prophet (Sayyads), or of Sufi saints, assuming a nobility that they have not themselves earned. Latif says clearly that the Friend is not interested in the social standing of the seeker.

> Cursed are these high-born
> Samo and Soomro queens
> Who carry themselves with airs

> Blessed are those born in Kinjhar
> Who humbly remember Tamachi
> In their hearts

> Among all queens the fisherwoman
> Was gifted the jewel
> In a single night

There is the hint of a secret communication (the exchange of the 'jewel') between Tamachi and Noori, which points to her representing the station of a saint or a prophet. Noori belongs to the world, to the human race, with all its flaws. She is a 'Gandhari'. And yet, the water from the dervish (guru) which cured her leprosy, has brought an ineffable light into her face and being. She stays in the world, yet she's not of it.

> Her hands among fish
> She does her work

> Yet she installed the king
> In her heart
> From the beginning

That's why he came
Himself
To reveal his secrets to her

A saint is said to be a benediction upon the entire world, on the whole human race, because his or her radiance brings peace to everybody and attracts many souls to the spiritual path. Latif even goes so far as to say that it was Noori who conferred a favour upon Tamachi, not the other way round.

Noori did a great favour to Tamachi
She climbed aboard his vehicle

From a low-born fisherwoman
She turned into a noble

All in Kinjhar celebrate this
What a great benediction it is

Noori confers a favour upon Tamachi in the sense that she becomes a bridge between him and her people. The human race is ignoble because it robs, steals, kills, exploits, lies, strives for power, and does not know how to love. Noori enables a 'redemption' for the rest of her community. This is expressed by Latif in terms of their taxes being forgiven by the king. In fact, in the story, the king confers the entire area of Kinjhar upon the fisherfolk, and remits all their taxes.

This is expressed both in a beyt and in a highly lyrical Waai by Latif. Kinjhar represents the entire world. The ripples of such an event spread far and wide.

You are a great King
Lord of the port

I'm a poor fisherwoman
Yet you are so close to me!

Relieve me and my people
Of our due taxes

~

Who will call her a fisherwoman
Who consorts with the King?

She has braided her hair
With the love of Samo

Those who wouldn't let her come near
Now bow down to her

She has braided her hair
With the love of Samo

Noori's charm has brought blessing
Upon the entire universe

She has braided her hair
With the love of Samo

The parallels with Prophet Muhammad are obvious and the baatin of the story is often interpreted specifically with reference to him. The Prophet was an orphan and not from a family of any importance. He was also well-known for his upright conduct and his humility. Yet he was chosen and raised to the station of a prophet. Latif may certainly be referring to the Prophet, especially when he mentions the redemption of the community. But it can also easily refer to any saint who becomes a beacon of light for the human race.

Latif hints at this otherworldliness of the saintly ones by flatly denying that Noori was actually a fisherwoman. (Here he speaks in metaphor.) In one sense, she both is and isn't. She's human and yet she's the Chosen One.

> She neither cuts nor sells
> Nor does she fill up baskets
>
> She gives no importance
> To the ways of the world
>
> She follows the ways
> Prevalent in Samo's house

> ~

> Hands, feet, conduct, appearance
> None betrayed her as a fisherwoman
>
> Like the central string of a surando
> She stood out from other queens
>
> She was queen in spirit since birth
> Samo recognized her
>
> He tied the red nuptial thread
> Round her slender wrist

Latif also comes to the part of the story where Tamachi and Noori spend time together on Kinjhar lake. The ecstasy of spiritual union ('haal'), experienced by prophets, saints and seekers, is described by Latif in extremely tender terms, as the union of two lovers who are out on the lake, in nature, together in a boat, passing endless hours absorbed in intoxicating proximity.

> Water below
> Flowering branches above
>
> Lotuses on the lake
> Fragrance in the air

Spring has finally come
To Kinjhar

~

I row the boat
He casts the net

Yesterday, the whole day
Was spent in the hunt

The coming of the king, Jam Tamachi, to the 'lowly' shores of Kinjhar lake is a cause of deep celebration. The king comes and the land is blessed. The king comes because the fisherfolk, in all their foul smelliness, have managed to produce a Noori. He leaves his queens behind.

As always, the lord favours the low. The oral traditions celebrate this grace in an exquisite beyt.

All the huts are abuzz
Jam Tamachi has come

Children are at play
At the shores of the lake

Talk of him and he was there
As if the moon had fallen into my lap!

13

Swallowed by the Vortex

Sur Ghatu and Sur Khambhat

The wise turn witless
Warriors begin to wilt
The vortex sucks
And they plummet
Powerless

All craft and expertise
Swept away

In the mid eighteenth century the present-day bustling metropolis of Karachi was a sleepy fishing village called Kolachi Jo Goth. It had been named after Mai Kolachi, the very first fisherwoman who had settled there. But the village was notorious in these parts for another reason. There was a whirlpool off its shores which was rumoured to be the home of a ferocious shark (or a whale or a crocodile, depending on which version of the story you chance upon), which lurked in the seawaters, ambushing many hapless sailors. This had struck terror in the hearts of fishermen, and was dubbed 'Kolachi jo Kun'.

Night has fallen
The oars are afloat
Empty turbans gather dew
The boat drifts

> No one comes back alive
> From the Kolachi vortex

About sixty kilometres from Kolachi, in the village of Son Miani
lived a fisherman named Obhayo who had seven sons. While six
of them were strong and able, the seventh and youngest, Moriro,
was a man of feeble strength. He generally stayed at home when his
brothers went fishing into the deep seas.

> Six brave ones set forth
> Their turbans proud
> And spears bright

> The sky darkened
> None returned

> Swallowed by the vortex
> Those magnificent men

We could say that danger lurks within our psyche. The
surface often conceals an underlying force—unedifying, self-
destructive—which arises from the depths of our subconscious
with frustrating regularity or, in calamitous moments, pulling us
under. Variously termed as the baser self, the ego, the mind or
the nafs, it is capable of spinning delusions in our perceptions of
ourselves and the world, dragging us into unwanted patterns of
thought and action.

> Inexorable
> The vortex grips like a vice
> Those who are caught
> Vanish

> No one comes back
> To speak of it

It is reported that the Prophet Muhammad once said after returning from a war that they had returned from the small struggle (jihad-e-asghar) to take on the big struggle (jihad-e-akbar). When his companions asked what the big struggle was, he replied, 'The struggle against the nafs.' A person who wages war against the baser self is a 'mujahid'. It is a deep and unfortunate irony that a 'mujahid' and its plural, the 'mujahideen', today are almost only understood as political fighters or as terrorists waging violent struggles in the outer world.

> The zeal to tackle the vortex
> Is what makes a true sailor!
> Till they kill the shark
> They do not rest

Meanwhile, we return to our story, to find such a 'true sailor'. The youngest brother, Moriro, was in deep mourning after the death of his six brothers.

> My feet drag on the shore
> Searching in the noon sun
> For those who did not return
>
> The anchors of my life
> Have sailed into the whirlpool

Though Moriro was of feeble health, he was gifted with intelligence and a resourceful spirit. He decided to avenge the loss of his brothers by trapping the shark.

To be a 'mujahid', to be able to outwit and subdue the ego, has been the central preoccupation of many spiritual traditions.

Moriro crafted an ingenious iron cage, covered with deadly spikes and fitted with long ropes. He himself sat in this cage and got his friends to lower him into the seawaters. Smelling the prey, the shark lunged for him, and its jaws were immediately impaled on the protruding spikes of the cage. Moriro tugged at the ropes as a signal to his friends, and two strong buffaloes began to pull the ropes out of the waters. Out came the cage, and along with it the dead shark. The bodies of the brothers were retrieved from its belly, and lie interred in a mountain graveyard two miles to the north of Karachi city. For many years, Moriro lived next to the tombs of his brothers as a caretaker.

It is clear that it requires not just brawn (conviction, enthusiasm and heroism) but also brains (awareness, technique, discernment and intelligence) to conquer the nafs. Perhaps we could say that it takes incredible 'mindfulness' to catch the 'mind' in its games.

> Hooking little fish in trifling ponds
> Won't prepare you for the shark!

> Gather your nets
> And make them strong

> You've been wading so far
> In shallow pools
> The great ocean
> Is yet ahead

Sur Ghatu is the shortest Sur in the Risalo and yet sharp in its impact. The word 'Ghatu' means 'ghaat karne waala', or 'one who strikes'. The term could be referring to the nafs, that shark or ego, the delusion that lies in wait, ready to ambush you when your gaze is not clear, when your consciousness not alert. However, it is generally understood to refer to the fisherman in Shah Latif's poetry, the hunter who strikes at his nafs.

> Questing for the shark
> They plunged in

> They faced the fathomless
> That deep unknown

Slaying the wily beast
They emerged
Jubilant

This is the true jihad—to face the fathomless, the unknown within our own selves. Getting to know the inner self begins with becoming alert about the nafs. In its basest form the nafs is termed as 'Nafs-e-Ammara' (the Inciting or Commanding Nafs) and it represents our instincts or appetites focused on the material or the carnal, which incite us towards grasping, lusting, consuming and hoarding, and which can pull the 'rooh' (soul) towards devastation in a spiritual sense (though materially one may flourish).

Yet the nafs is not only about carnal appetites, but also subtler appetites that are less obvious. Rumi says, 'The nafs has a rosary and a Qur'an in its right hand, and a scimitar and dagger in the sleeve.'[45] The needs of the nafs can drive us to insincerity and hypocrisy.

In his famous poem '*Maaya maha thhagini ham jaani*' (*Maaya's a great thug, I know . . . for priests she's an idol, for pilgrims a river*), Kabir shows the manner in which our egoic mind fixates on things that it wants. This craving subtly or grossly clouds our ability to see things clearly. So we are not only speaking here about lust and craving for material objects, but subtler fault lines in our psyche that crave attention, recognition, power, knowledge, that become our undoing.

To describe a person in the grip of a subtler form of nafs, Rumi uses the term '*khod-parast*' or 'one who worships the self'. He says that the idol of your self is the mother of all idols, and to regard it as easy to subdue is a mistake.[46]

The fishermen didn't return
They perished at sea

Oh sailors
Bear down on the shark
Attack decisively!

Where are your hooks?
Your nets?

The vortex foams
And gurgles ahead

It should be pointed out, though, in defence of the poor animal used as a negative metaphor, that the 'animal' instinct becomes 'base' only in a human being. This is because, unlike the animals themselves, human beings can devour the world, and still be hungry!

When twenty became twenty-five
And sixty became a thousand
The desire arose to get a million
When a million, trillion turned to a countless zillion
The desire arose to be lord of the earth

– Unknown Poet

This is the core instinct of the Nafs-e-Ammara, to never be sated, and keep driving us to grasp and consume in an unaware, unconsciously identified manner.

Living in the sandy desertscapes of Sindh, it is not surprising that the other animal Shah Latif chooses to represent the nafs is the 'camel' (a metaphor deployed in a similar vein before him by Rumi).[47] The beyts of Sur Khambhat move like the strokes of a brush, painting a moonlit desert canvas, in which the seeker is astride his camel, mocking or beseeching the moon overhead, while scolding and urging his camel on the path.

Night glows
On the desert sands
The path to my love is long
Don't slacken, O camel
Don't swerve

> Be unwavering
> Till you reach him

Unlike the shark, which needed to be hunted down and done away with, here there is a recognition that the animal is a necessity. The ego or nafs cannot be done away with. When sluggish and rebellious it can be your ruination, but when befriended, it can lead you to your goal.[48]

> Whisk me away
> To the home of my love
>
> I'll deck you with pearls
> And reins of silk
> I'll feed you sandalwood
>
> O camel, take me
> To my beloved tonight

This journey of taming the beast is a metaphor for '*tazkiyatun nafs*', the 'purification or cleansing of the ego-self'. It describes the movement of the nafs from its most primitive aspect—Nafs-e-Ammara—through distinct stages towards a progressive refinement. Commonly understood as the three stages of the nafs, a fuller delineation would consist of seven, but we will briefly outline four here.

When the nafs gets free of the mindless identification with its insecure and grasping instincts, conscience begins to awaken. It begins to struggle, repent, argue, criticize and cajole itself. This stage is called Nafs-e-Luwwama or the Self-Reproaching Nafs. The word 'luwwama' is derived from 'lom' which means 'to reproach'.

> O camel
> Shake off your stupor!
> Gallop on your way with speed

Bring me to my love
Just once

May the curse of a lover
Be on you
If you ignore my plea!

When our awareness becomes more aligned and subtle, we begin
to read signs, receive teachings from the phenomenal world, get
inspirations and insights. This is the Nafs-e-Malhama or the
Inspiring Nafs. The term 'malhama' is derived from 'elham'
(inspiration). The 'elham' or inspiration may appear anywhere, in
any moment, sometimes as lightning in the sky on a dark night, so
fleeting that we barely get a chance to apprehend the truth.

When lightning flashes
String your pearls, oh seeker
In the blink of an eye
Your world will be dark again

This is the voice of Ganga Sati, a woman saint–poet poet of Gujarat,
urging the progressing nafs, one could say, to 'act' upon the flash
of inspirations and insights that she has begun to receive. In the
imagery of Shah Latif the signs that call out to the camel, that
inspire it to shed its apathy, are of a different kind—sometimes a
taste, or even a visage . . .

Seeing the face of my love
The camel was transfixed

Now he's restless
In his shackles

~

The camel tasted
Something, somewhere

He is chafing
In his chains

We arrive eventually at the ideal stage of the ego, when the distractions caused by continual cravings come to a rest, one tastes the fruits of the path, a conviction develops, doubts and confusions disappear, and one moves decisively towards the Nafs-e-Mutmainnah, the Self at Peace or the Satisfied Nafs.

Flinging off nine fetters
The camel broke free at dawn
Breaking into a gallop
He set off on the road
To the beloved

This describes one simple arc in the poems of Sur Khambhat, in which Shah Latif outlines the journey of the camel-nafs from initial rebellion and resistance to eventually taking the path towards union with the beloved.[49]

Let us delve deeper by drawing on an image from another tradition.

From Tibetan Buddhism comes a powerful image describing the struggle with the self, and this time the animal metaphor is that of an elephant. There is an oral teaching beautifully explicated by Fernand Schwarz on a unique drawing based on an old Tibetan engraving.[50]

The engraving depicts the climbing of a path by a man and his elephant. The path turns five times, with each turn representing a conscious change in attitude on the part of the seeker. The man represents the seeker inside each of us, the consciousness that is struggling to evolve. He follows a black elephant swaggering on the path ahead of him, which represents the ego that we call mind, the temporal self, the personality. The elephant's black colour represents torpor and lethargy.

Having a heavy, lumbering animal as metaphor for something as intangible and quicksilver as the mind might seem like a curious choice, but it is significant. Schwarz says, 'The elephant leaves deep footprints in its wake, which are the actions and decisions, both good and bad, of the mind, which are deep and have many repercussions, *far more so than all the actions of the body or our speech*.' (Emphasis ours.) In other words, the karmic imprints of a recklessly uncontrolled mind are deep and significant.

Walking by the elephant-mind is a gesticulating monkey which represents distraction (literally the 'monkey-mind'). The walking man carries a sceptre or a hook, symbolizing attention. Attention is alert to the slightest distraction or loss of clarity and tackles it instantly. In his other hand the man holds a lasso, symbolizing memory. Memory is that faculty which follows the flitting thoughts and gently brings them back to the object of the mind's concentration.

At the start of the journey, the man is shown following the elephant, his tools of sceptre and lasso remain unused as the monkey clutches the elephant's trunk and steers it. But with each bend in the journey, the scenario begins to shift. The man draws closer to the elephant, he begins to wield his sceptre, he touches the elephant's head with the lasso, as the elephant-mind begins to turn white (a kind of 'purification'). Consciousness and the mind draw closer together. The seeker begins to lead the elephant, as he leads his thoughts instead of being led by them. The elephant follows without reins. At one point the seeker sits atop the elephant. The mind and the higher self are now linked. He has no more need for sceptre and lasso, as the tools become internalized. Finally the elephant-mind prostrates itself at the feet of its master, the inner being. The master commands and instructs, and the elephant listens.

By the side of the path is a beautiful fruit-bearing tree that represents all the things the seeker renounces, to embark on the path of stilling the mind (or one might say, purifying the nafs). These may be attachment to relationships and worldly objects, professional ambition, glory, social obligations and status, even knowledge and learning. All of these seem worth struggling for, as they hold the false lure of bringing fulfilment to our lives, but the seeker has learnt that quieting the mind is the only thing that will bring true stability.

Shah Latif strikes a similar note of caution about the distractive energies of 'worldly ties' in Sur Ghatu and Sur Khambhat when he says,

> Oh sailors!
> If you would conquer the shark
> Strengthen your strings
> Bolster your nets
> Cast away all worldly ties
> Then venture in
>
> ~
>
> The path is festooned
> With juicy vines
>
> Hold the camel close
> Always on a leash
>
> Tasting them
> He may go wild

In conversing with the evolving camel-nafs Shah Latif dwells extensively on this idea of 'taste', the gratification that our senses and mind crave. He distinguishes between different kinds of taste, bringing our awareness to the idea that we not only feed our body, but we also have the possibility of 'feeding' our soul, either giving it the nourishment it needs or depriving it.

The camel savours
No fragrant flowers
Or scented trees

Lusting after
Brackish brambles and weeds
He is gorging himself
And getting fat

~

I tie it near a tree
Laden with tender sweet buds

But when I'm not looking
The wretched animal
Still gobbles thistles and thorns

The ways of my camel
Perplex me

Slowly, the camel begins to transform his habits. When struck by love, he begins to lose interest in the usual gratifications of the world, begins to lose weight, begins to pine . . . Old tastes begin to give way to new ones.

The camel turns away
From the herd
And saline ferns

Now there's a turmoil
In his heart

~

Refusing to graze
Spitting out flowers
He crushes camphor underfoot

He's tasted sandalwood
My camel is full

This signals the 'spiritual transmutation of the senses', when we begin to tune into our *inner* senses. Then we start 'tasting' the fruits of practice, being nourished by them, 'touching' the teachings in our practice by altering our behaviour, 'hearing' and 'smelling' things on another level, and eventually 'seeing' things as they are.

The weight of the truth
Carry without a head

When truth calls out to you
Listen without ears

Behold your true beloved
As though unseeing

(Sur Khahodi)

When the rooh is fed on a different kind of 'taste', of the teaching, or the 'shabd' or the 'kalma', depending on which tradition you are referring to, its doors of perception open to a different kind of universe.

In a wondrous garden
Of priceless trees
Where two branches cost a million
And a leaf half a million
Chomping on a thick bunch
My camel feeds

The returns of cultivating an inner life are wondrous. Working day by day, moment by moment, with our fractious, unpredictable nafs, wooing it, quarrelling with it, cajoling it or pacifying it, in all cases

walking patiently with it on this long journey of life, we find at
some point perhaps that it has gradually transformed from being
our most embattled enemy into a precious ally, a prized friend.

One million, the camel's price
I'd pay ten times more

It's not a loser's bargain
To have this camel grace my home

~

One million, the camel's price
Pay ten million, it's still a steal
Do it now, says Latif
Strike the deal

This camel can take you
Where you most long to go

The very moment you
Saddle and mount
You find yourself cradled
In the beloved's arms

14

You Killed Me with a Glance

Sur Barvo Sindhi

Sometimes his doors
Are shut and bolted
Sometimes flung wide open

Sometimes I'm rebuffed
And turned away
Sometimes welcomed
And ushered in!

Sometimes
Not a single word
Sometimes
Countless intimate secrets

What can I say, my friends
That's just the way he is
My Friend

In this impassioned and short Sur, there are no middlewomen to broker the conversation. No Sasuis or Sohinis or Maruis or Moomals, and Latif has shed the tone of being their friend, guide and historian. He valorizes no khahodis, yearns for no yogis. He doesn't couch his laments in metaphors of herons and swans. He doesn't even speak to us, his readers, urging or cautioning us on

the journey of our lives as sailors, cotton spinners or musicians . . .
Here, it seems, Shah Latif speaks simply in his own voice (albeit a
woman's) and directly to his Friend.

> You did what you did
> And that's just as well, my love
> Though it was hardly kind to me

> You stole my heart
> Then slipped away

> Even if you're indifferent
> Did you have to be so hard on me?

> ~

> Won't you come, just once!
> I'll spread my lashes
> Like a carpet under your feet
> My tresses will cushion your bed
> I'll serve you forever

> ~

> Today again
> I'm blasted to pieces
> By my love

> This longing batters me
> Like a club smashing corn

How are we to 'read' these poems, and indeed all the poems of the
Risalo that strike this chord of feeling? Evidently they are 'utterances'
in an extraordinary 'state' of being, and for them to truly work on
our spirit, they must be received as such, in a commensurate 'state'
of longing. Perhaps the poems (especially when sung) are meant to
spark the longing latent within each of us. In one place Latif says,
about his own poems:

What you think are 'poems'
Are inklings from the unknown[51]
These words nudge me nearer
To my Friend

(Sur Sohini)

Evidently for Latif, the practice of his poetry—composing, expressing, singing—is a device to create intimacy with the Friend, it is an enactment or re-enactment of coming closer to that experience.

Control slips away
Reins not in my hands
But his

A mountain
Struck my chest!

He came as in a dream
And left me delirious
Says Latif

~

The desert heat blazes white hot. Quite magically we sit rather cool and ventilated, as a gentle breeze flows through the tall reed grass walls of a hut on stilts in the Jat village of Asari Vaandh. Umar kaka warms to another tale. This one originates from the region of Yemen, and we hear it with mixed feelings of wonder and revulsion. For it is a tale so visceral, that it is almost difficult to digest.

However, Umar Kaka feels that this love story may have an inner resonance, an implicit even if tenuous connection with the impassioned love poems of Sur Barvo Sindhi. And so we listen, and as we do, we allow our intuitions to take flight. As in a whimsical reverie, the poems of Sur Sindhi Barvo begin to weave themselves into this astonishing tale.

There was once a shehzadi, a princess, whose name was Shireen. She lived in purdah, secluded on the top floor of her palace. One day in a slightly distracted way she happened to spit out of her window, and was immediately horrified to see her spit land near the feet of a passing fakir. He looked up, saw her face looking down at him, and was transfixed. The tryst that was written into the destinies of these two people was sparked in that inadvertent moment, in a glance.

> The way a blacksmith forges
> A link into the chain
> My heart was interlocked
> With my love

She made a gentle gesture of apology to him. He dug his walking staff into the earth and sat down, looking up at the palace window, expectantly. Worried that she may have upset the fakir, Shireen glanced furtively down from the window once again.

> You have seen me
> Now don't look away, my love
> Having looked away
> Won't you look this way again?

> Eyes are meant to look
> Let them do what they do best!

> Gaze upon me
> With my countless flaws
> As I see you
> In your blameless beauty
> O Friend

In the gaze between lovers is the experience of being fully 'seen', with all the goodness we possess, but also with our flaws, our vulnerability met with a gentle gaze. If the beloved is our innermost self, this surrender is also in a sense a surrender *to* oneself, an embrace *of* oneself.

Oh beloved, come back!
A heart-to-heart
A meeting of the souls
Is what I long for

My faults forgiven
I'll be nakedly true
Come!
Let this long separation end

Shireen sent her servant girl to him, asking for forgiveness for her rude and thoughtless act, and offering him a few alms as a conciliatory gesture. But to their surprise, the fakir turned them down, saying he was now resolved to sit there unmoving, in a vigil for his love.

Oh beloved, my heart
Longs for you

Bring out your knife
Cut into my flesh
Don't worry about etiquette

One direct glance
From you
Would be mercy

The next day the servant went out to the market to buy mutton for the princess, only to discover that it wasn't available. The fakir intercepted her. He took a knife and chopped off pieces of flesh from various parts of his body, and convinced the girl to take them instead, making her promise not to reveal to the shehzadi the source of the meat. The meat was cooked. The shehzadi tasted the dish and liked it immensely. The servant girl could not resist and revealed the secret of the meat.

You called me
And killed me with a glance

You sliced me up
Farmed out my flesh
Leaving only bone
And then said—
Be calm

Slaying this poor wretch
Already so dead
You smiled

The shehzadi was stunned. Something shifted inside her. I cannot turn away from this, she thought. The 'baazigar'—that great trickster gambler—has dealt me this hand of cards, and now I must play the game. She looked down from the window again, and this time, with an altered gaze.

Sometimes near, but distant
Sometimes far, yet so very close
Beloved

Sometimes you elude my heart
Sometimes you just will not
Be erased

Like the curved horns of a bull
You are entangled
With me

Shehzadi Shireen declared to her parents that her fate was now tied to the fakir. Meanwhile, the fakir's body was festering with the wounds he had caused himself. He was in a critical state, and yet he remained unmoving, his gaze transfixed.

Separation
Makes deep gashes
In my flesh

I languish
Cast off, disowned

O lord
Bring me up close
To my faraway love

The shehzadi asked her parents to construct a special shrine with a small door and no windows, buried beneath the earth. In this she and the fakir sat facing each other. She then instructed her protesting parents to seal the door. She was adamant and equanimous. Her mind was made up. The fakir sat facing her. The door was sealed.

Crashing, crumbling
Dissolving, disappearing
The world scatters
In a moment

Your dear ones' feet
Stomp the earth
Over your head

In all moments we carry
A spade and a string
To dig and measure out
Our graves

Death, a mundane and ordinary destiny for millions, becomes an extraordinary event in the lives of just a few legendary lovers, and long after they are gone their stories keep being told and retold in myriad tongues.

It is rumoured in the lore that surrounds this legend that when, many centuries later, a Khalifa got the mazaar opened they found their bodies in exactly the same position as they had been in, when entombed.

'Duniya mein jo bhi aashik hone ka daava karte hain, vo Barvo fakir se seekh lein!' says Umar kaka, finishing the story. In other words, 'Those who lay claim to being great lovers in this world, should learn the art of love from Barvo fakir!' (and, we add mentally, Shehzadi Shireen!). For that is what the fakir's name was: Barvo (with means 'true' or 'good').

> True love
> Has vanished from this world
> 'Lovers' devour each other's flesh
> These days!
>
> What is real
> Is the fragrance, my friend
> Nothing else will stay
>
> Save a true few
> Most people are given
> To charades

While listening to the tale, apart from the images of butchery (common to many other tales and poems of Shah Latif) the other striking image that comes up repeatedly is the *gaze*, this almost unquenchable thirst in Barvo fakir's eyes, who keeps his eyes fixed at his beloved's window. When he is near death, he is asked what his last wish is. He says, simply, 'To *gaze* upon my beloved.' In a sense it is that very gaze that is subsequently enshrined and, as legend has it, remains unbroken to this day. Two lovers, buried alive, looking at each other.

'Enough! Now have some tea!' says Asibai, Umar kaka's wife, exasperatedly. The tea is laced with salty camel milk, and we have learnt over several visits that Asibai's earthy pragmatism is the perfect foil for Umar kaka's philosophic ramblings, of which she is always decidedly amused and a tad impatient.

The tea is drunk and we say goodbye and leave. But even as we drive away from the village in the evening cool, somehow the image of those unflinching eyes stays with us . . .

> No call to 'Be!' had rung out then
> No vista no visage
> No whisper of 'good' was there
> Nor the thunder of 'bad'
> From then, a thirst
> Crept into my eyes and soul
> Taking that first sip of love

'There is a deep thirst in our eyes,' Abdullah bhai had told us on another occasion.

He had spoken that day of the famous creation myth of Islam in which Allah uttered the words 'Kun-fayakun', literally, 'Be!' (kun) 'And it was!' (fayakun). But before he told them to arise and 'be', Allah gave all the roohs a sip of a special 'jaam', a drink. It was this sip of love—ishq or tawheed (oneness or unity of God)—which created a deep thirst in all souls. This image echoes in the special 'sip' of milk that Heer is given by Ranjha when her wedding procession is leaving the village. Latif mentions a special kind of water kneaded by the Potter into the 'clay' with which he crafted us.[52] A primal thirst—or, to use a contemporary idiom, an existential angst—planted deep in our bones.

Heer says her rooh was tied to Ranjha even before Allah uttered the words 'Kun-fayakun' to create this universe (Bulle Shah).[53] Sasui, Marui and Sohini all declare that their hearts were locked with their loves before that moment. In a different idiom, Kabir too evokes the idea of being a 'bairaagi' or a 'yogi' (a detached one) before all of creation happened.

This inkling of our origins, a harking back to pre-eternity, is an intimation of a time before all of creation, rather a time that was not 'before' but 'beyond' our linear idea of time. Perhaps legendary lovers speak of a love not *of* time, or *in* time, and so we do not really grasp it with our limited, linear minds.

'Kun-fayakun' evokes the idea of this universe as *continually* taking birth, being formed, taking shape and dying even in this very moment. If we could enter the quality of being that emerges from this understanding, Time may longer be a finite, sequential measure given to us to live out our lives. We could then stop clinging to moments . . . bartering, saving, remembering, anticipating . . . and in general, getting attached to them. If we could shed this pragmatism and enter the field of love, we might penetrate the veil, as Sufis do (becoming *ibn-al-waqt*—'sons of the present moment'), and be free.[54]

Mysteriously, then, what we seek would begin to seek us.

The Qur'an says, 'I remember those who remember me.' Bayazid Bistami says, till now I thought I was searching for Rab (God), but I realize now that Rab is searching for me! Kabir says that he no longer chants the name of Raam, rather, Raam chants his name![55] Shah Latif says to Sohini, those who search for Mehar, Mehar searches for them![56] The Buddhist master Dogen says, 'That the self advances and realises 10,000 things is a delusion. That the 10,000 things advance and realise the self is enlightenment.' One's thirst provokes a corresponding thirst; one's gaze calls for a gaze returned, like Barvo wooes Shireen with both his gaze and his flesh. Like 'quantum entanglement', this experience perhaps lies outside of space and time.

The sun has set on the Rann by now, and the highway is dark. But the tale continues to glimmer, inscrutable, and the feelings it evokes are ineffable, perhaps best not analysed, perhaps best only felt.

Like a reed shrieks when cut
I howl
Sundered from my love
Why brand my arm, doctor?
The pain is in my heart

15

My Beloved Came Thundering

Sur Sarang

Once Shah Latif and his friends were travelling through the deserts of Balochistan in the midst of a scalding summer towards Mecca on a Haj pilgrimage. On the way, they came upon a lake with some trees that provided some shade and relief. As they rested there, Latif witnessed a herd of cows come racing towards the lake waters, evidently dying of thirst. They gulped the waters deeply, two or three times, and once their thirst was quenched and they were at ease, they turned their backs on the lake and urinated in the very same waters they sought so dearly a few minutes ago.

This sight struck Latif very deeply. He decided to abandon his pilgrimage to Mecca. His friends were mystified, and they asked him why. Latif said, as long as the cows were thirsting, they yearned for the beloved. But the moment they attained their love, they lost all value for it. In that moment, he is said to have recited this beyt.

> Drink, but let thirst persist
> Eat, but let hunger remain
> That's when you will glimpse
> The miracle of Allah within

> (Sur Aasa)

Sarang—papeeha or the Indian cuckoo bird—is famed across many folklore traditions as a bird who 'thirsts'. In the intense summer months this bird sets up a plaintive cry, an incessant call rising higher and higher in pitch and intensity—'Peeyu! Peeyu!'—a sound uncannily similar to the word 'Piya' which means 'Beloved', and so the Sarang becomes symbolic of 'viraha' or 'separated love'.

The papeeha has a special kind of thirst, for she *rejects* ordinary rainwater. She never drinks the water gathered in shallow puddles. Instead she waits for a very special drop of rain. Only when the stars are aligned in a rare and particular constellation and if it happens to rain at that time, will the bird will fly upwards into the raining skies and take one drop into a slit in her throat (not her beak). *This* is the drop that slakes her being, and it is a very special taste.

Shah speaks of oysters living in the sea but thirsting for a drop of rain. He speaks of eyes, restless and searching, that will not be sated. He speaks of a thirst planted in us before all time, before all creation. This thirst, 'sikk' in Sindhi, is perhaps the most powerful and central image in Shah's universe of seeking—surfacing again and yet again in diverse metaphors, stories and Surs.

Imagine then that it is on *this* landscape of the Risalo that the monsoon arrives in Sur Sarang.

> My beloved came thundering
> Like a monsoon cloud
> Drenching those who thirsted
> Their whole lives
> With a true love

A pot, simmering for long, spills over. Sur Sarang truly is 'a spilling over', a celebration. The tones are exuberant, plentiful, luxuriant. The heart is full.

> The clouds are voluptuous
> The violin, sweet
> The monsoon, sudden
> Grains spill over
> Cream overflows

As zikr waters the soul
My dry and rusty heart
Is moist again

~

Clouds don't delight
As much as a glimspe of my love
Without her, the season is empty
And so is my heart

But look, here she comes
Like a thousand gusty monsoons
Filling me to the brim

One could well imagine the monsoon as the sky making love to the earth. The overtures of this seduction are in the games of hide and seek that clouds play—sometimes rumbling with empty promises of love; sometimes spraying a light caress sending shudders down the spine of the dry, parched earth; sometimes arriving to a thunderous, climactic applause. To this primordial love affair between earth and sky, humans have forever attuned their own love cycles, and Latif too, like many other poets, weaves into this monsoon opera the human theatre of longing for love.

'Rain' and 'Love'[57]
Echo each other

When ready to shower
Clouds set up a clamour
Lovers call out and cry

If you signal you are near
I'll turn into a monsoon cloud

~

Even today
Clouds from the north
Have tumbled and gathered
Like dark, wavy tresses
Hanging low

Lightning appears
Like a bride in the sky
Radiant, red

My love was far away
Suddenly she is near

The feelings are at once deeply spiritual *and* sensual. The landscape on which it's pouring is both inner and outer. The language both metaphor and detail.

A storm brews within
Outside the sky is blue

Longing is like lightning
It cracks open the heart

When the beloved dwells within
There is never a drought

~

The monsoon turns crimson
Molten like wax

Clouds burst into colours
The sky is etched
Delicately
In patterns of a shawl

'Bhit' is festooned with rain
Lake Kirar is full

There is delight simply in *noticing* the tactile beauty of the monsoon, and one beyt may differ from the other only in the slightest detail. That the skies turn inky black or silvery grey or then sometimes a bloody crimson . . . that the rain falls in fat drops, or in a light spray, or in torrential sheets . . . that the lightning is red like a bride, or exuberant like sunflowers, or delicate like a filigree . . . that the clouds are sometimes a murmur, sometimes a boisterous babble . . . sometimes like patterned scarves, sometimes majestic forts . . . This is not human language deploying the metaphors of the monsoon to convey other loftier meanings, rather here the monsoon is its own language.

Clouds build up in the sky
Like a city of forts

Music wells up
Bows play on strings

Last night the sky
Opened its heart
Filling Bhit to the brim

The beyts are filled with an evident tenderness and concern for the lives of ordinary farmers, their thirsting cattle. This is not just a Sufi's inner experience of the monsoon-beloved, it is as much a Sufi rejoicing together with the villagers of Sindh on the arrival of the lifegiving monsoon, feeling gratitude for its palapable benefits in the lives of those who till the earth, grow crops, graze cattle . . .

The season is here
The sky is murmuring
A cuckoo begins to sing

Farmers pull out their ploughs
Life brims with nectar
Ripples of joy abound

Today my beloved
Is wearing
The garments of a cloud!

~

Even today
Clouds from the north
Are turning dusky and dark

Rain falls in big drops
Cattle are drenched
Animals quenched
And the trees are positively
Exultant

~

My beloved hums
Like a monsoon drizzle

Bringing mercy
To the village of Jhok

Rain greens the land
The beloved's eyes are clouds
Of compassion

Evidently this elixir that showers on us from above, that cools, resuscitates and washes away the rust from our hearts is *rehmat* or 'grace'. 'Rain is called in some Islamic languages, particularly in Turkish and Persian, rehmat, "mercy" . . . where the clouds are described as messengers of God's mercy,' says Schimmel, describing how wide and extant this connection is across human cultures. 'The comparison of a king or a religious leader to a rich rain cloud was common in oriental poetry . . . The Mahabharata compares the *dharma* to the rain which makes everyone just and equal; but the most beautiful description of this kind is the hymn in honor of the Buddha in the *Saddharma Pundarika*, where he is seen as a large cloud, raining peace and blessings over the world.'[58]

The lightning portended rain
It filled the monsoon sky

Latif says,
The rain quenched the thirst of millions
Then it poured
Over Kaaba

There are many signals in Sur Sarang to read the monsoon as the lifegiving spirit of Islam, bringing relief and succour to thousands of seekers in the lands where it spread. This long beyt is recited with much gusto by lovers of Shah Sayeen, and is savoured for its striking evocations of a very concrete geography.

The monsoon turned
Amidst bolts of lightning
Crashing down on earth
Here and there

It crackled over Istanbul
Then turned towards the west
Glinting over the China sky
It shimmered in Samarkand

The storm swept to Turkey
Then Kabul and Kandahar

Rain thundered over Delhi
Also Deccan and Girnar

Glittering over Jaisalmer
The lightning flashed in Bikaner
A blustering gale blew over Bhuj
Drenching the dry desertscape

Then blessings rained down
On the town of Umarkot
Greening the low-lying plains

O Lord, let the land of Sindh thrive
Be ever prosperous and plentiful
O Friend, O Beloved
Let your benevolence shower
Over the entire
Universe

Specific religious conotations aside, the metaphor of rain speaks powerfully to all human hearts as a blessing, a benediction. The image carries with it all the human emotion of receiving protection, being looked out for . . .

Don't believe
What drops from the sky
At dawn is dew

Seeing our suffering
The night is shedding
Tears

(Sur Dahar)

Shah makes the skies complicit in our emotional well-being. The skies *care*. The image is a potent one, not just from the perspective of those who thirst and *receive,* but also as an image for one's own capacity to *give.* For the solace of love lies not merely in *getting* but becoming able to *give.* The water cycle mirrors that potential transformation.

We could imagine our sorrows as giving out heat, vapours coalescing into dense clouds of human emotion, pregnant with possibilities of love. Lightning arrives like a cataclysmic tear, renting open the clouds, causing them to dissolve with a relief of letting go. Sorrow leads to meltdowns. Then we shower out of our selves, offering ourselves with a generosity that perhaps only the metaphor of rain can evoke—an impartial, a non-partisan willingness to benefit *all* creatures, known and unknown.

> Light love within
> Smoulder
> Burn
> Blaze
> Let it flare to such fury
> That it melts you
> To water
>
> (Sur Ramkali)

~

And so once again we become privy in Sur Sarang to an intense conversation that Shah Latif builds up with a more-than-human world. Speaking directly to the elements he invokes in our hearts a reciprocal kinship with them, tangling us *emotionally* with the sky, the wind, the clouds and the rain . . .

Lovers of Shah's poetry outdo each other in impossible-sounding claims about the number of words in his vocabulary for elements from nature—116 names for the camel, 127 names for different kinds of grasses, 78 names for different kinds of clouds! Whatever be the real figures, reading and listening to Latif undoubtedly boggles the alienated modern mind, and a deep awe and even yearning arises in us, for this intimacy with nature. These poems slow down our discursive, hyperactive minds, stirring in us a tactile empathy with the material nature of things.

> Black clouds glow
> With silver lightning streaks
> Ah, joy!

> Clouds rumble softly
> Washing the rust
> From my soul

Often we hear a collective sigh, an 'ahhh', rippling through the gatherings in Kutch in response to the recitation of a Shah Latif beyt evoking the skies or the seasons. And we feel it rise up in our hearts too. A deep solace. A profound silence. A stirring in our bones of a memory. A time when human experience was inextricably embedded in nature.

> An alder leaf, loosened by wind, is drifting out with the tide. As it drifts, it bumps into the slender leg of a great blue heron staring intently through the rippled surface, then drifts on . . . As I watch, I too am drawn into the spread of silence. Slowly a bank of cloud approaches, slipping its bulged and billowing texture over the earth, folding the heron, and the alder trees and my gazing body into the depths of a vast, breathing being, enfolding us all within a common flesh, a common story, now bursting with rain.
>
> —David Abram

16

Why Did You Leave My Door?

Sur Pirbhati

The giver is only one
All the rest are beggars

Rains come in season
But you shower at all moments

Come to my home
Make this tainted one
Glow

The heart of Sur Pirbhati is contained in the idea of the 'manganiar'
or '*mangan-haar*' or '*maangne waala*', in other words, 'one
who begs'. The term refers to a community of musicians found on
both sides of the border between India and Pakistan, concentrated
in the Rajasthan–Sindh region. The 'manganhaar' is a wandering
minstrel, an oral historian, a bard who roams the streets and desert
lands with his surando[59]—a bow and string instrument—singing
stories and songs of kings, pirs and prophets, and asking for alms
in return.

But in the imagination of Shah Latif, is it surprising that the
metaphor rapidly spins outwards to make all of us 'manganhaars'?
The idea of being a 'beggar' may be uncomfortable to the modern,
secular mind. Perhaps several of us roam and strut about in
myriad delusions of being in control of our lives and destinies,

175

puffed-up with the arrogance of being 'givers', benefactors, protectors, pundits, what-have-you . . . But life and indeed death have a way of repeatedly bringing us to our knees, with our palms outstretched . . .

> O bard, don't let him fade
> For an instant from your heart
>
> Remove the broken strings
> String your violin with silver
> Woo him with tenderness

In the historical time preceding Shah Latif there was a famed king by the name of Sapar Khan or Sapar Sakhi who was the founder of a dynasty in Las Bela. Originally a Rajput, he and his tribesmen had migrated to Las Bela and were called the 'nine men' or Nau Marya or Nay Mard, who wrested power from the local Balochi chief.[60] Sapar Khan was famed in the region for his largesse and, according to popular lore, in an act of great generosity he once gifted a hundred pedigree Arab horses to a wandering bard. What is significant in this legend is that the minstrel's music was quite mediocre. But what moved Sapar Sakhi was the sincerity of the musician. Shah Latif may have found out about the fame of this king in his travels in Las Bela with the nomadic yogis. The image of a tryst between a bard and a king reappears in a very different way in Sur Sorath.

The living oral traditions of Shah Latif in Kutch have spun a backstory about Sur Pirbhati, and it was recounted, or rather ranconteured to us, by Abdullah bhai.

There was once in Sindh, a manganhaar who went by the name 'Saumang' ('one who would beg at a hundred doors'). At a very tender age, his mother died. Unable to take care of him, his father gave him up, and Saumang grew up in the household of his 'mama' (his mother's brother), his mama's wife and their little daughter.

As was the custom in those days, to cement the bonds between two families, the two young children, Saumang and the little girl, were bethrothed and promised to each other by their parents.

But Saumang's destiny began to unfold in accursed ways. First his father passed away and he was left completely orphaned. Then he contracted polio, lost the use of his legs, and became a cripple. He was brought up in his uncle's house like a cur, reviled and neglected.

One day, when Saumang had grown into a man, and his cousin had grown into a beautiful young woman, a neighbour reminded Saumang of the family's childhood marriage promise. Emboldened, Saumang went to his uncle to ask for the girl's hand. In response, he was thrown out of the house. Villagers sympathizing with his condition took care of the crippled musician.

The conscientious young girl had a mind of her own though, and decided that the childhood vow must be honoured. Who was the man that she had been betrothed to? She decided to meet Saumang and acquaint herself with him. She arrived at his room at dawn. Now the hours of early dawn, says Abdullah bhai, are considered deeply auspicious for practice, creativity, saadhna, meditation and prayer, as they are potent hours, 'when the doors of the giver remain open', and all true seeking finds fruition.

When the young woman arrived at Saumang's window and glanced in, she found him lying curled up, fast asleep on the ground, his home in disarray, his instrument hanging neglected from a peg. She was horrified, and she cried out:

> Your fiddle hangs
> Forlorn on a peg
> That is not the mark
> Of a musician!
>
> Your back is turned
> On the auspicious dawn

Who would call you a bard
If you can't honour your calling?

~

You dawdle and doze
The night away!
At midnight you didn't wake
To meet the giver

Last night his coffers
Were overflowing
He threw them open

True bards were helping
Themselves to gems

~

The morning star glimmers
Get up and sing!

The lord is watchful
He can see quite clearly
The truth of your heart

Saumang was struck. It was a bolt from the blue. He felt insulted and
wounded by the girl. But now he was even more keen to secure her
hand in marriage, so he limped over to the elders in the community
and asked for their help in the fulfilment of the promise. When the
village elders approached Saumang's uncle, he was defiant. He said,
'Excommunicate me if you like, but I won't give my girl.' When the
elders of the village reminded him of the sanctity of a promise, the
father of the girl laid down a condition. 'Fine!' he said. 'Get me a
dowry of a hundred Arab horses, and my daughter is yours!'

Now this was a very big ask. Even the richest among the villagers
did not possess a single Arab horse, let alone a hundred. Saumang

was in a quandary. To whom should he turn? Neighbours advised him to go the biggest benefactor in the region, with a reputation for unstinting generosity, who never turned anybody away empty-handed from his doors—Sapar Sakhi, the king of Las Bela.

The crippled bard began to drag himself slowly, painfully towards the city of Las Bela, which was a great distance away. On the way he passed through the region of Khaari Kutch, ruled by a local chief Ulad Jaam. The chief asked the musician where he was going. When Saumang said he was on his way to ask for patronage from the king of Las Bela, the local chief's chest swelled with competitive ego. He said, 'I am a big king myself! Do you think my generosity is any less than Sapar Sakhi's? Sing my praises and glory, and I will take care of you.'

So Saumang changed his path, stepped into Ulad Jaam's court, and started singing his praises. The local chief was pleased. Later when Saumang asked the Jaam for the gift of a hundred Arab horses, the chief laughed. This crippled musician had the nerve to ask for such an impossible gift? Saumang was thrown out of his kingdom by the scruff of his neck!

Saumang climbed down the steps of Ulad Jaam's palace, despondent and deep in thought. Why did he change his course? He was going to meet the fabled king of Las Bela. And here he was, thrown out of the court of a petty local chieftain.

This is perhaps that moment in the journey of our lives when we stop to ask ourselves: Where have we been doing all our 'asking'? Whose glories have we been singing? Where have we been peddling our wares? A moment that could be a path-changing one, when we ask ourselves: Are we seeking help in freeing our chains from those who are themselves in chains?

Kabir says, *Bandhe ko bandha mila, chhoote kaun upaaye? Kar bandagi nirbandh ki, pal mein lega chhudaaye.* One tied man meets another, who will set whom free? Bow to the unfettered, and in a moment you'll be free!

A conversation begins to unfold in Sur Pirbhati, between Saumang (the alms seeker, the *yaachak*) and the king of Las Bela

(the giver, the *daataar*), interjected with counsel in the voice of
Latif. The voice of the chastened musician is achingly vulnerable
and honest.

You are the giver
I a beggar

You are the wise
I a fool

Hearing your call
I slung this surando
On my shoulder

~

Oh bard, you forgot me!
Where were you yesterday?

Stumbling here and there[61]
Why didn't you come
To my door?

~

You are the giver
I a beggar

You are the saviour
I the fallen

You the philosopher's stone
I the iron

Touch my heart
Turn me to gold

~

Why did you neglect my door
And turn to others?

Is it any wonder that you face
These days of trouble?

~

O bard, go ask of him
Who gives wordlessly
Every day

False the doors of this world
Where you go abegging

They'll taunt you tomorrow
For what they give you today

How the story of Saumang and Sapar Sakhi ends is perhaps not relevant, nor do any of the beyts in this Sur have resonances with any 'happy ending'. Even Abdullah bhai seems to brush aside the end, with a cursory recounting of the crippled musician's arrival into the kingdom of Las Bela, the gift of a hundred horses, healers who cure him of his illness and the consummation of the marriage vow. The cripple, metaphorically, is transformed into a whole man. And this can only happen when we 'sing' (seek) and 'ask for alms' at the 'right' door.

~

Another story from a different land and time that has echoes of the story of this Sur could be shared here. Tansen was a famed sixteenth-century musician in the court of Emperor Akbar. From time to time Tansen would urge the king to travel to the jungles of Brindaban to listen to his guru, the hermit Haridas. But Emperor Akbar was dismissive of the idea. So besotted was he with the musical prowess of Tansen, he could barely imagine anyone superior to him.

However, one day the emperor was persuaded to make the journey. The emperor and Tansen set out on an elephant and after two days of travel they arrived in Brindaban, to find Swami Haridas seated in his courtyard deep in meditation. Tansen advised the king to stay disguised in the presence of his guru and not reveal himself. To instigate his guru to sing, Tansen started singing a song and at some point deliberately went off key. Jolted into his role as a guru and in order to demonstrate the right way to his disciple, Haridas began to sing, with the Mughal emperor crouched in the bushes, listening intently.

The song sent Emperor Akbar into a trance. Later, while they were returning home, Akbar turned to Tansen, and admitted, 'You were right, Tansen. You are a pale shadow of this sun. But why this huge difference? What makes his song so extraordinary?'

'The answer is simple,' said Tansen. 'I sing to please you, an earthly king. My guru sings for God, the King of Kings.'

This legend from the life of Tansen, however, tends to reinforce the common notion of creativity and expression, which is that if you sing for God, you are exalted as a singer, and your song becomes exalted to the heights of perfection. But Shah Latif is pointing us to a more humbling and humane truth, one that touches our innermost vulnerable core, which hides the shame of not being 'good enough'. He says:

> Be simple when you seek
> Don't brag, don't brandish your skills
>
> He lines up many gifts
> For those who cannot even sing
>
> ~
>
> Even if you know, stay unknowing
> This door is for the guileless

Only they may enter
Who think nothing
Of themselves

~

Maestros and masters
Strut his court
Posturing and preening

All human effort is flawed
Just say, you're the alchemy
I the ore

Rest your eyes on me
Turn me to gold

~

If maestros who dazzle
Came to know
How much he gives
To flawed but earnest ones

They'd abandon their practice
And smash their surandos!

The King of the Court does not look for excellence in our song. He looks for sincerity.

A story from the tradition tells us about the Persian Sufi Bayazid Bistami arriving at the door of Allah. Allah asks him, what have you brought for me? Bistami says, I have brought my 'pakeeziyat', my purity and piety. Allah is not impressed. He says, this whole world is not worth the wing of a mosquito to me, what will I do with your piety? Bistami apologizes and says, I've brought my 'tawwakkul', my complete faith and trust in you. Allah remains unimpressed. He says, when I declared myself your trustee and protector, wasn't that enough for you? Finally, Bistami gets it. He says, O Allah, forgive me. I have come in full surrender to you, with nothing at all, except my helplessness. Allah is pleased, and the doors open.

As long as our knowledge, our talents, even our spiritual deeds and merits, are adding to our ego, it's just another form of self-cherishing (to use a Buddhist idiom). True surrender requires an abdication even of spiritual merit. Our talents and our merits may swell our 'self' and they may bring us success in a world swarming with egos, but that which our heart most desires will elude us.

> I am closer to you
> Than the veins of your body
>
> I know all thoughts
> Jostling in your heart
> Oh manganhaar!
>
> I have no need of gold or silver
> Remember me in every breath
>
> Your tambura may be twisted
> The strings broken
>
> Even if your instrument is not in tune
> All I want to hear
> Is in your heart

17

Call of a Bald Mountain

Sur Khahodi

Where no bird flutters
A fire glimmers
Who but lovestruck yogis
Could light one there?

~

No sign of man
No footprint of bird
There the yogis come and go
Plucking wild fruit

There was once a cattle herder in Sindh who lost a few of his buffaloes. Searching here and there, following the fading footprints of his cattle, he wandered quite far into unknown territory. The sun was beginning to set and soon darkness would engulf the earth. Just as he was beginning to worry about his situation, the herder came across a man sitting beside a rock, slouched over. 'Have you seen two curved horn buffaloes cross this way?' he asked him. There was no answer.

The herder noticed the man was quite wiry and emaciated. Perhaps he was asleep? He went over and nudged him. The body keeled over. The herder sprang back in alarm, realizing that the man was not conscious. Was he in a trance? Was he dead?

Agitated, the herder went further up the rocky path as it climbed the hill, to look for help. And he came upon a surreal sight. Many

185

men were lying, or sitting about, utterly still, their bodies bags of bones, some with their eyes rolling upwards, some softly chanting 'Allah Hu' in whispers. What was this place? Where had he come?

'That is where you go if you are ready to give up the world,' said a villager he met later. 'The yogis are there in body,' he said, 'but their roohs are not. The name of that place is Ganjo Dungar, the "bald mountain".'

Sensing a secret
Yogis scour the stony hill
Abandoning fields of plenty

They seek nothingness
And arrive there
Lahoot

~

Perceiving a power
Yogis scale the craggy hill
Shutting their books of learning

They reach the place
Beyond all knowing
Lahoot

~

A touch of swirling dust
From that naked hill
The yogis give up their sleep

They search, struggle and find
Lahoot

'Lahoot' is an enigmatic word that can kindle heated conversations in the oral traditions of Shah Latif on this side of the border. What is it? A physical place? A state of mind? A mother's womb? A cave? A nothingness? Many theories and conjectures abound.

While there is indeed a famous cave in Balochistan with stalactites, which goes by the name Lahoot,[62] it is also said that Lahoot is a *makaam* (milestone) in the advanced stages of a tough spiritual journey, the first few stations being Nasoot, Malkoot and Jabroot, and last and final one being Hahoot.[63]

Umar kaka tells us that he has heard from knowledgeable sources that before seekers leave for Hinglaj, the famed pilgrimage site in Balochistan, they must cross these progressively rigorous fields of experience, which involve fasting, meditation and other austerities on the Ganjo Dungar. A diet of a single date a day with only a few sips of water. No shade from the blazing sun on the bald mountain. Nothing but a loincloth for cover in the chilly desert night. A pillow of stones.

> Khahodis don't dawdle
> They labour for the fruit
>
> Their reward is nothingness
> They plunge further
> Lahoot

The word 'khahodi' means 'those who search for food in the mountains'. These yogis wander in wastelands and make a home on the Ganjo Dungar, scouring the hill for wild fruit for sustenance. The 'wild fruit' is a metaphor for the 'ism-e-azam' or the Great Name, the Word which can be found within.[64] The mountains, jungles and valleys are the inner landscapes of seeking, which are tricky and tough to traverse.

> Khahodis don't disburse gifts
> Among the sleeping

If you want a taste of the wild fruit
Wake up
Tackle the mountain

Others say the term 'khahodi' means 'snake charmers'. The snake is
our nafs, our ego or the mind. The wild animals these yogis confront
on the naked mountain are sensory delights and egoic delusions—
kaam, *krodh*, *lobh*, *moh* and *ahankaar* (lust, anger, greed,
attachment and arrogance). The yogi learns on the bald mountain
the rigours of how these animals can be hunted down, how the
snake of the ego can be charmed or subdued into submission.

The jungle of desires
Is razed to a field of ash
Thieves scatter, scrambling for cover

The thirsty meets her thirst
Face to face
For the first time ever

Sur Khahodi is an invitation to nakedness. The mountain which
beckons is bald. The jungle of desires is stripped—razed clean to an
utterly empty field where the scurrying mind has no cover, where
all distractions have burnt away, where the scariest confrontation
occurs. A moment when you meet yourself.

Better a desolate place
Where I find only
You

I turn away
From noisy dens where
A thousand tales are told

~

Better a pitch-black night
That makes me
Lose the way

Not only does the world fade
I do too

All memory gone
Of me
And you

Curious tales are told about the kind of people attracted to Ganjo Dungar. Only a crazy person would venture on this path. The mountain is bald, but it is a mountain, with a peak. Kabir speaks of this in many poems as 'shoonya shikhar' or the 'peak of emptiness'. In another poem he says, 'Go there, nowhere.' What kind of fullness may be found in such an emptiness? Where do we arrive, in going nowhere?

Shah Latif had himself set out on such a quest. It is said that he visited the Lahoot cave along with the Nath Panthi yogis with whom he wandered in his early twenties. In fact, it was on the Ganjo Dungar near Hyderabad—this very bald mountain—that he first met the Nath Panthi yogis, indicating that the yogis of Sur Ramkali and the khahodis of Sur Khahodi are kindred, if not identical, spirits.

The rare traveller sets foot
On this quirky path

Mobs jostle and mill about
But don't take it—
The fast lane to the Beloved

The sun was filtering through the reed huts of the Jat village of Asari Vaandh, as Umar kaka warmed to yet another story, making us wonder if it was the sun or the story that lit his handsome eyes. Stories are the stuff of this tradition. Stories and poetry. Slippery like snakes! Charm them and you will get their essence.

At one time, the Badshah of the famed city of Thatta in present-day Sindh in Pakistan was a man named Peer Pathho. One morning, as the sun filtered through silken blinds in luminous shafts into his resplendent bedroom, the Badshah stirred from his bed, arose and went to the hamaam, the royal bathing quarters. His queen had woken up before him and gone to the kitchen to explain something to the servants about the morning meal. Meanwhile, a servant girl came into the bedroom to dust and clean. She gazed longingly at the velvet and satin covers of the royal bed. She touched them cautiously, wistfully. Ah, so pliant and soft! Knowing that the king and queen would be busy for a while, she was tempted. Exhausted as she was with many hours of work, the very moment the poor girl's head touched the royal pillow, she fell fast asleep.

'How dare you!' shouted the Badshah, lashing the girl awake with swift strokes of his whip! 'How dare you sleep in the place of my queen?'

The startled girl sprang out of bed, and then, rather curiously, laughed! Outraged and incensed, the Badshah fumed, 'Leave alone apologize, you dare to laugh?' Then the girl suddenly began to weep! The Badshah was mystified and enraged in turn.

The girl pleaded with the Badshah to show mercy. 'It was not my intention to sleep,' she stuttered. 'But Badshah, you know that sleep is such a stubborn thing, it will come over you when it has to, it takes no heed of the setting! Even if your neck is in a noose, sleep could take over, and then this was your royal bed. Please forgive me . . .' she trailed off.

The Badshah calmed down. He asked, 'But why did you laugh? And then why did you weep?' The girl looked furtively this way and that, wishing she could escape. 'Don't ask me that!' she cried with folded hands. The Badshah persisted, sensing the unfolding of a secret.

> Those who took
> The crazy, crooked road

Reached far and heard
What was never heard before

Eventually persuaded to speak, the servant girl said softly, 'Badshah, I realized that the punishment for sleeping on this bed for a few minutes was a few whiplashes. And you gave them to me, and it was over. And so I laughed out of relief.'

'And then? Why did you weep?'

'Then I thought of you, Badshah, and I began to weep for your fate. I thought of what kind of punishment lies in store for you, for sleeping on such a bed for an entire lifetime!'

The weight of the truth
Carry without a head

When truth calls out to you
Listen without ears

Behold your true beloved
As though unseeing

As the import of the words of this slip of a girl began to dawn on him, the Badshah started to weep. He held his head in his hands. The queen and the princes gathered around, and so did worried ministers and courtiers. The servant girl stood by, watching.

Black night, bright day
We know dark from light
This way

But where my beloved stands
There is no other

No form
No colour

'Find someone to take my place,' said the Badshah, turning away.

'Where are you going?' asked the distraught elders.

'I don't know, but I am resolved to leave the palace. I hear the call of a "bald mountain" . . . the Ganjo Dungar. This servant girl made me hear it . . .'

Ganjo, the sacred hill
Draws them
With its fragrance

Shedding all garbs,
Visages and masks

They arrive into nakedness
Lahoot

One is compelled to reflect on the metaphoric palpabilities and mysteries of Lahoot. Perhaps we can find a glimpse of it, taking an unexpected turn into a busy back alley of a city. Perhaps we can come upon it travelling on a train, dissolving into unprepared tears, struck by the song of a blind bard. Perhaps we sense it most intimately, when life strips us naked, defenceless, and brings us to our knees.

But then again, perhaps we never find it. We spend our lives assiduously avoiding an encounter with it, its call and its fragrance. The Lahoot we carry within.

18

The String, the Dagger and the Head

Sur Sorath

I was a mighty king.

One day I heard the distant strains of music come wafting into my palace. It was a mere beggar, a wandering minstrel passing by the high walls of my palace. He played a beautiful string and bow instrument—a surando—whose strings were made of dried deer intestines. The music pulled at my heartstrings. I had him summoned to my court and asked him to play for me.

He played once more. It rent my heart. I held out for a while, but then the barriers broke and my eyes couldn't hold back the tears. It was as though my whole existence was being shattered. And still, the beggar played on. He did not stop. He showed no mercy. He had a secret quest to fulfil.

When the music ended, there were eternities of silence. I was hardly able to speak. He had told me something extraordinary through his song.

Slowly, the world returned. I took a deep breath. Gathering myself, I pronounced, 'Ask, O *chaaran*,[65] for whatever you desire. Anything you ask for shall be yours.'

'Consider well, king, before you make such a promise,' he said. 'I'm not so easily appeased.'

Affronted, I drew myself up and proclaimed with confidence, 'Ask, chaaran. You shall not be disappointed.'

The beggar turned a clear gaze upon me and said, 'Then listen, king. I ask for your head.'

A hush descended over the court.

He said again, 'This is my price, king. This is what you have to pay.'

I did. I cut off my head.

Placing faith in Allah
He came this way

He does not ask for wealth
This beggar
He asks for my head

Cut quickly now
I cannot wait
Another second

~

The king beheaded himself. The queen wailed, the courtiers were stunned and the city of Junagadh was plunged into mourning. This is the story of Beejal and Rai Diach. Beejal was the bard, Rai Diach, the king of Junagadh in present-day Gujarat, renowned for his generosity and patronage of the arts. The folk tale to which this episode belongs is lengthy, with many complicated twists and turns. But Shah Latif culls out the baatin, the hidden import, in just this one episode of the tale.

Junagadh is the world, which is to be left behind, mourning and weeping. Beejal is the murshid, the guru, who asks for the impossible price. Rai Diach is the disciple yearning for the truth. His body is the royal palace, where Beejal plays his instrument. And the price Beejal demands for his music is the king's head, his *khudi* (sense of self), which blocks him from Khuda (God).

Placing faith in Allah
The beggar plucked his chang[66]

Entranced jungle animals
Joined the gathering
May the lord not disappoint
Beejal in his quest

Beejal came with a clear purpose. The music that he played was not accidental. Rai Diach recognized Beejal's intent. He had perhaps been waiting for him all his life. He couldn't wait to fulfil the master's command.

He desires and demands heads
Accepts nothing less

The poor are killed
The rich are not spared
He tramples on royalty
Takes away their breath

At dawn or dusk
That maestro
Spares nobody

The head is heavy with the self, the 'I', the ego. It is the symbolic seat of everything that separates us from others and brings us into conflict with each other. In the verses of Sur Sorath and Sur Kalyan, in poem after poem, Latif tells us to take note—there is no love, nor any use in talking of love, without cutting off the head.

The gallows are the bedroom
Of true lovers

To turn back or hesitate is a shame
Their love belongs to open fields

The vow to embrace death
Is a sign of true lovers

(Sur Kalyan)

The price for love seems very high. And yet the ego we cling to
so fiercely, the individuality that we prize and cherish so much, is
not really of such great value as we imagine, says Latif. Rai Diach
saw instantly that his head was a burden, that in fact the bargain
favoured him.

This head is worth nothing
Compared to your voice
Your notes

This wretched head doesn't even
Know how to bow

Yet it is all I have to give
A humble, paltry gift

This head is not
Worthy of you

~

Into his inner chamber
The king invited the minstrel
No woman servant
Could enter unbidden

The king offered him
A bejewelled Arab steed

The beggar, says Latif
Turned down the prize

Your royal head
Is what I want

~

In the utter solitude
Of the palace's secret room
The king and the musician
Became one

The king invited Beejal to play his music in a secret chamber of his palace, where even his special *daasis* or female servants (the senses) could not reach. Evidently, one must retreat to a special place within oneself to listen to this music—in order to truly listen, perhaps for the first time.

Music is the great figure for this union. Again and again, in his poems, Latif returns to the power of music. Mehar's bells, the yogis' singis, Beejal's surando, they all have devastating effects on the one who is primed to hear them. You cannot hear this music in a state of separation. Music works on your being, and brings you to a place where you are ready to lose the self.

They struck a wondrous deal
The string
The dagger
And the head

But is this all you came for, minstrel,
From so far away?
My head's not worthy of you

The fuller tale recounts how Beejal was sent as an undercover assassin by King Anerai of a neighbouring kingdom, who coveted Rai Diach's queen, Sorath. In another version of this tale, Rai Diach himself uses aggression to marry Sorath, even though she was betrothed to Anerai.[67] King Anerai lays siege on the kingdom of Junagadh in an attempt to reclaim Sorath, but finding the fort impregnable, he resorts to the stratagem of sending Beejal. This could be a metaphor for the impregnability of Rai Diach's ego. His mighty fortress can only be breached by song. Only the power of music can melt its bastions.

> In a high palace, the king
> Down on the ground, the bard

> But the strains of his surando
> Penetrated the palace walls

> ~

> The beggar entered the palace
> Bearing his instrument
> He struck up his melody
> And fortresses fell

> O Beejal, your music
> Resounds everywhere
> The cry has gone out in the city
> You've asked for the king's head!

Abdullah bhai recounts to us a quirky story from Rumi's *Mathnawi* about a merchant in Persia who owned a caged parrot from Hindustan. One day, he was setting out for trade towards the Hind. He asked the parrot, among all others in the household, if he could bring something back for it. The parrot told his master: 'If you see any of my brothers, tell them of my plight—how I'm caught in a cage in a foreign land—and bring me back their message.' The merchant, curious, agreed. Many months later, the merchant returned. The parrot asked him, 'Well, did you see any of my brothers? Did you give them my message?' The merchant replied, 'Yes, I saw many of them on a tree. When I told them what you'd said, one of them was so stricken that he flapped his wings miserably and died on the spot!'

To the merchant's amazement, as soon as his own parrot heard this, he too flapped his wings and dropped dead. The merchant was shocked. He took the dead parrot out of the cage and threw it into the street. Who wants to keep a dead parrot?

Imagine his surprise when the 'dead' parrot revived at once and took flight. As he flew away, he shouted: 'I understood my brother's message. To be free, you must die while you're still alive!'

> The surando struck
> A murderous chord
> In a flash the king
> Saw the truth of the bard
>
> Whipping out his dagger
> He chopped off his head

'Cutting off your head' is to be 'dead' in this sense, while still alive. Then absolutely nothing in the world has power over your heart. You are dead to the world, but your heart and mind are free. In a yogic sense, this death is the state of samadhi, when breath is suspended and the body appears inert and lifeless as in death. In the normal waking state, one is alive in the body but dead to the larger truth. In the state of union, the body dies to the world, but the self awakens to the nature of reality.

This story ends overtly in a tragedy. Sorath, too, kills herself in the wake of the king's death. But the inner tale, the baatin, speaks of a different truth. Such a death is life itself.

> Sorath died, peace descended
> In all places a hush
>
> The king pitched his tent
> In lands elsewhere
>
> The music plays forever
> For those who cross over
> The king rests in accord

19

Those Who Plunge, Emerge

The Woman's Voice

Those who plunge, emerge
That's how it's always been
Submerge in the rampant river
And meet with Mehar

(Sur Sohini)

Passionate and tragic love legends have long inspired Sufis in their poetic expressions. Perhaps they found that the range of emotions experienced by human beings in their yearning for worldly beloveds *(ishq-e-majaazi)* were a powerful metaphor in which to express mystical longings of a different kind *(ishq-e-haqeeqi)*. But why have they largely chosen to speak in the voice of the heroines and not the heroes of these legends? Why, indeed, must Shah Latif speak in the female voice?

Sufis of the Indian subcontinent have especially invoked the female voice as the quintessential seeker's voice, and this trend dates back at least to the time of Amir Khusro in the thirteenth century. Devotional songs to God by a female subject, in the doha and geet forms, seem to have been popular even before this time. In the poetry of the early Sufis of the Arab-speaking world, according to Annemarie Schimmel, there was no mention of worldly love at all. In later Arabic Sufis, a man pines for a woman (who personifies divine beauty)—Salma or Hind—traditional heroines of pre-Islamic poetry. In the

Persian tradition the two lovers are imagined as male, and only in one tale, it is a woman, Zulaikha, who pines for her male beloved Joseph. It is really only in the Indian Sufi and Bhakti tradition of Kabir and others that the human soul is always personified as a woman, in Hindu myths, legends, Islamic literature and folk mysticism.[68]

This may have something to do with the broader Indic understanding of Consciousness (Purusha, Shiva) as 'male' and Manifestation or Nature (Prakriti, Shakti) as 'female'. This is personified most strongly in the figure of Krishna in play with Radha (his principal consort) and other 'gopis' (his female playmates). Krishna represents God while Radha and the gopis represent the human soul. From this point of view, all human beings are 'female'. Indeed, some later Sufis have even written odes to Krishna.

A conventional prayer or worship of a (male) deity morphs easily into the expression of a 'female' soul longing for mystical union with God, or a mureed (spiritual seeker) feeling devotion and surrender towards his murshid (spiritual guide). In this hugely popular composition by Amir Khusro, we find him taking on the character of a woman, with 'feminine' delicacy and detail, talking to his guru as a lover and husband.

> You stripped me of all markers of identity
> With just a glance

> My fair, delicate wrists adorned with green bangles
> You took them in your grasp
> With just a glance

> I give my life to you, Oh my cloth-dyer
> You dyed me in yourself
> With just a glance

> I surrender to you, Oh Nijam
> You made me your bride
> With just a glance

Khusro often addresses his poems to a *sakhi* (female friend or companion), connoting the intimacy of one female friend talking to another. Kabir evokes a similar feeling when he speaks to his *heli* (a shorter form of *saheli*) or *sajni* (female friend), as Latif speaks to his *shartiyun* ('female friends' in Sindhi). Sometimes the poems suggest a daughter confiding in her mother (Heer often speaks of her yearning for Ranjha with a cry of '*Maai ni*' and a lot of Latif poems cry out directly to the mother). Whatever be the relationship, common to all these kinds of address is one woman speaking her heart out to another.

Perhaps the fabric of female companionship enables the sharing of all kinds of emotions—longing, vulnerability, torment, abandonment—or tales of secret trysts, the excitement of anticipation, the ecstasy of union. In nearly all societies, through most of known human history, men have had a limited scope for sharing such emotions, especially for the expression of vulnerability, and thus they do not have a 'voice' in which to say all this. In fact, given the nature of gender socialization in our society, men perhaps don't even allow themselves to *feel* these emotions, leave alone struggle to find a vocabulary in which to express them.

One of the most powerful emotions male poets express through the woman's voice is that of 'surrender'. It is only through surrender of the egoic, separate self that the Beloved can be met. Though much has changed since the thirteenth century, even within our present socio-cultural realities such self-renunciation is seen to be easier for the female than for the more egotistical male. Indeed, a woman in traditional South Asian society has ample training in 'renunciation', especially around the institution of marriage. She has to give up a lot for it—her childhood home, her friends, her parents, her social context, sometimes even her first name. For the Sufi, these acts of letting go and leaving behind become powerful motifs for the shedding and stripping that is needed in order to meet with the Beloved.

Bulle Shah evokes this loss of self and identity joyously in the voice of Heer:

> Chanting Ranjha! Ranjha!
> I became Ranjha myself
> Call me only Ranjha, friends
> Don't call me Heer any more!

Shah Latif echoes this experience in the voice of Sasui when she realizes she herself is Punhu, or Sohini when she realizes she is Mehar, or Moomal when she sees only Rano all around her in an explosion of light. Losing one's identity can be glorious.

The celebrated qawwali singer, late Nusrat Fateh Ali Khan, said:

> I'll tell you something, something about Bulle Shah. When his Sheikh, his mentor got annoyed with him, got weary of him, Bulle Shah went away to spend twelve years among the dancing girls. He adopted the dancing girl's identity, the female voice, and returned to dance, dance like a dancing girl before his mentor, to woo him, to win him back! . . .
>
> [When the] . . . Sufi poets . . . present themselves as the female . . . there is elegance in it . . . a humility in the female voice, which is lacking in the male voice . . . they found their spirit, their soul, the essence of what they wanted to say in the female voice.[69]

All of this raises several questions. Does such a practice only reinforce gender stereotypes? Is it yet another instance of the convenient appropriation of the female voice and qualities by male poets (and singers) in the safe elevated realms of spiritual seeking and poetry, while eschewing those qualities in the grounded realms of worldly life?

Or could we interpret it, in our own historical moment, as a challenge in some ways to the strict male–female binary set up in our society? Does it offer a more open and fluid reading of gender roles and possibilities?

Both views seem possible.

In our travels in Kutch, for instance, we saw how the use of the woman's voice by Latif *has* indeed been appropriated by patriarchy. Thus a simplified reading of the Marui legend easily makes it all about the valorizing of female chastity. A Moomal or a Leela is at times almost denigrated in the oral traditions (for their 'mistakes' or 'weaknesses', typically ascribed to women by patriarchy), with comparisons to the grave or to the devil, respectively. The fashioning of the Beloved as always male and the seeker as always female, and the willing devotion and submission of the female lover to the male Beloved, can be and often *is* seen as reinforcing male superiority. So the gendered nature of the metaphor is perhaps fundamentally problematic, given the very real and material consequences of patriarchal structures.

And yet there is a code that these stories and verses seem to embody, their veiled import or baatin, which challenges social normativity at multiple levels. Yet again, we come to a place not of strict binaries, but of paradox. It is not a question of a strict 'yes' or 'no'; it is both. There is a code in this poetry that upholders of convention will not be eager to read; it is legible only to lovers and seekers . . .

Sohini abandons everything for love and breaks the norms of conventional fidelity. Mehar gives up a life of business and profit to choose the life of a cowherd, then a fakir. Brushing aside the concerns of her friends and family, Sasui takes off into the desert and has an intensely personal and wild communion with the elements. Sasui and Punhu's union (one Brahmin, the other Muslim) was not sanctioned by social norms in the first place. Ramkali leaves her father's royal palace to go in search of the yogis. Marui manages to resist the advances and threats of a powerful king purely through the strength of her spirit. Tamachi, the king, abandons the majesty of his court and goes fishing in the lake with Noori (of the 'low', 'foul-smelling' fishermen's caste) where they have the most intimate communion.

These poems accord their women a subjectivity that might be denied to them in social terms. These women seriously challenge conventional values—of middle-class security, comfort, or pragmatism ('being practical'), for example. The woman here is autonomous, strong-willed and on a powerful, destabilizing quest—quite the contrary to the traditional picture of woman as idealized by patriarchal cultures: keeper of the home, a picture of docility and domesticity, in short, a woman 'who knows her place'. The female protagonist depicted as the seeker is itself a powerful statement of agency and autonomy accorded to the woman.

> I'll put vermilion in my hair
> But can't line my eyes with kohl
> In my eyes lives my beloved
> How can anyone else enter there?

This is Kabir speaking in the role of a bride. She applies vermilion to signify her status as a married woman but refuses to adorn her eyes with kaajal, reserving that special place for her *true* beloved—an assertion of inner autonomy and selfhood.

In a Baul poem addressing the male seeker, the poet Shashanko Goshai says: 'Seek the woman within.' Parvathy Baul, a woman practitioner in the Baul tradition, says that the same principle applies to women: to develop the *purushatva* or masculine principle within themselves. Though this kind of formulation is still couched in the language of a traditional gender binary—of 'courage' as male and 'surrender' as female, for instance—nevertheless it encourages the spiritual seeker, whether male or female, to embrace other qualities within themselves than what their culture sanctions, in order to approach wholeness.

Latif's women display many qualities conventionally attributed to men—Sasui's unflinching courage in setting out alone upon a vast, barren desert; Ramkali's love of knowledge; Marui's steadfastness and resolute strength of will; Sohini's rebellion and flying in the face of social norms in order to be true to herself; and most of all the autonomy and self-sufficiency signalled in their discovering the beloved within.

But the point is not to celebrate or appreciate only conventionally 'male' values. The conventionally 'female' ones need to be reclaimed and their incredible strength needs to be recognized as well. Especially a culture like ours, in which 'equality' can sometimes seem to mean an equality of egos, could benefit from an appreciation of qualities such as the ability to love, nurture and care, to give oneself completely and fully (to 'take the plunge'), and the ability to transform oneself (not remain rigid or fixed), which in the end is what the spiritual quest is all about. Radha becomes Krishna, who then worships her in certain traditions. Sohini must take the plunge and emerge as Mehar. Moomal does not even go to Rano anymore, but finds the gardens of Kak within her own self.

Latif's women embody qualities conventionally attributed to women as incredible spiritual virtues, not as a weakness. Leela, Noori and Moomal may not be defiant or rebellious like a Sohini or a Sasui, and yet they are still the seeker, because they introspect, aspire, reach out, and ultimately transform themselves. Sasui and Sohini are even more compelling because they embody both—the surrender and the strength, the giving up of themselves and the courage of the solitary quest. And in the end surrender, giving oneself up, taking the plunge, losing one's identity, is strength. It requires incredible courage.

All these qualities, whether deemed 'male' or 'female', resonate powerfully for us as women and men in modern times and changing contexts. The traits that have traditionally been labelled as 'feminine'—selflessness, devotion, surrender and the unremitting capacity to give—remain as compelling as ever. It's true that delimiting these qualities as 'feminine' has aided patriarchal cultures in exploiting women and curtailing their agency and self-expression. But surely the time has come now for us to reclaim these values as 'superior' to those that our current societies are structured upon (power, competition and self-aggrandisement); to not confuse submissiveness with the power of 'surrender'; to recognize that integrating these qualities would be much more deeply empowering for us as a human race.

So perhaps it is time now for men to openly embrace these qualities and clothe them, as beautifully and compellingly, in the male voice (longing for a female beloved?). Perhaps a poem will arise now, in the male voice, expressing vulnerability and surrender as a man; and male poets, singers and listeners will feel the freer for it.

20

The Six Manazils

Roads of Return

manazil
a stopping place; a day-long journey; an arduous task;
one flight of a building; one section of the Qur'an;
final destination

As we prepare to leave the land of Kutch, and our tangible journeys draw to a close, Abdullah bhai unexpectedly opens out a new road for us in his inimitable, conversational style.

We know the four obligations of Islam to be namaaz (prayer), roza (fasting), zakaat (charity) and haj (pilgrimage), he says. But inner spiritual work calls for something more. Citing the well-known Islamic theologian Muhammad Ghazali (or al-Ghazali), he tells us that if we choose to walk on the path, there are six milestones to be crossed.[70]

We were deeply moved by what he described, and these 'six manazils' have stayed with us, vibrant and present, since our return from Kutch.

1. shukr (gratitude)

So many blessings
Can I even count them?

They're more than
The grains of sand in the desert!

– Marui (Shah Latif)

Marui, trapped in a fort in Umarkot, speaks only of the enormous debt of gratitude she owes to her land, to her people, and even to Umar who, by imprisoning her, gave her the opportunity to seek and recognize freedom. When we realize that suffering is the path, even difficulties inspire only gratitude.

Many thanks
To my sorrows
They never left me
Even for a moment!

– Sasui (Shah Latif)

Abdullah bhai points out how there is so much to be grateful for. Where does one even begin? Gratitude for having life, a human form, for the water in the womb that nestles us, for the milk that is ready and waiting for us in the mother's breast, for the air that we breathe and water that we drink and food that we eat. All simple, miraculous things that perhaps we learn too quickly to take for granted.

2. sabr (patience)

Slowly, oh heart, slowly
Things take shape slowly
The gardener pours a hundred water pots
But the fruit appears in season

– Kabir

This is the power to wait, to forbear, to abide—as an active choice, not as helpless fatalism or a last resort. It is the capacity within us to endure.

Don't weep, don't shout, don't shed tears
Whatever comes, live that fully
Such equanimity brings joy in its wake

– Marui (Shah Latif)

One milestone points the way to another. The practice of gratitude releases the restlessness of wanting and the sense of entitlement. Patience arises. The practice of patience leads to trust and acceptance.

But each step on the path also gets more difficult. If sabr calls upon our powers of endurance, tawakkul asks for even more.

3. tawakkul (trust)

Whirlpools roar and crash
The river looks fearsome
She flung herself in
With no hope of saving her skin
With the grace of Mehar
She crossed over

– Sohini (Shah Latif)

Trust is Sohini jumping into a swirling river each night. Trust is Sasui setting out into a barren white desert, alone without water or food in hand. Trust is Rai Diach cutting off his head to honour the word of his guru. Trust is letting go of the need for control, trusting that something higher guides you as well as the world.

Trust gives enormous strength.

4. razaa (acceptance)

Tu Allah ki razaa mein raazi ho ja, is how Abdullah bhai explains it. To accept the will of Allah; to become one with it. To know the moment for struggle, and the moment for surrender. To realize that nothing happens exclusively by your will. To understand that nothing here is yours to take credit for—not your relationships, not your property, not your achievements, nor life itself. Because so much has been given to you—as a gift. And as much shall be taken away one day. Then why cling to it? Why quarrel with what happens?

> Nothing in me is mine
> It all belongs to you
> I give to you what's already yours
> What can I say is mine?

> – Kabir

5. mukhlis (devoted to the truth)

> The mind can hold either 'me' or 'God'
> One sheath can't accommodate two swords

> – Shah Latif

> When I was, Hari wasn't
> Now Hari is, I am not
> The path of love is narrow
> Two can't walk on it

> – Kabir

Gratitude, patience, trust and acceptance bring you here, where there is no 'you'. Personal concerns and ambitions fade and recede. One accesses a state of non-attachment. The 'I' is not the focus of actions, truth is. One becomes devoted to the truth, rather than to the self.

With the fifth step, the seeker becomes one-pointed, one-minded, one-seeing. To be mukhlis means to be utterly sincere and pure, free of ego-compulsions, to be loyal or faithful exclusively to the truth. Abdullah bhai describes it as seeing the one in everything—in your mother, in the murderer out to kill you, in the stranger. There are no easy differences. No friendship, no enmity; no love, no hate; no attachment, no resistance.

> Kabir, in the marketplace, wishes everyone well
> No special friendships, nor enmity's spell

– Kabir

6.   ikhlaas (non-self)[71]

> Deluded, I forgot
> I myself am Punhu
>
> I wasted all this time
> Searching for him
>
> No knowledge
> Is worth anything
> Without a glimpse of
> The beloved within

– Sasui (Shah Latif)

As we mull over these six milestones and their meanings, there is the flickering recognition that all this goes much beyond the realm of the mind, beyond the urge for mental control of the world. In fact, the path starts with let-go.

What we ordinarily call knowledge is the everyday mind's limited understanding of a perceptual world. The path takes no heed of this. It asks us to enter another paradigm.

The redness of my beloved
Spreads in all directions
I set out in search of red
I became red myself

– Kabir

When you arrive into the sixth and last station, there is no 'experience' to be spoken of, because there is no actor left, because 'you' have become *that*. Sasui becomes Punhu and Sohini becomes Mehar. Rai Diach merges with Beejal and his music. At the end of the search, there is no seeker left, nor any beloved.

Paanehi pase paan ke, paanehi mehboob
Paanehi khalkiyo khoob, paanehi taalab tahinjo

I saw myself
I was the Beloved
I made this world
I myself seek it

– Shah Latif

Selected Poems from Shah Jo Risalo

1

Sur Kalyan and Sur Yaman Kalyan

I'm in love with one
Who carries daggers!

I press ahead
In the field of love

My head's on the chopping-block
Now slaughter me, beloved

(YA 135/16)

~

The gallows are the bedroom
Of true lovers

To turn back or hesitate is a shame
Their love belongs to open fields

The vow to embrace death
Is a sign of true lovers

(YA 132/5/8)

~

I look for the head but can't find the torso
I look for the torso and can't find the head

Hands, wrists and fingers chopped
And dropped who knows where

When oneness is the bride
The groom is cut to pieces

(YA 122/13)

~

The beloved's knife
Cut right to the bone

For Allah
Lovers gladly
Chop themselves
To pieces

(YA 135/13)

~

He is This and he is That
He is death and he is life

He is the beloved's body
And its breath

He is enemy and well-wisher
Both here and there
Also hiding in the heart

He is the one looking at himself
In his own light

(YA 127/21)

~

He himself is the great, the glorious
Himself is the graceful

He is the face of the beloved
And its incredible beauty

He is the teacher
And the student is he

He himself is his thought
Manifested

This whole reality and truth
Can be grasped only from within

(YA 125/19)

~

I saw myself
I was the Beloved
I made this world
I myself seek it

(YA 126/20)

~

Don't call him lover, you fool
Nor call him beloved
Call him neither Creator nor creation

But this can be understood
Only by those
Whose faith is unflinching

(YA 124/17)

~

The many came from the one
Both of these
Belong to the same truth

There is only the One
Nothing beyond or outside

I swear upon Allah
That only Allah exists

And all the sound and fury of the world
Which appears not to be him
Is also him

(YA 124/18)

~

What is the secret of sound?
Listen, if you want to know
The word and the echo are one
They only appear as two

(YA 127/22)

~

'Slaughter' and 'Search'
Begin with the same letter
Both belong to the road!

Set out
Experience them
They bring good health

(YA 228/10)

~

The gallows call out, friends
Who'll walk with me to their end?

Only those may come
Who chant the name of love

(YA 131/3)

~

The gallows call out to lovers
Don't hold back

If love truly fires your loins
Cut off your head
Then dare speak the name of love

(YA 132/4)

~

One cup, two drinkers
Love doesn't function like this!

Those who fall prey
To the game of numbers
How will they attain to love?

Existence arranges it so
That they remain deprived
Of the experience of union

(YA 187/1)

~

One palace, one million doors
Countless windows in between
From wherever I look
The Beloved is before me

(YA 127/23)

~

If you crave one sip
Go to the wine-maker's distillery

Cutting, chopping, tearing into shreds
Chunks and bits of bone and flesh
All this is done by him

If at the end you get
Even a small portion of his wine
It's still very cheap, says Latif

(YA 137/21)

~

Some in the front
Some in the rear
Many heads lie here
Near the chopping block

If you can offer your head
You, too, will be accepted
Don't think it's a small thing

Can't you see on the ground
All these heads lying around?
This distillery uses
Heads as fuel!

(YA 136/17)

~

This Mokhi is a suspect character!
She belongs to a lowly caste
She hands out cupfuls of poison
And kills many a healthy man!

(YA 194/13)

~

All the healthy men are dead
Mokhi, may you never die!
But, tell me, how is it
That you live without your customers?

(YA 194/14)

~

All the healthy men have died
Mokhi, may you die too!
Who will drink your outrageous potion
Now that all the drunks are dead?

(YA 194/15)

~

The world is full of 'I', 'I', 'I'
It's hard to comprehend
This spell of self-enchantment
Cast by the magician

(YA 204/9)

~

You flinch if a thorn pricks you
How will you bear being stabbed
In the face by love?
Why do you even aspire to love?

(YA 228/7)

~

You are the beloved
You the physician
You are the pain and you the remedy

Oh master, this suffering
You give it and you take it away

Medicines are effective
Only if you want them to be

(YA 160/4)

~

You are the beloved
You the physician
To call out to you my sole remedy

Only you can assuage
The pain in my heart

(YA 159/2)

~

You are the beloved
You the physician
You are the hot iron rod!
You are both guide and lord

I'm amazed why
So many 'doctors' exist
To boss over us

(YA 160/3)

~

While the doctor tries to treat my pain
The beloved strikes

He cuts further into the wound
And brings it all to naught

(YA 160/5)

~

You argue with the physician endlessly
But will not follow the means
Prescribed by him

If you'd implement his advice
You'd be healthy instantly

(YA 167/1)

~

Understand well, oh seeker
Whatever is given by him
Is given in all mercy

Never consider it an unkindness
If he wants to kill you
Consider it a special favour

He unites his favourites to him
In this manner

(YA 235/10)

~

The slaughterers are the saviours
The saviours are slaughterers
He is the one who slaughters me
And he is the balm for my soul

(YA 151/20)

~

Those struck with iron arrows
Groan piteously
Their wounds ooze blood

Those who have been coloured red
In the field of love
They writhe and moan

They bandage themselves
Treat their own wounds

At least one night must be spent
With such wounded ones

(YA 162/12)

~

Go ask the moth
What it means to burn

They hurl themselves into fire
With no concern for their lives

Their innards are pierced
With spears of love

(YA 177/9)

~

If you want to be called a moth
Come, extinguish the fire!

This fire has roasted many
You must roast the fire

Seek the truth
Extinguish the flame
But never spell out
Your inner secret to others

(YA 178/10)

~

The Sufi is not sectarian
He is beloved of no one

He is always at war within
But shows nothing on the outside

Those who wish ill to him
He is their greatest well-wisher

(YA 202/4)

~

Give something to a Sufi
And he is unhappy

Give nothing
And he is thrilled

Call him a Sufi
Who keeps nothing for himself

(YA 201/3)

~

Stuffed with desire
Yet you call yourself a Sufi

To be a Sufi is no bed of roses
Take off your 'Sufi' headdress
And put it in the fire

(YA 202/6)

~

The Sufi belongs to every place
Like the blood in each vein

He apprehends the ultimate truth
But never speaks a word of it

To speak easily of these things
Would be a crime for him

(YA 201/2)

~

Wretch, how did you become a Qazi
By a mere study of letters?

You guess and you speculate
Dole out opinions and beliefs
But truth is nothing like this!

Go ask Satan
About the taste of this drink

(YA 209/21)

~

With all their surface talk
These mullahs mislead people

All this blabbering
Takes them further away from God

The beloved is closer than the breath
Yet they don't look for him

They don't understand
The secret of breath

They scream and cry
Like ghosts devoid of flesh

(YA 216/38)

~

They read endlessly
Nothing enters their heart
The more they read
The deeper they sink

(YA 212/27)

~

Oh mother, that mullah is a mess
Like bile bursts in the stomach!
He senses the truth of Allah and yet
He rolls around in the sludge

(YA 216/39)

~

Mullahs, shrine-keepers and pimps
They're all of the same ilk
They've sucked Allah dry
Like marrow from the bone

(OT)

~

Don't call them 'mullahs'
They're hunters who sell
Sacred verses like pig's meat
They're a disgrace, says Latif

(OT)

~

Don't call them 'mullahs'
God made them into donkeys
They beg and thieve to fill their bellies

Long after they're dead
God will still be angry

(OT)

~

Don't call them 'mullahs'
They're blind as bats
Leave them to their debates
They read, but grasp nothing

(OT)

~

The Many are in search of the One
The way to it is beauty
This is the teaching of Rumi

First, lose yourself
Then, lay eyes on the beloved

(YA 205/13)

~

Your body is the mosque
Your heart the inner chamber
For contemplation

Don't just fast ritually
Behold the invisible within
At all moments

Know yourself
From the inside out

Allah stands before you
Present in every person

(YA 215/34)

~

How will a single heart
House both Self and God?
There isn't space for two swords
In a single sheath

(YA 239/22)

2

Sur Pirbhati

Your fiddle hangs
Forlorn on a peg
That is not the mark
Of a musician!

Your back is turned
On the auspicious dawn

Who would call you a bard
If you can't honour your calling?

(YA 246/1)

~

How can you slumber?
You should weep and sing
Every hour of the night

Seize this moment
Tomorrow your fiddle
Will cease its sound

(YA 246/2)

~

You dawdle and doze
The night away!
At midnight you didn't wake
To meet the giver

Last night his coffers
Were overflowing
He threw them open

True bards
Were helping themselves
To gems

(YA 247/4)

~

The morning star glimmers
Get up and sing!

The lord is watchful
He can see quite clearly
The truth of your heart

(YA 253/17)

~

Only they can be called minstrels
Who play without pause

Violins over their shoulders
They roam the barren wild
Searching for the path
Where mirages shimmer

(YA 247/5)

~

O bard, go ask of him
Who gives wordlessly
Every day

False the doors of this world
Where you go abegging

They'll taunt you tomorrow
For what they give you today

(YA 254/19)

~

Be simple when you seek
Don't brag
Don't brandish your skills

The emperor had the horses
Ready for you last night!

He lines up many gifts
For those who cannot even sing

(YA 249/8/15)

~

Even if you know, stay unknowing
This door is for the guileless

Only those may enter
Who think nothing
Of themselves

(YA 249/9/14)

~

Don't be greedy when you ask
O bard
Or you'll be thrown a mere gem
And dismissed

(YA 249/9A)

~

The bard should declare himself
A cripple and a fool

No one took anything
Along after death

Only a poor cripple
Is invited
To the lord's palanquin

(YA 250/9B)

~

The naïve and artless seeker
Prostrates
Praying to Allah
In a simple tongue

The whole city sleeps
He alone wakes
Calling out from his heart
In the only way
He knows

(YA 251/12)

~

Maestros and masters
Strut his court
Posturing and preening

All human effort is flawed
Just say, you're the alchemy
I the ore

Rest your eyes on me
Turn me to gold

(YA 256/23/8)

~

If maestros who dazzle
Came to know
How much he gives
To flawed but earnest ones

They'd abandon their practice
And smash their surandos!

(YA 248/7)

~

You are the giver
I a beggar

You are the master
I a cur

Asking for you I set out
Hanging this fiddle
On my shoulder

(YA 256/24)

~

You are the giver
I a beggar

You are the wise
I a fool

Hearing your call
I slung this surando
On my shoulder

(YA 257/25)

~

Oh bard, you forgot me!
Where were you yesterday?

Stumbling here and there
Why didn't you come
To my door?

(YA 252/15/5)

~

You are the giver
I a beggar

You are the saviour
I the fallen

You the philosopher's stone
I the iron

Touch my heart
Turn me to gold

(YA 257/26)

~

Why did you neglect my door
And turn to others?

Is it any wonder that you face
These days of trouble?

(YA 255/20)

~

The giver is only one
All the rest are beggars

Rains come in season
But you shower at all moments

Come to my home
Make this tainted one
Glow

(YA 257/27)

~

O bard, don't let him fade
For an instant from your heart

Remove the broken strings
String your violin with silver
Woo him with tenderness

(YA 255/22)

~

I am closer to you
Than the veins of your body

I know all thoughts
Jostling in your heart
Oh manganhaar!

I have no need of gold or silver
Remember me in every breath

Your tambura may be twisted
The strings broken

Even if your instrument is not in tune
All I want to hear
Is in your heart

(OT/Waai)

3

Sur Aasa

I look for a limit
But you are out of the box
Your beauty beyond speech

Length or breadth
Cannot capture you!

Here
Lovers fret and chafe
Restless with ardour

There
The beloved is indifferent
Unimpressed

(YA 268/1)

~

To hell with duality
Save me from that fate
Strip me of this 'I'
So that you may find yourself

(YA 269/3)

~

241

If in your eyes
You still see your self
There is no surrender

Lose the self
Then chant, Allah-u-Akbar!

(YA 275/12)

~

All obligations to
Pray, plead, prostrate
Are shed

In the realm of the real
No rituals exist

(YA 272/9)

~

I forgot the zikr
I abandoned namaaz
A falcon's talons
Have gripped my heart

(YA 275/12A)

~

If with the first light of day
The beloved is not beheld
Pluck out these eyes
Feed them to the crows

(YA 280/1)

~

If with the first light of day
The beloved is not beheld
Feed these eyes to the crows
Bit by bit

(YA 280/2)

~

Somewhere, something
These eyes saw
Now they wander
They cannot rest

(YA 282/8)

~

Somewhere, something
These eyes saw
Ecstatic
They cannot sleep

(YA 282/9)

~

My eyes went today
And met with him
My love

Turning bloodshot
Now they sparkle like gems

(YA 282/10)

~

Every day these eyes
Laugh and weep
Eager to get a glimpse

They've found him
A thousand times
Yet they crave the joy of search

Even when fulfilled
Eyes thirst
To gaze upon the beloved

(YA 283/13)

~

I scrambled to stop these eyes
But they leapt across the sleeping world
And went to meet with him

They came back delighted
Landing me in trouble

(YA 284/15/18)

~

They love a good fight, these eyes!
Once started, they just won't stop

Clouds gather heat in the sky
They don't shower delicately

These tears burst
Like the monsoon

(YA 284 16/17)

~

Eyes get angry at eyes
They suffer miseries

They've learnt how to love
Now their tongue's got sharp

Eyes laugh, cry, get upset
And then again
Are mollified

(YA 284/17/15)

~

Hammer the nails of insight
Into your eyes
Surrender these fragmented
Breaths to him

Latif says, surrender
Each atom of yourself

Heart and eyes have been butchered
For the beloved

(YA 292 12/6)

~

They didn't confer with me
These eyes
Before falling in love

They entangled themselves
Where there are no entreaties
Or remedies

My wrecked heart longs
And waits
And melts into nothing

(YA 285 21/20)

~

They didn't take my consent
These eyes
Before falling in love

They've strayed into
A dangerous market
Where no one haggles
And the price is steep

You offer your life
To close the deal

(YA 285 19/19)

~

Reverse your gaze
Go against the grain

People plunge downwards
But you should soar to the sky

Look only inward
To reach for the beloved

(YA 285 22/21)

~

Keep your eyes exactly there
From where you can see him

Don't look at anyone else
He gets easily upset, your love

(YA 286 23/22)

~

His back is turned to me
But even in this view
I take delight

Now he turns his face to me
My body comes to life
The blood pounds
In my veins

(YA 286/24)

~

O my love
How will my eyes rest
Without you
Their patron, their prize?

I'm as patient as the earth
Even if you lay beyond
Sunrise and sunset
I would still walk to you
On the feet of my eyes

(YA 288/Waai)

~

Don't look with the eye
Of worldly love

Those who seek open-eyed
Find him missing

Only they behold him
Who close their eyes

(YA 289/ 2/1)

~

Don't befriend
These physical eyes
Don't scatter your glances
Here and there

Look intently, inquiringly
On the road to reality

(YA 290/6)

~

Neither being, nor non-being
These are mere turns of thought
The beloved's brilliance
Has gone beyond seeing

(YA 291 10/4)

~

Come sit in my eyes, my love
I'll shut my lids and hide you
The world will not see you
Nor I see anyone else

(YA 293 16/10)

~

Eyes search, find joy
No joy without these eyes
The joy and the search
Both I find within my self

(OT)

~

Beloved, your eyes
Flash like silver shards

The one for whom I kept awake
Fell asleep at fall of day

Tears flow from my eyes
Soaking my bed

(OT)

~

I and my love are one
You are my sanctuary
Beloved

Where these dark eyes will meet with yours
That place is still far ahead
Beloved

In that marketplace of eyes
Will mine fetch a good price
Beloved?

(OT/Waai)

~

Love with deep love
This love is not so simple

Hide even your hiding
So distraction
May not see you

(YA 295 19/13)

~

Reason is stunned
You are beyond its grasp

How would the blind
Bear witness
To a beauty such as yours?

(YA 298/ 29/23)

~

Reason is astounded
And shatters to pieces

How would the blind spot
Your signals of love?

(YA 299/30/24)

~

Reason is baffled
And skulks in shame

Staggered by your immensity
It's no longer cocky

It cannot bear
The sight of you

(YA 300/31/25)

~

Blind men quarrel
Over a dead elephant
Groping and prodding
Unable to understand
Unable to see

Those with real sight
See the shape of the beast
With the light of insight
They illuminate us

(YA 300/33/27)

~

I myself am the one
For whom I was pining
Delusion, disappear!
I've got a true glimpse
Of the beloved

(YA 309/8)

~

'I', 'You', 'Us', 'Them'
Free your heart of these four!
The flames of suffering
Won't touch you then

(YA 310/9A)

~

Shush, be quiet!
Restrain your eyes, ears, lips
Drink, but let thirst persist
Eat, but let hunger remain

That's when you will glimpse
The miracle of Allah within

(YA 310/9B)

~

When the redness
Of my beloved's eyes
Seeped into mine
The whole world transfigured!

Shot through and through
An ecstatic red

(YA 316/21)

~

I hid my heart's woe
Even from my breath

My love was secret
Till an outburst of tears
Betrayed me

(YA 320/26)

~

Countless rivers within
Turn and churn

I whirl and swirl
But let not even a sigh
Betray me

(YA 321/30)

~

The tale of love
Cannot be held captive
In the throat

Lakes overflow
When the river is in spate

(YA 321/29)

~

The self is a veil
Obscuring you from yourself
Watch out, be vigilant
'You' are in the way
Of union

(YA 321/31)

~

The beloved tied me up
And flung me into the sea
Standing on the shore, he said
Watch out, don't get wet!

(YA 324/38)

~

Body, the rosary
Breaths, the beads
Their hearts, damboors

Their veins vibrate
To the chant of oneness

Awake when asleep
Even their slumber
Is worship

(YA 329/46)

4

Sur Barvo Sindhi

Like a reed shrieks when cut
I howl
Sundered from my love
Why brand my arm, doctor?
The pain is in my heart

(YA 334/2)

~

Like an elephant trunk hangs low
Touching the earth
My head stays bowed
My body prostrates

That's how I get close to him
Says Latif

(YA 335/3)

~

Control slips away
Reins not in my hands
But his

A mountain
Struck my chest!

He came as in a dream
And left me delirious
Says Latif

(YA 336/5)

~

Won't you come, just once!

I'll spread my lashes
Like a carpet under your feet

My tresses will cushion your bed
I'll serve you forever

(YA 336/6)

~

Won't you come, just once!

Our souls would meet
In the hidden
Corners of the mountain

(YA 336/7)

~

Oh beloved, come back!
A heart-to-heart
A meeting of the souls
Is what I long for

My faults forgiven
I'll be nakedly true
Come!
Let this long separation end

(OT)

~

There are no remedies for love
What can I say or tell?
Fate planted this branch
Now it's watered by my tears

Hang in there, oh heart
Even though he left
Just yesterday

(YA 336/8)

~

You did what you did
And that's just as well, my love
Though I hardly expected this

You took my heart
In your possession
Now what's left for me to give?

What words can describe
This torment
Nesting in my heart?

(YA 337/8A)

~

You did what you did
And that's just as well, my love
Though it was hardly kind to me

You stole my heart
Then slipped away

Even if you're indifferent
Did you have to be so hard on me?

(YA 337/9)

~

Sometimes near, but distant
Sometimes far, yet so very close
Beloved

Sometimes you elude my heart
Sometimes you just will not
Be erased

Like the curved horns of a bull
You are entangled
With me

(YA 338/11)

~

You called me
And killed me with a glance

You sliced me up
Farmed out my flesh
Leaving only bone

And then said—
Be calm

Slaying this poor wretch
Already so dead
You smiled

(YA 339/12)

~

People crave wealth
I crave my love
For whom I'd relinquish
The world

Just a mention of him
Makes me rapturous
What would I do with a glimpse?

(YA 339/13)

~

Sometimes his doors
Are shut and bolted
Sometimes flung wide open

Sometimes I'm rebuffed
And turned away
Sometimes welcomed
And ushered in!

Sometimes
Not a single word
Sometimes
Countless intimate secrets

What can I say, my friends
That's just the way he is
My Friend

(YA 340/17)

~

With oomph and elan
My beloved takes the ramp
The earth itself sighs, bismillah!
Strewing kisses on the path
In a hush, angels stand by
Awed, astonished

No one can hold a candle
To the beauty of my love

(YA 342/19)

~

He is the beloved of my eyes!
Here and there, he's everywhere
Where should I turn my gaze?

Yet I climb hill after hill
Searching for the way

Says Shah Latif, friends
Allah will bring me to him

(YA 344/Waai)

~

Oh beloved, my heart
Longs for you

Bring out your knife
Cut into my flesh
Don't worry about etiquette

One direct glance
From you
Would be mercy

(YA 346/2)

~

Beloved, it's not right
That you kill me
Then don't ask how I am!

Not a drop of blood
Left to bleed
Yet my thirst for you
Is strong

I whisper secret prayers
For your mercy

(YA 347/3)

~

The way a blacksmith forges
A link into the chain
So my heart was interlocked
With my love

(YA 347/5)

~

Today again
I'm blasted to pieces
By my love

This longing batters me
Like a club smashing corn

(YA 348/8/11)

~

Crashing, crumbling
Dissolving, disappearing
The world scatters
In a moment

Your dear ones' feet
Stomp the earth
Over your head

In all moments we carry
A spade and a string
To dig and measure out
Our graves

(YA 348/10/8)

~

Today my beloved came home
Like fulfilment

Sorrows were wrung out
By joys
Like a washerman
Beats dirt from soiled cloth

(YA 350/12)

~

Where did you learn the art
Of butchery, my love?

Use a sharp knife
Spare me the blunt

Open up these wounds
See how deep it cuts
Your sorrow

(YA 353/3/10)

~

Separation
Makes deep gashes
In my flesh

I languish
Cast off, disowned

O lord
Bring me up close
To my faraway love

(YA 354/3A)

~

It's easy to call yourself a lover
The real test
Is in the doing

(YA 354, 4/3)

~

True love
Has vanished from this world

'Lovers' devour each other's flesh
These days!

What is real
Is the fragrance, my friend
Nothing else will stay

Save a true few
Most people are given
To charades

(YA 354 5/4)

~

You have seen me
Now don't look away, my love
Having looked away
Won't you look this way again?

Eyes are meant to look
Let them do what they do best!

Gaze upon me
With my countless flaws
As I see you
In your blameless beauty
O Friend

(YA 355/7/6)

5

Sur Rip

Sorrows have no hands or feet
Yet they march forth from my heart
In column after column
Laying siege on my body
Who but I can survive this?

(YA 421/3)

~

Pain sprouts like grass
Spreading across the land
When he departs
Like a retreating monsoon

(YA 422/4)

~

He lit a flame in me
Now it rages like a fire
What hope of it being put out
When he fans it himself?

(YA 422/5)

~

While I sleep
Sorrows encircle
Gripping me like a vine

Gasping, restive
I wake up

(YA 422/8)

~

Weep, but alone

Let the pain of your absent love
Fill your pores to the brim

As lotus fruit ripens
Submerged
In deep waters
Make your roots grow strong

(YA 423/10)

~

Clouds crowd my head
Rain pours from my eyes

Last night
A deluge of sorrows
Swept me away

Oh beloved, look out for me
Relieve me of my grief!

(YA 425/17)

~

Rain is born in me
Why do I need clouds?

Every moment of the day
My sky is overcast

(YA 425/18)

~

I remember you
In details
I converse with
Your memories

My very veins vibrate with love
Beneath my skin
Like rabaab strings

(YA 426/22)

~

My heart knows no ease
Yet censure cannot tame it

Forlorn, by the roadside
I'm covered in sorrows
Like a dust-laden tree

(YA 427/23)

~

All night I'm at work
Quieting my restless heart

But then dawn breaks
My love calls out
And I'm back on the rack again

(YA 427/25)

~

My beloved left
My body hanging
On the gallows as he went

Even the wretched trees
Awash with my tears
Have begun to shine

(YA 431/4)

~

The sky is clear
But a storm blusters within
Clouds burst with rain
When pregnant with love

Eyes that hold the beloved
Cannot afford to blink

(YA 432/5)

~

My beloved is a splendorous stole
Made of sensuous silk
He sends my heart galloping
How can I forget him?

(YA 433/9)

~

Water dredged up from a well
Comes all mixed up with sand
So too are he and I
Inseparable

(YA 433/11)

~

Put a lid on your love
Keep it secret like a potter's kiln
If your fires escape
How will the pot be baked?

Go learn from a potter the art
Of holding your fire within

(YA 434/15)

~

Learn the ways of love
From the potter's kiln
Not a wisp of smoke escapes
To betray the fires within

(YA 435/17)

~

Like water swirls and eddies
When an oar cleaves through it
My mind churns with endless plots
Of how to meet with him

(YA 433/10)

6

Sur Karayal

He soared into the sky
Crying, Allah is One!

Hurtling into the hurricane
Which tests all birds
The swan emerged
Unscathed

(YA 442/1)

~

Shaking off the company of cranes
She flew into the blue
Seeking the lake
Where her beloved lives

(YA 442/2)

~

Her gaze piercing
The swirling sea waters
She stands still

Scouring the depths
She finds pearls to thrive on

(YA 442/3)

~

In the perilous deep
You will find the swan

To wallow in the shallow
Is the way of herons

(YA 443/5)

~

Clear waters are now murky
Muddied by the herons
Swans stay away
Embarrassed

(YA 444/7)

~

Taste just once
The company of swans
You'll never hitch yourself
To herons again

(YA 446/12)

~

In the lake, one swan
Fifty hunters lurk on its banks

The solitary one
Rides the waves
O Allah, with your grace

(YA 447/18)

~

O beautiful bird!
Drink pure waters
And fly across the sea

A whirlpool lies ahead
Only herons would
Fear its wrath

Plummet into the exacting waters
Don't die the death
Of a coward

(YA 446/14)

~

The lake is the same
But the birds that alight
Are different

Those generous birds
With open hearts
Who danced on branches
Chirped and sang

They have all flown away
To the other side

(YA 452/28)

~

Rapt in meditation
Do not be amazed
By what you see

Drop the hollow talk
Stay far from those who go
'Me', 'me', 'me'

When you mingle with the true
Union draws near

(YA 444/8)

~

Rapt in meditation
Do not be amazed
By what you see

Dive deep
And deeper
Where the water is clear
And pearls are found

Leave behind the shore
There's doubt and confusion
On its dusty paths

(YA 445/9)

~

An age ago, the lake turned dry
Yet footprints glisten
Of the swan who walked this way

Can herons hope to emulate
The gait of a swan?

(YA 447/16)

~

Lotus roots go deep in water
While the bee wanders in air

Yet both their needs
Are met by Allah

The power of their love
Brings them together

(YA 449/22)

~

Lotus roots go deep in the water
The bee roams in the open air

They are exemplars of love
They drink, and drink deep
Yet their thirst remains

(YA 450/23)

~

When the world sleeps
The swans soar
Plunging into the deep
To find pearls

What ploy of hunters
Could bring them harm?

(YA 451/25)

~

Swans will all be swans
Not a single false one in them
When they alight
To pass the night
The lake turns fragrant

(YA 451/27)

~

No peacock survives
No swan

My world is overtaken
By lying, thieving herons

(YA 452/29)

~

I searched the lake
I peered in vain
For my beloved Karayal

That flamboyant bird
Of swaying step
Did not return

So dear to my heart he was
The bird that has flown

(YA 453/32)

~

Fly back, O beauteous swan
You are remembered
Wistfully on this side

Steer clear of hunters
Rapaciously
Plotting your end

(YA 447/17)

~

The world's undependable
A bogus game, a bitter taste

Birds bustle on trees
Chirping and chattering

Don't they hear it coming
The lash of the falcon?

(YA 458/ Waai)

~

Don't underestimate
The baby cobra
One bite
Can immobilize
An elephant

(YA 454/1)

~

Even peacocks stay clear
Of these venomous vipers
Their expert bite
Frightens whole herds
They migrate to other lands

(YA 455/5)

~

O snake,
Don't tangle with snake charmers!
My foot covers your hole
How will you emerge?

Enter this lair
At your own peril

Remember, it belongs to those
Who set fire to Junagadh![72]

(YA 456/7)

~

Night fell
The peacocks gathered

They lunged for the snakes
Killing them in great numbers
They drank down their poison

(YA 457/9)

~

The snakes
And the peacocks
Are locked in mortal battle

Who will retreat?
This is the decisive moment

(YA 458/11)

~

Courtesy will vanish from this world
Close on its heels, decency
Dignity will disappear
And with it, humility
Trust between men will dissolve

The day swans sit in conference
With crows, says Sayyad
Nothing will remain

(OT)

~

Beware of the bird-catchers
They swarm the shores

The decoy tricked you
You alighted
Where you shouldn't have

(YA 448/19 & 20)

~

It was a decoy
That lured you to your death
It had no life no flesh
It was merely scrap and hay

(YA 449/20)

~

Crows descend
A cawing clamour
Fills the world

Sensing the changing wind
They left

The swans flew away
To distant lands

(OT)

~

Oh foolish swan
Why hobnob with herons?

Seek lucid waters
Shake off the sludge

Before you know it
You'll be mired in the muck

(YA 446/13)

~

Why tarry on the shore?
Why walk the path of hordes?

Come into the garden of Oneness
Dive into the soul of Shariat
Walk the way of Haqiqat
In the company of swans

With the murshid's words as your guide
Cleanse your heart
Let go of the self

When 'you' disappear
Who will the hunter grasp?

(YA 450/24)

~

The bird and the cage are one
One, the lake and the swan

When I looked within
I saw the one who causes pain

That bird-catcher hunter
Who roams
My own being

(YA 453/31)

7

Sur Sarang

Clouds don't delight
As much as a glimspe of my love
Without her, the season is empty
And so is my heart

But look, here she comes
Like a thousand gusty monsoons
Filling me to the brim

(YA 501/3)

~

Even today
Clouds from the north
Are turning dusky and dark

Rain falls in big drops
Cattle are drenched
Animals quenched
And the trees are positively
Exultant

(YA 502/8)

~

Even today
Clouds from the north
Have tumbled and gathered
Like dark, wavy tresses
Hanging low

Lightning appears
Like a bride in the sky
Radiant, red

My love was far away
Suddenly she is near

(CS 22/6)

~

Even today
Clouds from the north
Loom into peaks

Lightning's promise in season
Is never empty

O love, come back!
The days of brooding
Are over

(MD 117/245)

~

The sun peeps cautiously
Obscured by clouds

Lightning shouts
Congratulations
I bring news of rain!

O heart, hold steady
Your love will soon be here

(YA 526/3)

~

In a flash, there he was!
The rust in my heart
Washed away
My longing to see him
At rest

(YA 505/17)

~

'Rain' and 'Love'
Echo each other

When ready to shower
Clouds set up a clamour
Lovers call out and cry

If you signal you are near
I'll turn into a monsoon cloud

(YA 516/6)

~

O cloud!
If you learnt your job from my eyes
You'd never run dry

(YA 507/20)

~

The sky is clear
But my eyes are rain-laden clouds
Just the thought of my love
Can get them going

They burst into tears
Recalling the absent one

(YA 508/22)

~

Black clouds glow
With silver lightning streaks
Ah, joy!

Clouds rumble softly
Washing the dust
From my soul

(YA 512/34)

~

The monsoon turns crimson
Molten like wax

Clouds burst into colours
And the sky is etched
Delicately
In patterns of a shawl

'Bhit' is festooned with rain
Lake Kirar is full

(YA 514/1)

~

Monsoon clouds bustle
Like a boisterous crowd!
A gale is gathering
From the north

Lightning blooms in the sky
Like flowers flashing

Glowing fields
Springing grass
Brimming lakes

(YA 514/2)

~

Clouds build up in the sky
Like a city of forts

Music wells up
Bows play on strings

Last night
The sky opened its heart
Filling Bhit to the brim

(YA 515/5)

~

The clouds are voluptuous
The violin, sweet
The monsoon, sudden
Grains spill over
Cream overflows

As zikr waters the soul
My dry and rusty heart
Is moist again

(YA 519/3)

~

The season is here
The sky is murmuring
A cuckoo begins to sing

Farmers pull out their ploughs
Life brims with nectar
Ripples of joy abound

Today my beloved
Is wearing
The garments of a cloud!

(MD 118/249)

~

Like a cloud laden with rain
The beloved is full of grace

He showers mercy
On lands that have too long
Been dry

(YA 521/8)

~

My beloved hums
Like a monsoon drizzle

He brings mercy
To the village of Jhok

Rain greens the land
The beloved's eyes are clouds
Of compassion

(YA 525/1)

~

A storm brews within
Outside the sky is blue

Longing is like lightning
It cracks open the heart

When the beloved dwells within
There is never a drought

(YA 532/16)

~

My beloved came thundering
Like a monsoon cloud
Drenching those who thirsted
Their whole lives
With a true love

(MD 119/252)

~

The lightning portended rain
It filled the monsoon sky

Latif says,
The rain quenched the thirst of millions
Then it poured
Over Kaaba

(YA 505/18)

~

The monsoon turned
Amidst bolts of lightning
Crashing down on earth
Here and there

It crackled over Istanbul
Then turned towards the west
Glinting over the China sky
It shimmered in Samarkand

The storm swept to Turkey
Then Kabul and Kandahar
Rain thundered over Delhi
Also Deccan and Girnar

Glittering over Jaisalmer
The lightning flashed in Bikaner
A blustering gale blew over Bhuj
Drenching the dry desertscape

Then blessings rained down
On the town of Umarkot
Greening the low lying plains

O Lord, let the land of Sindh thrive
Be ever prosperous and plentiful

O Friend, O Beloved
Let your benevolence shower
Over the entire
Universe

(YA 529/11)

8

Sur Khambhat

Oh accursed moon!
Why do you rise so soon?
Be off so I can keep my tryst
In a pitch-black night

(YA 541/8)

~

O moon
Full of fuss and frills
You rise

No matter how hard you try
You're outshone by my love
In a single moment

(YA 542/10/11)

~

O moon, what to speak
Of you and him?

You glow, but only at night
My beloved is shining
All the time!

(YA 543/12)

~

O moon, I'll be frank
Though you may quarrel or sulk
Your two eyes, and third your nose
Aren't a patch on my Beloved's!

(YA 543/13)

~

O moon, may I be frank?
Though you may get peeved

Sometimes skinny
Sometimes stout
You rise
Your face glaring light

Yet, you just can't match
The effulgence
Of my love

(YA 544/14/17)

~

The beloved's forehead
Glows with kindness
Lighting up homes
Of those who yearn
For him

O sun and moon!
Your daily visitations
To our homes
Pale in comparison

(YA 538/2)

~

Eighty-four moons may shine
And countless suns may blaze

But without my beloved
The world is only
Darkness

(CS 4/6)

~

With playful drunken eyes
When my beloved gazed around
Sun's rays paled, the moon wilted
Stars beat a hasty retreat
Jewels lost their sparkle
Seeing a beauty so wondrous!

(YA 545/15)

~

O my love
On the weighing scales of my heart
When I put you on one side
And the moon on the other

The moon was light as nothing
And yours hit the ground

(TSS 292)

~

Oh moon
You see him
From your perch in the sky
Give him these words and tears
'May I never be bereft of you!'

(YA 539/3)

~

O moon
Cast your first glance on him
Give him news
Of helpless ones who wait
Eyes fixed on the road

(YA 552/1)

~

O moon
Glow in his courtyard
Touch his feet
Speak my thoughts softly
To him

(YA 554/5)

~

O moon
Take my messages to him
Tied safely in the hem of your skirt

Bow your head
Then tell him how I am

Be humble in his presence
For he is
The refuge of the world

(YA 554/6)

~

O moon
Rise and gaze upon my love
So near to you
So far from me

He dozes softly
In the cool night air
Perfume wafting from his hair

If I set out on foot
The road would be long
My father won't give me a camel
Or I'd be with him
Before dawn

(YA 555/7)

~

Night glows
On the desert sands
The path to my love is long

Don't slacken, O camel
Don't swerve

Be unwavering
Till you reach him

(YA 557/12)

~

Whisk me away
To the home of my love

I'll deck you with pearls
And reins of silk
I'll feed you sandalwood

O camel, take me
To my beloved tonight

(YA 562/20)

~

O camel
Shake off your stupor!
Gallop on your way with speed
Bring me to my love
Just once

May the curse of a lover
Be on you
If you ignore my plea!

(YA 560/14B)

~

Oh camel
Get up, get going
The path is straight
No hurdles, no turns

Don't grumble or groan
Bring me to my love
This very night

(YA 561/16)

~

The path is festooned
With juicy vines

Hold the camel close
Always on a leash

Tasting them
He may go wild

(YA 567/32)

~

The camel savours
No fragrant flowers
Or scented trees

Lusting after
Brackish brambles and weeds
He is gorging himself
And getting fat

(YA 569/38)

~

I tie it near a tree
Laden with tender sweet buds

But when I'm not looking
The wretched animal
Still gobbles thistles and thorns

The ways of my camel
Perplex me

(YA 562/18)

~

The camel shuns the herd
Nor grazes on tender buds

Struck by the arrow of love
He crawls along
Unmindful of his life

(YA 564/25)

~

The camel turns away
From the herd
And saline ferns

Now there's a turmoil
In his heart

(YA 564/23)

~

Refusing to graze
Spitting out flowers
He crushes camphor underfoot

He's tasted sandalwood
My camel is full

(YA 565/27)

~

The camel tasted
Something, somewhere

He is chafing
In his chains

(YA 568/34)

~

Seeing the face of my love
The camel was transfixed

Now he's restless
In his shackles

(YA 566/28)

~

Nine chains
Ten ropes
Fifteen leashes
Tie the camel down

But it springs up
Pierced by a memory of love
And clambers free
Breaking all fetters

(YA 573/45)

~

Flinging off nine fetters
The camel broke free at dawn
Breaking into a gallop
He set off on the road
To the beloved

(YA 572/44)

~

In a wondrous garden
Of priceless trees
Where two branches cost ten million
And a twig half a million
My camel feeds!

(YA 573/46)

~

In a wondrous garden
Of priceless trees
Where two branches cost a million
And a leaf half a million
Chomping on a thick bunch
My camel feeds!

(YA 573/47)

~

One million, the camel's price
I'd pay ten times more

It's not a loser's bargain
To have this camel grace my home

(YA 574/48)

~

One million, the camel's price
Pay ten million, it's still a steal

Do it now, says Latif
Strike the deal

This camel can take you
Where you most long to go

The very moment you
Saddle and mount
You find yourself cradled
In the beloved's arms

(YA 575/49)

9

Sur Sri Raag

Desire is in your hands
Destiny in his
He's the one to shipwreck you
He alone, to the rescue

Only he can deliver you
Dry upon the shore

(YA 603/17)

~

Waters heave
In the endless fathomless

Don't leave me alone!
Don't let my little boat crash

(YA 588/11)

~

Wise ones are wakeful
Stocking their boats
With the cargo of surrender

They sail swiftly
Through the storm

(YA 598/6)

~

Submit to the ocean
Depths conceal wondrous things
Just a few of those gems
Will make your coffers brim

(YA 597/3)

~

Some tackle the deep
And find the pearl
Others loiter in shallow waters
Hoarding shells

(YA 597/3A)

~

Stars orbit ceaselessly
Rivers flow endlessly
Why then do you stop seeking?

Content with mere morsels
That fall into your lap
When will true riches
Be yours?

(YA 649/9)

~

Quit your frolic on the shore
Befriend the ocean instead

Endless waves rise from its depths
Many jewels glitter there

(YA 649/9A)

~

Divers plunge deep
Touching the very bottom
They find jewels
Come up with their hands full

(YA 600/9)

~

They soar high
On the crests of waves
And plunge deep
Into whirlpools' depths

Divers scour the sea
To find rubies and gems

(YA 600/10)

~

Waters seep in
Your boat is creaky, leaky
Don't take on this burden

Today is fading, life's escaping
Think about tomorrow

(YA 611/5)

~

I traded in trinkets
Not jewels
I filled my boat with dross
What but your grace
Can help me now?

(YA 586/7)

~

You bought cheap salt
But want to barter it for musk?
Your house is in peril

If you drive a false bargain
You'll lose all your goods
And the profit to boot!

(YA 609/1A)

~

The jewel is shattered in its box
Whole, it was worth a million
It's worth nothing
In pieces

(YA 632/20)

~

Thieves lurk
Where a true gem is found
The wise guard it well
And carry it safely away

(YA 632/21)

~

Don't offer pearls to one who
Doesn't know them from trinkets
When you find a real jeweller
Then reveal yourself

(YA 627/7)

~

The knowers of gems are gone
Where once master craftsmen
Carved and sparkled jewels
Today they hammer iron

(YA 630/15)

~

Not knowing the mysteries
Of swimming in the deep
The fools
Wear big turbans
And head to the sea

(YA 647/3)

~

The boat has holes
The mast is weak, ropes hang loose
Water trickles in

A skilled sailor charts his old vessel
Through these
Treacherous currents

(YA 612/6)

~

The boat sinks, then surfaces
Its pegs crumble
The lazy oarsman has fled
Letting pirates take the helm

Magnificent ships have gone under
Look out for my frail one, Allah

(YA 614/11)

~

You cannot sleep at the helm
Yet arrive safely on the shore!
All night you nod and doze
It's the day of reckoning
Tomorrow

(YA 615/14)

~

Don't doze!
The coast is treacherous
Waves foam and froth
Like milk curdling in a jar

How can you sleep
In so much peril?

(YA 618/18)

~

Oh lazy man
The currents will consume you
Wake up, seek refuge

Count yourself lucky
The sea didn't swallow you
Yesterday

(YA 639/3)

~

Oh boatman
The currents covet your boat
Watch those waves closely, sailor!

The sea can swallow you
In one gulp

(YA 640/5)

10

Sur Khahodi

Sensing a secret
Yogis scour the stony hill

Abandoning fields of plenty
They seek nothingness
And arrive there
Lahoot

(YA 713/1)

~

Perceiving a power
Yogis scale the craggy hill

Shutting their books of learning
They reach the place
Beyond all knowing
Lahoot

(YA 714/2)

~

A touch of swirling dust
From that naked hill
The yogis give up their sleep

They search, struggle and find
Lahoot

(YA 714/3)

~

A mere whiff
Of the fragrant hill
Draws the yogis on a quest

They refuse rest
Till they encounter
Lahoot

(YA 715/4)

~

Piercing the enigma
Of the inscrutable hill
They shed all trappings
And enter the void
Lahoot

(YA 715/5)

~

Khahodis don't dawdle
They labour for the fruit

Their reward is nothingness
They plunge further
Lahoot

(YA 707/20)

~

Ganjo, the sacred hill
Draws them
With its fragrance

Shedding all garbs,
Visages and masks

They arrive into nakedness
Lahoot

(YA 715/6)

~

Khahodis don't disburse gifts
Among the sleeping

If you want a taste of the wild fruit
Wake up
Tackle the mountain

(YA 705/16)

~

Where no bird flutters
A fire glimmers
Who but lovestruck yogis
Could light one there?

(YA 709/23b)

~

No sign of man
No footprint of bird
There the yogis come and go
Plucking wild fruit

(YA 718/10)

~

The jungle of desires
Is razed to a field of ash
Thieves scatter, scrambling for cover

The thirsty meets her thirst
Face to face
For the first time ever

(YA 726/9)

~

Better a desolate place
Where I find only
You

I turn away
From noisy dens where
A thousand tales are told

(YA 728/13)

~

Better a pitch-black night
That makes me
Lose the way

Not only does the world fade
I do too

All memory gone
Of me
And you

(YA 728/14)

~

The rare traveller sets foot
On this quirky path

Mobs jostle and mill about
But don't take it
The fast lane to the Beloved

(YA 723/4)

~

Those who took the
Crooked, crazy road
Went far and heard
What was never heard before

I have witnessed them
This way

(YA 724/5)

~

Snakes swarm
On the path of the world

The other way
Is full of reward

Only those shall know it
Who walk on it

(YA 725/6)

~

The weight of the truth
Carry without a head

When truth calls out to you
Listen without ears

Behold your true beloved
As though unseeing

(YA 729/16)

~

Black night, bright day
We know dark from light
This way

But where my beloved stands
There is no other

No form
No colour

(YA 728/15)

11

Sur Ramkali

Yogis there are of two kinds
Nooris and Naaris
Those who've reached the light
Illumined
And those still on the way
Burning

They've lit a fire in my soul
I can't live without them

(YA 741/1)

~

They played their singis
And effaced themselves
This is the way of the yogis
I can't live without them

(YA 756/36)

~

They seek no one's company
Nor let anyone seek theirs

This is the way of the yogis
I can't live without them

(YA 747/15A)

~

I treasure their music
They've gone beyond language
No talk
Only ecstasy
I can't live without them

(YA 745/9)

~

Their music rips off
The shroud over my heart
Their singis snared me
I am disconsolate
I can't live without them

(YA 746/14A)

~

Gathering their egos in piles
They made a bonfire
Their singis slay the self
They were my guiding light
Through the stormy seas of life
I can't live without them

(YA 748/17)

~

Their camp is forlorn
No music fills the dawn

Grief grips my heart
While they've moved on
I can't live without them

(YA 748/19)

~

I call out, I weep
I mourn their desolate dens
Their music has stabbed me
With inklings of eternity
I don't know where they are!
I can't live without them

(YA 749/20)

~

Tie me up in ropes
And take me along!
Their singis spilt out secrets
Plunging daggers in my heart
I can't live without them

(YA 745/11)

~

The naked seekers of Shiva
Take delight in Dwarka
And head off to Hinglaj
To see the Goddess
Hazrat Ali leads them on!
I can't live without them

(YA 752/28)

~

They've merged the part
With the whole
They've built their abode
Beyond time and space
I can't live without them

(YA 756/35)

~

Their music hides a secret
With the power to destroy me

More exquisite than the pipes
That camel riders play
Or even their flutes

Sweeter than
The cattle bells
That drove Sohini crazy

More agonizing
Than the strings of the fiddle
That sliced off the king's head

Nothing like it has been heard
In Hind or Sindh

Those who hear its melody
Know how rapturous it is
They step into ecstasy
Dissolving their selves

A peerless music
That God himself applauds
What can I say?

Bells may enchant goats and sheep
But this pierces the human heart

Says Abdul Latif
This music brings back to life
Even the dead

(YA 758/Waai)

~

Forget what is past
Begin right away
Die today, yogi
Tomorrow's too late

(YA 845/11)

~

They fill their warehouses
With hunger
The yogis care not for food
They guzzle down thirst

Latif says, the Lahootis
Have reduced themselves to less
Than a blade
Of grass

They went into the desert
And found the oasis

(YA 841/1)

~

The yogis roasted their selves
Demolished identity

No sin, no virtue
Only tears of blood

And you stand there asking
Their caste?

(YA 774/11)

~

Delusion has deluded many
Delude delusion itself!
Wake up at midnight
Burn yourself to ashes
Oh naked yogi!
Don't disgrace your tribe

(YA 857/36A)

~

Where there is no sky, nor earth
No light of moon, nor trace of sun
There the yogis congregate in hordes

Duality cast aside
They meet the lord in nothingness

(YA 861/45)

~

No cloak, nor loincloth
Their huts abandoned
And empty
They encounter the lord

(YA 843/3A)

~

If you want to be a yogi
Cut off all ties

Hitch your heart to them
Who are unborn
And never will be born

Then, seeker, you will step
Into the field of love

(YA 779/2)

~

If you want to be a yogi
Let go of all thirst
Become the slave of a slave

With the sword of patience
Your own identity slay
Then call yourself a yogi!

(YA 780/4)

~

If you want to be a yogi
Kill your brother
Leave your wife
Make love to your mother

Rise up from your slumber
Then call yourself a seeker!

(OT)

~

If you want to be a yogi
Fire an oven in your heart

Roast and burn your lungs,
Liver and kidneys

Only then will your name feature
In the lord's good books

(OT)

~

If you want to be a yogi
Take a swig of non-self

Hold fast to emptiness
Let the ego slip away

Then you will earn, seeker
The reward of Oneness

(YA 781/7)

~

Light love within
Smoulder
Burn
Blaze
Let it flare to such fury
That it melts you
To water

(YA 788/20)

~

Be the one who praises
Don't seek to be praised
It's a big disease
To garner praises for oneself

Those who flee the world
Avoid all flattery
And walk inconspicuously

(YA 828/21)

~

If we fretted as much for God
As we do for food, money or fame
The path would be clear
All worries would disappear

(YA 844/6/4)

~

Their heads gather dust
Their hair turns grey
They've smoked their selves away

The yogis unite
With the guru within
They don't need to put on
Outer shows anymore

(YA 811/6)

~

Any old fool
Can get their ears pierced
You need to cut off your head!

Latif says, associate
With true yogis and seekers

'Allah brings light
To whomsoever he favours'

This path is for those
Who can renounce both worlds

(YA 800/9A)

~

The ears fitted on your skull
Don't hear too well
Use your inner ears
To heed the call

(YA 789/22)

~

These ears are fit for an ass
Sell them off!

Get yourself another pair
The message awaits
Hearing

(YA 789/23)

~

Fine clothes on the outside
And rags within
They search like an ass

Finery within
And rags on the skin
Their search leads to God

(YA 856/857 34/35)

~

Whose fibres are dyed
In the colour of Hari
What need
For fancy clothes?

The yogis, says Latif
Are happy in rags

(YA 853/26)

~

Those who wander aimlessly
Never meet Allah
Allah greets his seekers
Within their own hearts
Latif says, their chains
Fall away from their bodies

True yogis go neither to Kabul
Nor to Kashmir
Those who walk the path of truth
Meet the beloved within

(YA 803/10)

~

True yogis don't set off on pilgrimages
They clean their hearts of dirt

Strip themselves of sleep
And weep with thoughts of Raam

(YA 813/9A)

~

The yogis have wonderful ways
Neither afraid of hell
Nor hankering for heaven

Neither infidels, nor Muslims
A single prayer on their lips
'Make me your slave!'

(YA 801/9C)

~

The beloved's face
Is the mihrab
All of creation a mosque

No Qur'an
No right, no wrong

They've claimed a knowledge
That staggers the intellect

Say, to which direction
Should they bow and pray?

(CS 18/51)

12

Sur Marui

Am I not your truest love?
Hearing those words
I answered, yes!

In that instant
My heart was pledged
To him

(YA 935/1)

~

I remember him
Since the day of the promise
To love him, and him alone

That memory is immutable
He's called 'neither born,
Nor birthing'

What can Marui do?
Sooner or later she will die

With that vow
Etched in her heart

(YA 990/1)

~

No call to 'Be' had rung out then
No ether, no flesh
No Adam, no form
It was then, in that moment
That I met with you
My lord

(YA 937/6)

~

No call to 'Be' had rung out then
No moon, no sun
No virtue, no sin
Just one
Only one

It was then, says Latif
That Allah unfurled the riddle
I grasped the mystery
I saw, I felt
His presence

(YA 938—939/7)

~

Destiny captivated me
Why else would I be here?

Fate brought me to this place
But heart, body, breath
Belong to them

Oh King, let Marui return
To her people!

(YA 939/8)

~

I'll wreck this palace of delights
Bereft of my kin
I'll burn it to cinders!

All things return to their origins
So I long to return

I'll set eyes on Maleer again
My homeland calls

(YA 941/14)

~

Herdswomen don't wear silk
Rough gowns please them more
Than fancy shawls or brocade

O Soomra, I choose the wool blanket
Over your gilded offerings

Let me die of shame if I abandon
The legacy of my ancestors

(YA 951/1)

~

Desert women
Wear black bangles
Gold for them
Is a harbinger of woe

With my people
Penury is a privilege
And hunger, happiness

(YA 954/10)

~

Happy those born in their homelands
Who have the desert as their shelter!

The Golra creeper and the Gugryan bush
Offer them protection
My people roam in such jungles

It's as if the wilderness itself
Was made into my bridal bed

(YA 956/15)

~

They feast on sour desert trees
And camp amid dunes

In spite of this their homes
Are always open to guests

They give them cupfuls of milk
O Umar, I belong to them!

(YA 957/17)

~

So many prisoners
Wander about in chains
Reconciled

I alone chafe and writhe
The sword of my love
Dangles overhead

(YA 964/12)

~

King, I've lost my beauty
That enviable splendour
A smoke rose up in the heart
My face has become black!

(YA 969/3)

~

Their faces are full of light
Who live in Maleer

Some lucky ones have returned
Their crimes forgiven

I'm a cursed one
My beauty destroyed

(YA 971/10)

~

The nomads are happy
Spring rains are here

Trees, creepers and bushes
Are in bloom

Truh, the bitter creeper
Has been emptied into the manger
For the goats
People savour the desert fruits

Given this, why would Marui
Stay in palaces
Instead of her grasslands?

(YA 984/3)

~

They are joyful with little
And live content

And yet they are physically
Strong and resilient

They wrap their bodies
With rough blankets
And move without
Heaviness of ego

In Maleer you can feel
The power of the herds-folk

(YA 985/6)

~

There is always surplus
Among these happy people who
Have nothing

They can eat a local Daura
Tree branch as food

They who have business
With trees and bushes
Are never weak or deprived

(YA 985/5)

~

Such a fine needle
Knits my heart to my Maroo
An unbreakable bond!

My brittle body and bones
Are with you, king
But my heart's in the desert

(YA 987/12)

~

The oyster is born at sea
And yet it craves the rain

This two-layered creature
Refuses the bitter seawater
As well as the sweet river

The pearl is formed when
You can stay thirsty in deep water

(YA 1010/14)

~

Learn steadfastness
From the oyster, friends

It refuses all kinds of water
And lives in hope of rain

(YA 1011/15)

~

Allah, let a camel rider pass
So I can dispatch my message

My trapped heart is theirs
Though they may not remember

The ink stains my hands
Will no one deliver my letter?

Tears do not let me write
They wash away all the words

(MD 235/622)

~

These are ever festering wounds
I yearn for union
Separation has destroyed me

King, my memory dwells on them
Who dwell in the desert
My eyes thirst for
The sight of my people

(MD 243/647)

~

Allah let it not be
That I live my life out in this prison

My body in shackles
Weeps night and day

Let me get back home
Then let my days
Come to an end

(OT)

~

Allah let it not be
That I die in this prison

The woes I suffer in shackles
Spare my people that grief

With Allah's grace, says Latif
Let my country be settled

I will reunite with my people
Then let my days
Come to an end

(OT)

~

Once I've left Maleer
What will the rain do?

My friends have abandoned
Their spinning wheels

Let the lightning flash
Only when I return home

(OT)

~

Lightning strikes, Umar
It makes me sad

Rain is falling at home, I see
Flashes of lightning
Crown my Maleer like a groom

(OT)

~

If only I could go to my country
See the huts of my Maroo

I yearn for my folk
I writhe in my iron chains

I ask about my home
From camel-riding wayfarers

(OT)

~

I see a dream, Soomra
I am in my own country

Passing around sweet berries
From the fruit trees

Herding goat kids
With a stick in my hand

(OT)

~

I see a dream, Soomra
I am going home

Plucking fruit with my people
Off the trees
Amid the sand dunes

I still have a hope, Soomra
Of returning to my land

(OT)

~

How can I forget?
The goodness of my Maroo
The joy of their companionship

Scrubbing my head with river mud
How they washed my braids
How can I forget?

The goatherds abandoned the village
Leaving me burning
How can I forget?

Friends, Latif says
It's raining in the land of the Maroo
How can I forget?

(OT/Waai)

~

Those who move about barefoot
On clean ground

They drink rainwater
And cover themselves with wool

They live among bushes
Without fear of danger

They are free of thoughts of self
And hence worriless and carefree

They who are blameless and meek
Umar, don't bring them grief!

(YA 956/16)

~

So many blessings
Can I even count them?
They're more than the grains of
Sand in the desert!

(YA 1031/39)

~

I thank those beautiful days in jail
Trapped in my tower I wept
Endlessly, out of longing

Tears of remembrance
Washed away
My earthly desires

Love released me
From the illusory
Shackles of captivity

(YA 1016/8)

~

Don't weep, don't shout, don't shed tears
Whatever comes, live that fully
Such suffering brings
Joy in its wake

Latif says, your chains
Are gone!
Burn these fetters
Your imprisonment is over

(YA 1034/51/48)

~

Marui has vanished from Maleer
Nor is she in Umar's fort

There's no trace of Punhu in Kech
Nor any seeker left in Sindh

The magic palace is bereft of Moomal
No yogi meditates on Ganjo hill

Sohini leaves no chafing husband
To find her Mehar within

No saint is met, these days
In mausoleums or burial grounds

There are no murshids or wise men left
In the smoking charnel grounds

(YA 1028/29A)

13

Surs Sasui Aabri, Mazuri, Desi, Kohiyari and Hussaini

How did you fall in love
With a stranger?
How did you get so entangled?

O stupid Sasui! Why did you love
The man of the mountains?

Did you imagine the love
Of a Brahmin and a Baroch
To be a game?

(CS 12/12)

~

I slept in love, but now love
Doesn't let me sleep

I wasn't awake when he came
The one for whom
I stayed awake through my sleep

Friends, how could I forget
That sleep and love
Don't go together?

(MD 160/387)

~

Oh eyes!
You didn't stay awake
In a vigil for your love
Now you weep, shedding
Tear after tear!

Eyes that droop at dawn
Will suffer much torment

Eyes that brim with sleep
How will they see their love?

Eyes heavy with slumber
How will they meet their love?

Rivers overflow every day
Spilling down cheeks

You were happy to dream
As they left and went their way

Says Latif, oh my friends
If only I could meet with him!

(Sur Khahodi, YA 734/Waai)

~

Big boulders are my bed
And rocks the bed-linen

Wherever I stop for the night
Animals are my companions

By the power of his love
The mountain becomes
My bridal palanquin

(CS 12/34)

~

If I revealed just a little
Of my true suffering
Animals would be struck dumb
Mountains rent asunder
All vegetation scorched
Nothing more would ever grow

(YA 1323/5)

~

My destination isn't clear
And I've carried no water
The mountain path is cruel
The desert sun harsh

Beloved, come to me here
Where I'm most alone
With my grief

(MD 128/279)

~

A blistering wind rose
Scorching the whole world

The sky rained sighs
Birds cried out
Fluttering on Punhoon's trail

Cattle were aghast
Shepherds saddened
Animals went into mourning
Giving up their breath

The whole desert grieves
For Punhu

(CS 8/9)

~

The setting sun turns red
As Sasui sheds tears of blood

There is no wayfarer
To whom she can turn

Dazed, perplexed
She walks on

(CS 8/38)

~

Trees, stop growing!
Mountains, don't be so tall!

Eyes, stop weeping
So I can see the footprints
Of my beloved

(YA 1179/6)

~

Blisters burn
My gait is unsteady

There is no question
Of turning back

But truly speaking, my spirit flags
The cruel mountain
Broke it apart

(CS 8/39)

~

The mountain weeps
For the wretched girl
The deer mourn
Wandering about they cry,
Her pain has wounded us!

(YA 1208/13)

~

Trees and shrubs
Howl in anguish

Pausing under their shade
She had infected them
With her grief

(YA 1208/15)

~

Her love wounded
Even those without blood

Boulders, stones and rocks
All wept and died
For her

(YA 1208/16)

~

You caught fire
Now don't stop burning

Fan the flames
Till they singe the sky

Forget all things
Raze your world to
Nothing

(CS 8/65)

~

Don't wail without a true cry
Don't walk without a true gait
Don't burn without true fire
Don't weep without true tears

(MD 139/320)

~

Burn as long as you live, Sasui!
There is no rest without burning
In heat and cold, keep walking
This is no time for loitering

(YA 1352/17)

~

O harsh mountain
You splice my body
Like a woodcutter saws a tree
My fate is tangled with you
Else why would I be here?

(YA 1302/1)

~

O mountain, if I ever
Lay eyes on my beloved
I'll complain about you

You loom menacingly at dawn
Confound me with your twisting paths

And you do me no favour
By erasing his tracks

(YA 1302/2)

~

O mountain
Why don't you speak?
Tell me if my beloved
Passed this way yesterday

Was he part of the vanishing
Caravan of camels?

(YA 1303/3)

~

O mountain
Grant solace
To the miserable

Take special care of those
Bereft of their love

Oh, stone!
Why do you bring
Such pain to my feet?

(YA 1304/7)

~

O mountain
Tears on the cheeks
Of those who grieve
Never dry

They melt the stones of Pab
Like the horde of sorrows
That wrecked my being

(YA 1305/11)

~

The mountain burst into flames
When it brushed against my pain
Oh friend, the earth was scorched

There is no more hope
Of joy in my mind

(YA 1387/16)

~

The mountain and the girl
Sat together and wept

Sobbing, silent
Not speaking of their love

(YA 1306/15)

~

Between me and him
A mountain
Rough and steep

Those who cling to life
Are daunted, dismayed

I invite death as escort
And cross over

(YA 1189/9)

~

The step she took
When she could take no more
Brought her to him

With one
Exhausted stride
She crossed the Pab mountain

(CS 8/80)

~

The camel men were devious
They kidnapped my love

But his scent wafts to me
From every tree

Wild animals
May eat my flesh
But my bones will keep marching
Towards him

(YA 1234/26)

~

The camels
Their drivers
And Punhu's brothers
They're all my foes!

Also the wily wind
Which wipes out his tracks

My foe, the setting sun
Which darkens my way

My foe, this rocky path
That hurts my feet!

Foe, that malicious moon
Why does it rise so late?

The day darkens
The birds come home
Chattering in their nests

Only I trudge on
Madly
Among the hills

(YA 1234/27)

~

Don't leave me Jat
I am yours

Ari Jaam's camels
Eluded my grasp

Punhu, don't ever keep
Your bed apart from mine

(OT)

~

Camels, mountains and Punhu's brothers
These three gave me grief
But the same things turned to bliss
As grounds for union with him

(MD 151/366)

~

He's not found by sitting on your ass
He's not found on a soft, warm bed
He's found by those
Who walk the path and weep for him

(MD 136/309)

~

Shedding the garbs of
Greed and avarice
Set out stark naked
The beloved is not found in sleep

(YA 1170/3)

~

Leaving all your clothes behind
Set out stark naked
Those who walk with nothing
Reach farthest

(YA 1170/4)

~

Those who bedeck themselves
Remain forsaken
Those who set out with nothing
Find union

(YA 1171/5)

~

Advance towards him with your heart
Don't try to scale mountains
I found him within me
The man of mountains, the king of Kech

(MD 130/286)

~

Advance towards him with your heart
Leave your head behind!
Those who realised themselves
Dwelt with the beloved

(MD 130/287)

~

Make this pilgrimage
With your soul
Not your foot

O Sasui!
Don't trudge in his tracks
Your heart must move
And do the walk

(CS 8/25)

~

If I move, he is far
If I am still, he is here

Why did I wander
So far and wide for him?

(YA 1366/11)

~

If I move, he eludes me
If I lie still, I'm in his arms

What kind of love is this
Oh my Baloch?

(YA 1366/12)

~

The joy that is in separation
Is not found in union
By visiting me, the beloved
Distanced me from him

(YA 1377/12)

~

Don't take the name of love
Love's feet run somewhere else

Keep the company of sorrows
Trade in longing and separation

(YA 1461/46)

~

Sorrows have cared for me
Cares have brought me up

I thirst not for happiness
I'm a fruit of the sorrow-vine

(YA 1425/16)

~

Let me search and search
But never find
Let there be no meeting

I don't want to lose
This intensity of longing
In union

(MD 181/464)

~

Sorrow showed me the path
To the beloved
This beautiful pain
Made me one with my master

(MD 175/439)

~

They who have love in their hearts
Are thirsty even in water

Drain the cup of thirst
Let thirst increase thirst

Punhu, only if you were the bartender
Would I quench my thirst
With the deep drink of thirst

(MD 125/270)

~

Oh grief
I long to grow in you
I would trade a million joys
And my head besides
In exchange for your caress

(YA 1382/4)

~

Most have a handful of sorrows
I have many rooms full
Before I could spread my wares
Buyers left the marketplace

(YA 1389/21)

~

Friends there are so many
But they seek only comfort

Grief sticks with me
Through the wild and steep

The sorrow that Punhu gave me
My true companion
My only guide

(YA 1307/18)

~

Entangle with the world
And he is far
Disentangle, and he is close

He is met
By those who carry
Nothing but non-existence

(YA 1171/4)

~

Go away, life
You are the beloved of many

Come to me, death
In your embrace I encounter
My beloved

(YA 1189/10)

~

Die, and then live
And you will bask in his radiance
Follow this advice
And you will find him

(YA 1186/1)

~

If you wish to die tomorrow
The beloved will come tomorrow
Or never at all

It has never been
That one living in comfort
Found him

(MD 144/339)

~

Punhu's presence
Sometimes darkness
Sometimes light

The path to him is streaked
With many colours

First I'm singed with soda
Then he steeps me in the dye

(YA 1318/10)

~

Punhu's presence
A dark cloud
A flash of lightning

Tears pouring
I walk to him

(YA 1318/11)

~

Even at midnight
She marches on

Climbing the tops of trees
With courage and grit

No kin for support
Just her voice
For company

Her piercing calls
Echo far and wide

(YA 1219/14)

~

Scrambling onto tree tops
She peers the horizon for Punhu

Her wails echo
Over the rocky land

A rare woman
Who ventured so far
Into barren lands

(YA 1219/15 & 16)

~

A cry rang out in the void
Was it a koel?
Reverberating through the land
It was the call of love

(YA 1219/17)

~

A cry rang out in the void
Was it a crane?

Emanating near some spring
It was the call of love

(YA 1220 19/20)

~

A cry rang out in the void
Like the chord of a violin
Or was it a woman?
It was the call of love

(YA 1220 20/21)

~

Her wails pierce the midnight air
Rocks quake
Threatening to crack

All creatures
Cry out in distress
This is the state of those
Struck by love

(YA 1207/12)

~

In a cloudburst of tears
I come, hoping for a meeting

If I walk night and day
Surely I will meet him?

O Allah, bring me to him
As you do rain to a parched deer

Mother, I cannot rest
Says Latif, this quest
Leads to my beloved

(Sur Khahodi, YA 712/Waai)

~

I haven't met my love
A thousand suns have set
Let me see him once
Then give up my breath

(CS 9/46)

~

I haven't met my love
The sun is dangling upside down
The fault is mine
I let him slip through my fingers
He didn't take me with him
To his country

(OT)

~

I haven't met my love
The sun has reached its setting
I will light on this dark mountain
A lamp for my Baroch
I want no life
Without him, my friends!

(OT)

~

I haven't met my love
This day too has passed
Love took me
This maddened, blind creature
Death came on the road
With the beloved's name on my lips

(OT)

~

I haven't met my love
And you are setting, sun
Take this message to my love
Go tell them in Kech
Wretched thing
She died on the path

(OT)

~

Abject one, wear a crown of sorrows
Batter yourself in this barrenness

Dig your grave here, and your beloved
Will come to you with good news

(MD 147/349)

~

Death came
And shook the sleeping Sasui
She awoke thinking
Has Punhu sent a messenger?

(OT)

~

The hut is right by the river
But fools die of thirst!

He is closer than the breath
Yet he isn't felt

You don't know your own breath
And therefore whine like a beggar

(MD 126/273)

~

O foolish girl
The man you seek
Is not in the mountains

The oasis you seek
Is in your heart

You ask strangers
For the way to him?
Why not ask yourself

(CS 8/20)

~

Your love lies within you
Go back home
Look for him there

Don't go running
In outward directions

(YA 1066/5)

~

Sasui, you carry within you
That which you hunt outside

Wandering does not lead to Allah
He is discovered secretly
Seated in the self

(YA 1067/7)

~

Diving into myself
I spoke with my soul

There were no more mountains then
Nor lack of Punhu
I became him

So long as I was Sasui
Life was full of grief

(MD 133/300)

~

Deluded, I forgot
I myself am Punhu

I wasted all this time
Searching for him

No knowledge
Is worth anything
Without a glimpse of
The beloved within

(MD 134/303)

~

I myself am Punhu
Sasui has no more charm

The trees are full of this song:
The world is an image of God

This mad one has etched him
On her heart

(MD 134/302)

14

Sur Kamod

You a great King, I a fisherwoman
The site of all imperfection

Your high queens
Look so elegant

Seeing them do not forget
This low smelly one

(YA 1469/1)

~

You a great King, I a fisherwoman
Full of grievous defects

Fish stains and scum
Stick fast to my dress

Seeing this do not neglect
This low smelly one

(YA 1470/3)

~

You a great King, I a fisherwoman
Full of a million flaws!

You know quite well
The state of my being

Seeing this do not forsake
This low smelly one

(YA 1470/5)

~

You are a great King
Lord of the port

I'm a poor fisherwoman
Yet you are so close to me!

Relieve me and my people
Of our taxes

(YA 1471/7)

~

Kinjhar looks aflame!

Where is this light coming from
At this hour of the night?

There is neither cloud, nor lightning
Nor the blaze of the sun

It was the veil lifting
Just a little from her face

The fisherwoman has climbed aboard
Her boat

(OT)

~

All the queens dressed up nicely
To woo Tamachi

But behold their surprise
He moves among fisherfolk
With a net in his hands!

(YA 1484/6)

~

No trace of pride
Or vanity in her heart

Her eyes her only ornament
Yet she captured his heart

They all stood in front of the king
Her art alone was successful
In attracting him

(YA 1477/20)

~

Noori picked out a fresh lotus fruit
And presented it to Tamachi
In front of all the queens

Samo returned the gift with love
And raised her above
Everyone else

(YA 1476/19)

~

Noori's humility is unparalleled
Samo fell in love with that
All those who were queens
Were left behind

(YA 1477/21)

~

Cursed are these high-born
Samo and Soomro queens
Who carry themselves with airs

Blessed are those born in Kinjhar
Who humbly remember Tamachi
In their hearts

Among all queens the fisherwoman
Was gifted the jewel
In a single night

(YA 1479/26)

~

Her hands among fish
She does her work

Yet she installed the king
In her heart
From the beginning

That's why he came
Himself
To reveal his secrets to her

(YA 1478/22)

~

Noori did a great favour to Tamachi
She climbed aboard his vehicle

From a low-born fisherwoman
She turned into a noble

All in Kinjhar celebrate this
What a great benediction it is

(YA 1485/8)

~

Who will call her a fisherwoman
Who consorts with the King?

She has braided her hair
With the love of Samo

Those who wouldn't let her come near
Now bow down to her

She has braided her hair
With the love of Samo

Noori's charm has brought blessing
Upon the entire universe

She has braided her hair
With the love of Samo

(YA 1488/Waai)

~

She neither cuts nor sells
Nor does she fill up baskets

She gives no importance
To the ways of the world

She follows the ways
Prevalent in Samo's house

(YA 1475/17)

~

Hands, feet, conduct, appearance
None betrayed her as a fisherwoman

Like the central string of a surando
She stood out from other queens

She was queen in spirit since birth
Samo recognized her

He tied the red nuptial thread
Round her slender wrist

(YA 1478/23)

~

Water below
Flowering branches above
My beloved close to me

All my desires were met
Not a single one unfulfilled

(YA 1483/3)

~

Water below
Flowering branches above
Profusion all round

In the swirl of water
A hint of Tamachi

The northern wind blows gently
Water rocks the boat
The lake has become a cradle

(YA 1484/4)

~

Water below
Flowering branches above

Lotuses on the lake
Fragrance in the air

Spring has finally
Come to Kinjhar

(YA 1484/5)

~

I row the boat
He casts the net

Yesterday, the whole day
Was spent in the hunt

(YA 1485/7)

~

Young and old fisherwomen
All are called by him

He is neither Born nor Birthing
Such is his uniqueness

This is the greatness
Of the throne of Tamachi

(YA 1487/10)

~

Fisherfolk have nothing
Except smelly baskets of fish

People are embarrassed
Of even brushing against their dress

But Sama embraces them freely
And presents them with gifts

(YA 1472/10)

~

Clean your huts
Jam Tamachi has come

Put aside your worries
Light up your courtyards

Kinjhar is full of bliss
Samo has become its benefactor

(YA 1487/12)

~

All the huts are abuzz
Jam Tamachi has come

Children are at play
At the shores of the lake

Talk of him and he was there
As if the moon had fallen into my lap!

(OT)

15

Sur Moomal-Rano

Yesterday the Yogi was met
A beggar-like fellow

A shawl on his head
Lovely rosary round his neck

The fakir showed us a vision
And wounded our hearts

(YA 1494/1)

~

Yesterday the Yogi was met
Glowing like the moon

An abundance of longing
Was awakened in our hearts
By the fakir

(YA 1494/2)

~

Yesterday the Yogi was met
In the early morning hour

His beauty was radiant
But he wept tears of blood

One who gets entangled, he said
With one named Moomal
There's no escape for him

(YA 1495/3)

~

Yesterday the Yogi was met
An ash-smeared beggar

A glowing green shawl
Slung over his shoulders

Tell us, oh fakir, they cried
The truth about this Moomal!

(YA 1495/4)

~

The yogi glowed crimson
Like the rising sun
A fragrance wafted
From the hair on his head

Oh, to lay eyes on the place
That dyed this mystic red!

(YA 1496/7)

~

The sheen on the yogi's face
Emanates from the glaze of love

He was born like a moth
Now he burns like the sun!

He has returned from Kak
The maidens there
Have made him bloom like this

(YA 1498/9)

~

O yogi
Talk to us of Moomal
Who makes you weep tears of blood?

Tell us, O wanderer
Of the unbearable beauty
Your eyes beheld!

(YA 1500/1)

~

Moomal's eyes are fierce tongs
In a single glance
They capture all men

Would-be lovers arrive . . .
Whoever comes is cut down!

(YA 1502/5)

~

Moomal's eyes are machetes
Hacking down princes and kings

Royal graves litter
The banks of Kak river

(YA 1501/2)

~

Kings, warriors, noblemen
All are called to Kak

Everyone goes
None has ever returned

All of them rode
With great enthusiasm
To their doom

(YA 1503/6A)

~

The yogi roused them
And created a deathly difficulty

The banks of Kak, he said
Overflow with passion

If you were to go there, seekers
You would behold
Mighty rivers of love

(YA 1504/7)

~

Let's go, let's go
Let's go to Kak!

Where love overflows
And consumes all else

All can behold
The beloved

(YA 1504/8)

~

Let's go, let's go
Let's go to Kak!

Where lovers leap with abandon
No rules nor restraints

All can behold
The beloved

(OT)

~

Let's go, let's go
Let's go to Kak!

Where love flourishes and grows
There is neither day nor night

All can behold
The beloved

(YA 1504/9)

~

Let's go, let's go
Let's go to Kak!

Where the big cauldron
Has been set on boil

That colour has dyed millions
Like the red of the betel leaf

(YA 1504/10)

~

Oh camel, you've been raised
To make the journey

Step carefully, says Latif
On the slippery slopes of Ludano

Your tussle is with Moomal
Morning and evening
Night and day

Heed the advice of your master
And you'll be able to pick
The lotuses of Kak

(YA 1505/11)

~

Those ascetics who blossomed
In the colours of Kak
That hue never leaves them

It's a bitter drink
Of joy and intoxication
Drunk by those mad ones

Those who seek Ludano
Fulfilment is experienced
Only by them

(YA 1514/4)

~

Kak could not hold the ascetics
Wealth meant nothing to them

Even princesses were left behind
Such was their state

The girls tried hard to woo them
But they migrated to another land

(YA 1520/17)

~

The four friends came to Kak
Rano alone threw the betel nut

He entered Kak
Where Moomal dwelt

He passed Kak's lotuses
And marched ahead

(YA 1507/15)

~

Don't be so distant, Rana
Don't be upset
Enough upsetness already!

Relieve me of my flaws
Do justice to my heart

There is no parallel, says Latif
To the beauty of the beloved

Cover up my darkness
And fill me with delight

(YA 1538/10)

~

Moomal had shot many
With her arrows

Now she herself is struck
In the head
With the arrow of Rano's love

(YA 1516/9)

~

I heard your reproach
And lost myself

Millions came to Kak
With their treasures and wares
Only Rana removed my doubts

Kak has no meaning for me
Come back quickly, my love!

(YA 1523/21)

~

Kak is scorched, trees are burnt
All manner of pleasure
Is reduced to cinders

Since you left, oh beloved
My heart is rocked by wave
After wave of longing

Come quickly now
To fulfil all the promises
You made to me

(YA 1540/14)

~

Friends, Rana has laid waste
To my heart
He has made it a desert

My insides have been blown
To bits

I feel my heart is no longer
Inside my chest

(YA 1557/7)

~

Friends, Rana has laid waste
To my heart
My life is a ruin

He has hacked and chopped
My mind into pieces
My whole body trembles

I feel my heart is no longer
Inside my chest

(YA 1557/8)

~

I was stark naked
The Beloved covered me up

He clad me with his name
And transformed me into a cloud
Of blessing over Kak

(YA 1566/8)

~

Which way should I turn my camel?
There is radiance on all sides!

Within lie the gardens of Kak
Within lies Ludano

There is Rano
Just Rano
Nothing else

(YA 1577/6)

~

I've packed up my bed,
    says Latif

I've set it down
By the banks of Kak

I've left everything behind
And merged into Moomal

I've solved the riddle
And now am at ease

(OT)

16

Sur Leela-Chanesar

There is a blot on my heart
Strangling me slowly

For Allah's sake, don't go!
I'll burn that necklace in the fire
In your very presence

(YA 1586/1)

~

I'll set fire to the pearls
Hurl the necklace into a pit!

If you consent to relent
I will consent to everything

Only merging with you again
Will relieve me of my taint

(YA 1587/2)

~

I'll set fire to the pearls
Hurl the necklace into a pit!

Oh Leela, you beauty, says Latif,
How did you fall into complacency?

You know the King is proud
A powerful monarch

His majesty extends
As far as the eye can see

That master, the apple of your eye
Your traded him for some pearls!

(YA 1587/3)

~

The sorcery of the pearls
Consumed me completely

I thought they'd be mine
Forever
Kunru outwitted me!

(YA 1589/7)

~

Those pearls were not real, Leela!
The necklace was a trap

Real gems lie further
These ones are all fake!

This falseness has misled many
And caused them
Estrangement

(YA 1590/8)

~

What you thought was a string of pearls
Turned out to be a noose of sorrows

Chanesar has cast you out
Embraced the servant girl instead

Oh, how can one bear such discord
With the beloved?

(YA 1590/9)

~

The glamour of the gem
Gave rise to arrogance

You quibbled with Chanesar
And caused this rift

The page has been turned
Estrangement
Your punishment

(YA 1588/5)

~

The glamour of the gem
Made you arrogant

This ass called arrogance
Has ruined millions

Chanesar has turned away from you
Estrangement
Your punishment

(YA 1588/6)

~

You were so intelligent!
But you misjudged your husband

Did you think a necklace
Would make you more alluring?

Put on a thousand ornamentations
Yet the Friend despises falseness

He tests the worth of your heart
Like a jeweller examines diamonds

(YA 1597/3)

~

No adornment on the arms
No necklace round the neck
No doing up of hair

No lining of the eyes
No making up of cheeks
No reddening of lips

When I was as plain as plain can be
The beloved accepted me completely

(YA 1590/10)

~

Gold bangles and bracelets
Shining red necklace
Oiled and perfumed hair

Oh, the cruel irony
Now he pays no attention to me

(YA 1591/11)

~

Why are some wives
Abandoned by their husbands?

Pride alienates the Partner

(YA 1600/10)

~

Let me not be 'Wife'
Since it creates vanity

Better rejection and estrangement
Which will make him remember me

(YA 1601/11)

~

I thought sharing his bed
Was enough to please him

He works differently
A servant is more dear to him

(YA 1598/4)

~

My bed is now hers
She sleeps with you

Wrapped up in our sheets
In the palace where we lived

Chanesar, I did not expect
Such harshness from you!

(YA 1593/16)

~

Eyes wet with tears she departs
Having readied her camel

Loaded with her luggage
The camel sat in Chanesar's courtyard

Leela cried out
Someone tell him I'm leaving!

(YA 1593/18)

~

Smarter than all my friends
Renowned for my cleverness
Now I can't even
Raise my head

(YA 1598/5)

~

Lord, let me not be clever!
Cleverness brings grief!
He was kind to me
Only in my simplicity

(YA 1598/6)

~

Don't argue with him, Leela
Don't show yourself off

The Friend belongs to no one
Neither to me nor to you

I have seen many favourites
Left weeping at his door

(YA 1604/18)

~

If you wish to please the beloved
Please him with your tears
Leela, let entreaties flow
This is the path of humility

(YA 1605/20)

~

All are married women
All wear necklaces

To meet the beloved
They dress themselves up

But he attends to those
Who come to him with humility

(YA 1609/4)

~

Chanesar already knew
The story and its end

The necklace was just an excuse
For what then happened

(YA 1591/12)

~

After countless errors
This wretch has come to your door

If you reject me now
I have nowhere to go

For God's sake, lord
Forgive me my follies

(YA 1610/6)

~

Leela, rise up!
Sweep your courtyard
Be stricken not with grief

Offer yourself and your ancestors
In sacrifice to the beloved

(YA 1613/14)

~

Leela, be stricken not with grief
Get up and clean the house
The beloved is at your doorstep!

He has returned to the one
Who is low
He stands just outside
Your courtyard

(YA 1614/15)

17

Sur Sorath

Placing faith in Allah
He came this way

He does not ask for wealth
This beggar
He asks for my head

Cut quickly now
I cannot wait
Another second

(YA 1621/3)

~

Placing faith in Allah
He came from far away

You soar higher than the sky
I merely crawl on the earth

How might I woo you, king?
I covet your head

(YA 1621/4)

~

Placing faith in Allah
The beggar plucked his chang

Entranced jungle animals
Joined the gathering

May the lord not disappoint
Beejal in his quest

(OT)

~

He desires and demands heads
Accepts nothing less

The poor are killed
The rich are not spared
He tramples on royalty
Takes away their breath

At dawn or dusk
That maestro
Spares nobody

(YA 1633/14)

~

This head is worth nothing
Compared to your voice
Your notes

This wretched head doesn't even
Know how to bow

Yet it is all I have to give
A humble, paltry gift

This head is not
Worthy of you

(YA 1640/11)

~

In the utter solitude
Of the palace's secret room
The king and the musician
Became one

(YA 1629/4/3)

~

The beggar entered the palace
Bearing his instrument

He struck up his melody
And fortresses fell

O Beejal, your music
Resounds everywhere
The cry has gone out in the city
You've asked for the king's head!

(YA 1638/4)

~

In a high palace, the king
Down on the ground, the bard

But the strains of his surando
Penetrated the palace walls

Into his inner chamber
The king invited the minstrel

No woman servant
Could enter unbidden

The king offered him
A bejewelled Arab steed

The beggar, says Latif
Turned down the prize

Your royal head
Is what I want

(YA 1629/3/6)

~

The giver witnessed
The beggar's great act

The bard came and strummed
The strings cried out

That musician's string
Had been talked of long before

Friends, says Latif,
Ask for the Lord's care

(OT/Waai)

~

They struck a wondrous deal
The string
The dagger
And the head

But is this all you came for, minstrel,
From so far away?
My head's not worthy of you

(YA 1650/10)

~

The surando struck
A murderous chord
In a flash the king
Saw the truth of the bard

Whipping out his dagger
He chopped off his head

(YA 1651/11)

~

It's been plucked
The flower of Girnar!
The city shudders with sobs

Hundreds of women
Beat their chests
Along with the queen

Offering up their heads, they cry
'Our king left us last night!'

(YA 1651/12)

~

Sorath died, peace descended
In all places a hush

The king pitched his tent
In lands elsewhere

The music plays forever
For those who cross over
The king rests in accord

(YA 1652/15)

18

Sur Sohini

The jingling of his flock's bells
Stirs me deeply
How can I sleep?

Ten times a day I pine for him
I'll wear the chains of his love
Till death

(MD 104/200)

~

So long since I saw him
I wonder how my sweetheart is
Eyes overflow with love
They burst into rivers and seas

(MD 113/232)

~

So long since I saw him
I wonder how my sweetheart is

The pain of his love
Entwines me like a creeper

(MD 113/233)

~

So long since I saw him
I wonder how my sweetheart is
A thousand suns have set
Lying in wait for him

He, whose absence
Was intolerable even for a second
Has not been seen for years

(MD 113/234)

~

To long for that shore
To plunge into water
Is the lot of besotted ones

Ten times a day
Dam admonishes me

But reason, judgement, shame
Have all been gutted
In the fire of love

(MD 103/197)

~

Don't carry even yourself along
Leave all support, Sohini

Only love helps traverse
Such turbulent waters

They get across swiftly
Whose ardour is their support

(MD 101/192)

~

Those who long for Mehar
Mehar longs for them
Bolsters are a burden
For ones who burn with love

(MD 102/194)

~

What you think are 'poems'
Are inklings from the unknown
These words nudge me nearer
To the beloved

(CS 7/77)

~

May God keep him!
May God protect the goatherd!

He's my ornament, my pendant
The glow of my skin

Let others call it what they will
Whether disgrace or taint

(MD 104/202)

~

Every day Dam taunts me about Mehar
I spread out my arms
And take in all the barbs

Let everyone say what they will
I'll keep the cowherd's company

(MD 106/208)

~

Friends mock me
They like to taunt and jeer
O crazy river, you hear
The true state of my being

(MD 111/226)

~

Sohini's impure
Without her beloved
Only with the cowherd
Can she become pure

(MD 114/236)

~

Whirlpools roar and crash
The current is unpredictable

She threw herself in
Forgetting everything

She tackled the waves
With joy, says Latif

(OT)

~

Whirlpools roar and crash
The river flows in fear

She came and leapt
Where she stood no chance

With Mehar's help
With his grace she'll get across

(OT)

~

Don't go Sohini, the river is in spate
In this dark night
What draws you to the whirlpools?
If Dam were to awaken
He'll question us about you

(OT)

~

What can Dam do?
She asked the village girls

For ages love-wrecked women
Have had business with whirlpools

I sacrifice these bones and flesh
On my beloved Mehar!

(OT)

~

Dam, your days will end soon
Yet you sit and blabber away!
The fish lunge for my bones

But how can I break my promise
To the one who lives on the island?

(OT)

~

Watchful of the currents
Sohini grips her pot
And plunges in

'A head sacrificed
At the feet of the Friend
Is just as well'[73]

This is the test of love
Union, the prize

Allah, may you take them across
Who keep trysts
In the dead of night

(YA 1666/11)

~

The river is fearsome
The whirlpools roar

How will my frail heart
Bear these onslaughts?

Oh my guardian, look out for me
Pull me out of the deep

(OT)

~

Dark night, frail pot, pools of blackness
No sign of moon, river in tumult
For his sake Sohini steps out
In the middle of the night

This must be God's will
Or who would jump
Into this manic maelstrom?

(MD 107/212)

~

Dark night, frail pot, no way to swim
Yet she flung herself in!
She did not wait, nor hesitate

The stormy river turned around
Love turned it into higher ground

(MD 108/213)

~

Standing at the edge
They cry out, 'My love!'
But they love only their lives

Some claim, 'I'm all yours'
But wet only their big toe

He comes to those
Who plunge in with a smile

(MD 100/188)

~

Those who hear the bells
Of Mehar's buffaloes
Why talk of guru
They would break a promise
To God himself!

(OT)

~

Neither here, nor there
Poor girl's in the thick of it

He waits on the other bank
Swirls of water engulf her

Dive deeper, don't think!
He's kind to those who drown

(MD 108/214)

~

Don't leave the house, Sohini
Or don't return!
Smash duality
Take hold of oneness

(MD 110/220)

~

Perish close to Mehar, Sohini
Don't think of return!
Don't reveal to Dam
The radiance of your sweetheart

(MD 110/221)

~

Take care of your own affairs,
No one stop me!

I threw myself in
At midnight I leapt
No one stop me!

In this dark night
My soul whirls in these waters
No one stop me!

Day and night, in every moment
Dam doesn't let go of me!
No one stop me!

(OT/Waai)

~

On land and in water
Every living thing, every creature
The flowers and the trees
Cry out in concert
We are God
We are the light of God

They should all be hanged
According to the Shariah!
They are allies of Mansur
How many will you execute?

(YA 1773/1)

~

It's a blessing the pot cracked
It was a barrier, a block

My breath resounds
To infinite sound
My being becomes a drum

Everything I had is laid
At the feet of the beloved
Union is the prize

(MD 100/189)

~

The pot shattered
Lovestruck Sohini died
No buttress remained

This is when she began to hear
The sound of Mehar

(MD 101/191)

~

No river nor lake nor ocean
Was cause of Sohini's death
The longing in her eyes
Made her drown for Mehar

(MD 116/242)

~

Beloved, Sohini, river
All three are one
The water itself is me
This is the mystery of mysteries

(MD 102/195)

~

Those who plunge, emerge
That's how it's always been
Submerge in the rampant river
And meet with Mehar

(MD 105/204)

19

Sur Ghatu

Inexorable
The vortex grips like a vice
Those who are caught
Vanish

No one comes back
To speak of it

(YA 1803/3)

~

The wise turn witless
Warriors begin to wilt
The vortex sucks
And they plummet
Powerless

All craft and expertise
Swept away

(YA 1803/1)

~

Night has fallen
The oars are afloat
Empty turbans gather dew
The boat drifts

No one comes back alive
From the Kolachi vortex

(YA 1803/2)

~

Six brave ones set forth
Their turbans proud
And spears bright

The sky darkened
None returned

Swallowed by the vortex
Those magnificent men

(YA 1804/4)

~

My feet drag on the shore
Searching in the noon sun
For those who did not return

The anchors of my life
Have sailed into the whirlpool

(YA 1805/8)

~

No smell of fish
In the market
No scales on the road

No fresh supply
Fills the fish stalls

Baskets lie bare
Buyers return empty-handed

(YA 1806/11)

~

They would have returned
If they were close by

They must have drifted
A long way off

Fishermen call out to the sea
None respond to the call

(YA 1806/13)

~

The zeal to tackle the vortex
Is what makes a true sailor!
Till they kill the shark
They do not rest

(YA 1807/14)

~

Hooking little fish in trifling ponds
Won't prepare you for the shark!

Gather your nets
And make them strong

You've been wading so far
In shallow pools
The great ocean
Is yet ahead

(YA 1808/17)

~

Oh sailors!
If you would conquer the shark
Strengthen your strings
Bolster your nets

Cast away all worldly ties
Then venture in

(YA 1808/16)

~

The fishermen didn't return
They perished at sea

Oh sailors
Bear down on the beast
Attack decisively!

Where are your hooks?
Your nets?

The vortex foams
And gurgles ahead

Latif says, O friends
Grace will take them across
The wide and treacherous sea

(YA 1809/Waai)

~

Questing for the shark
They plunged in

They faced the fathomless
That deep unknown

Slaying the wily beast
They emerged
Jubilant

(YA 1807/15)

Notes

1. Kabir is probably one of the most popular and influential 'nirgun' mystic poets of India, who lived in the town of Varanasi in north India in the fifteenth century. His poetry thrives in a living tradition of songs and sayings that are woven into the psyche of millions of people, especially in north India.

2. Mekan Dada was a mystic *yogi* and saint–poet from Kutch who lived between 1667 and 1730 AD. His pithy duhadaas (two-line verses, another term for dohas) are acerbic and biting, often castigating listeners for their caste prejudice and small-mindedness. He was a nomad figure who traversed the lands around Saurashtra and Kutch with his two pet animals in tow—a donkey called Laliyo and a dog called Motiyo.

3. A 'beyt' (literally 'house' in Arabic) is a two-, three- or four-line rhyming composition, sung in a free-ranging style without a beat. Shah Abdul Latif Bhitai composed most of his poems in this literary form.

4. This story was recounted to us by Sahib Bijani of the Sindhology Institute in Adipur, Kutch and is mentioned in Advani, p. 32. Evoking a similar sentiment is this poem in which Kabir says:

If you say I'm Hindu, I'm not
Say Muslim, I'm not that either
Both contain that mystery
I play in both of them

5. Sayed, Durreshahwar, p. 9.

6. Albinia, pp. 88–95.

7. The well-known thirteenth-century Sufi poet, Amir Khusro, puts it this
    way:

    Khusro says, the river of love
    Flows in strange ways
    One who escapes drowns
    One who drowns gets saved

8. Albinia recounts how she comes upon this striking image of Sohini on
    the colourful frescoes inside a tomb in the desert sands of Sindh, pp.
    91–92.

9. This image takes inspiration from Najm Hosain Syed's insightful
    exposition of the symbolism of the river in Sufi poetry, Syed
    pp. 131–41.

10. Part of the legend says that Mehar used to catch fish and cook it for
    Sohini when he would visit her at night. One night, when he was
    unable to catch any fish, he cut out a portion of the flesh of his own
    thigh, cooked it and brought it to Sohini. After that, he was unable to
    swim across the river to meet Sohini, and Sohini started to cross the
    river instead.

11. Kabir echoes this moment in a poem:

    She who sought, attained
    Entering into deep waters
    I, a fool, feared drowning
    And stayed put at the shore

12. A moment from the legend of Heer–Ranjha evokes a similar feeling:

    Oh mother, I set out in search of Ranjha
    But I couldn't find him
    I found God instead and not my Beloved
    God's no match for my Ranjha!

13. This poetic phrase echoes in a Kabir song sung as a qawwali by
    Fariduddin Ayaz and Abu Mohammed:

It's just as well my pitcher shattered
I'm free of all that hauling water!
The burden on my head is gone
It's just as well my prayer beads scattered
I'm free of all that holy chatter!
The burden on my head is gone
(trans. Homayra Ziad)

14. Kabir echoes this moment in a poem:

    A pot in water, water in a pot
    Inside, outside water
    The pot crumbles, water merges with water
    This is an untellable tale!

15. This song has now become famous thanks to Coke Studio Pakistan (Season 9) and is most likely a poem by Fazal Shah Sayyad.
16. Advani, p. 31.
17. Quoted in Shangari, p. 57.
18. The gibbet used to be placed by the side of the road in those times.
19. Quoted in Agha, p. 188.
20. Hallaj does this, too, combining the image of the cup-bearer with the executioner. Schimmel, 1976, p. 199.
21. *Risala-i-Haq-Numa*, quoted in Shangari, p. 165.
22. Kabir says:

    Either taste the nectar of love
    Or keep your precious pride
    No one has ever heard of
    Two swords in a single sheath

23. Schimmel, 1975, pp. 107–08.
24. Ajwani, p. 80.
25. In a similar poem, Kabir subverts the derogatory casteist meaning of the word 'untouchable', and turns it into an exalted value. *Hey pandit, tell me where untouchability came from? . . . We eat by touching, we wash by touching, from a touch the world was born.*

So who's untouched? asks Kabir. Only she who's free from delusion.
Hess, p. 55.

26. This description of God is from a verse in the Qur'an.

27. Some Kabir songs too make a reference to that original promise
of 'remembering' made inside the womb which on being born we
promptly forget. Here is a Kabir song urging us to wake up, and recall
that original promise:

Your first sleep was in your mother's womb
Hung upside down
You made a promise there to meditate
But you forgot on coming out
Now you've been born
Wake up now, oh traveller, wake up

28. Kabir says:

You were so strong, swan
So light was your gait
You're stained now in dirty colours
You've taken too many lovers

Ajoyoddyanath Pakrashi, a Baul poet, uses the same image of
'forgetting one's true love' and being entangled with 'foreign loves',
in this song:

These cravings and desires
Are foreigners, they're not your own
In love with strangers, you forget
The one who's truly yours

29. 'Mysticism contains something mysterious, not to be reached by
ordinary means or by intellectual effort, is understood from the root
common to the words *mystic* and *mystery*, the Greek *myein*, "to close
the eyes".' Schimmel, 1975, p. 3.

30. The opposite view is also held, which says that Latif left them of his
own accord.

31. 'Mihrab' is an Arabic word for the semicircular niche in the wall of a mosque that indicates the qibla, that is, the direction of the Kaaba in Mecca and hence the direction that Muslims should face when praying.

32. Kabir says:

Kabir, you're better off losing
Let the world win
The winner will be taken by Death
The loser will land at Hari's door

33. Kabir says:

The mind is restless, like the endless waves of the ocean.
But pearls form spontaneously, only where the waters are still.

34. This story is based on the writings of Albinia (pp. 79–89), Naeem (2018), Schimmel (1969) and Sayed (pp. 9–11).

35. Sayed, p. 9 and Advani, p. 30.

36. Naeem writes that 'At the time when Sufi Shah Inayat began educating and preaching in Jhok, most mystics, Sufis and *syeds* of Sindh had become purely worldly landlords, forgetting their professional obligations . . .', but Shah Inayat was not one to preach 'patience and contentment, rather than changing the worldly circumstances', and it was his 'firm belief in the fundamental demand of Muhammadan equality' that made him recognize that equality was not possible only with a distribution of wealth, but more importantly through an equitable distribution of resources, i.e., lands and workshops. Hence the land that had been given free of tax to Shah Inayat's ancestors, he decided to offer to farmers in the surrounding region for an experiment in collective farming. First part of web series, 25 October 2018.

37. Schimmel, p. 152.

38. *'You have saved me from the fetters of Being–May God grant you good recompense in both worlds!'* Schimmel 1969, p. 163.
    'You have released me from the chains of existence / May Allah bless you now and in the Hereafter', Naeem, Third part of web series, 28 October 2018.

39. Schimmel writes that 125,000 Sufis were slaughtered as per local legend and according to Alice Alibinia's oral history, it was 25,000. Schimmel, 1969, p. 151, and Albinia, p. 82.
40. Sayed, Durreshahwar, p. 10, and Albinia, p. 95.
41. Albinia, p. 88.
42. Shackle, pp. xxvi–xxvii.
43. Kabir says:

> The fisherman casts his net
> But what will he catch
> If the fish itself melts into water?

44. Kabir says:

> Water does not stay in high places
> It runs to lower ground
> He who strives to be high
> Goes thirsty

45. Quoted in Schimmel, 1975, p. 114.
46. In fact, gross attachments and addictions are easier to recognize in ourselves than subtle ones. Kabir says:

> Everybody gives up gross cravings
> No one renounces the subtle
> Peers, sages and prophets
> The subtle devoured them all
>
> The one who caught the subtle
> The gross was gone by itself
> Says Kabir, that true seeker
> Was free of all her woes

47. 'Rumi compares the struggle of the intellect with the *nafs* to the attempts of Majnun to turn his camel in the right direction, towards the tent of his beloved.' Schimmel, 1975, p. 113.

48. Kabir says:

Lose to your mind, and lose the game
Win it over, the game is won
Astride your mind, you ride to Raam
Driven by it, you meet your end

49. Schimmel designates varying stages of the Nafs to different women characters of Shah Latif—so Leela is Nafs-e-Ammara and later Nafs-e-Lawamma, a grasping lower self, who later becomes repentant. Noori or Marui are clearly Nafs-e-Mutmainah, souls utterly at peace. For a fuller discussion see pp. 175, 181, 187–88; 1975.

50. This oral teaching is based on a drawing that was inspired by the oldest known image in the tradition, an engraving by Blo-Bzang Don-yod (1602–78), forty-second abbot of the Tibetan monastery of Gda'-Idan.

51. The specific term he uses for his poems here is 'aayats', which are literally 'signs' or verses of the Qur'an.

52. Sur Rip, Agha, p. 435/19.

53. Shangari, p. 79.

54. 'The Sufi has been called ibn-al-waqt, or "son of the present moment", he gives himself completely to the moment and receives what God sends down to him without reflection about present, past and future.' Schimmel, 1975, p.130.

55. Kabir says:

I don't turn the beads of a rosary
My lips don't chant the name of 'Raam'
My Raam is chanting my name
I have found my ease

56. Quoted in Shangari, p. 84.

57. The poem plays with the two words 'meehan' (rain) and 'neehan' (love) which have the same ring.

58. Schimmel, 1976, pp. 256–60.

59. Surando is a stringed musical instrument played with the use of bow by folk musicians in the Kutch and Sindh regions on both sides of the border between Pakistan and India.

60. Agha, p. 243.
61. The story of Sur Pirbhati can also be read within the tradition in a very Islamic way (though not by Abdullah bhai), in which the king of Las Bela is Allah, and the lesser chieftans like Ulad Jaam are the lesser Hindu gods of temples and idol worship, Pirs and Aulias of the Sufi traditions who have their dargahs and shrines where people throng and worship, asking for boons and wishes. Exactly the kind of worship that orthodox Islam frowns upon.
62. Schimmel, 1976, p. 221.
63. According to Schimmel the 'planes of humanity' are signified by Nasoot, and 'angelhood' by Malkoot, leading then to 'divine power' signified by Jabroot, to finally arrive into 'divinity' signified by Lahoot. Schimmel, 1976, p. 229.

   Shangari describes this understanding using terms from yogic philosophy, saying, 'In the inner journey of Sufi dervishes the first stage consists of three milestones—Nasoot, Malkoot and Jabroot. The yogi who is trapped in the section of his body beneath the eyes, is a "naari". The second stage is "Allah Hu". The power and influence of "mann" (mind) and "maaya" (ego-delusion) is exerted in these two stages. Crossing these, the yogi arrives into the third stage, which is Lahoot, where his soul attains freedom from the claims of body and mind, and that yogi is called a "noori". This yogi has recognised the true self as distinct from body and mind.' Shangari, p. 307.
64. Shangari, p. 299.
65. 'Chaaran' is a specific caste of wandering bards from Gujarat and Rajasthan.
66. The 'chang' is a kind of Jew's harp or Mouth Harp, played by musicians in Kutch and Sindh. It has a metal frame with a flexible metal tongue attached to it. The entire frame is held in the mouth of the musician, and the metal tongue is plucked with the finger to produce a note in a single pitch, with multiple overtones.
67. Agha, p. 1616.
68. Schimmel, 1976, p.173.
69. Abbas, pp. 68–69.
70. Abdullah bhai seems to be referring to what is considered Ghazali's last book *Minhaj al-Abidin*, or 'The Path of the Worshipful Servants to the Garden of the Lord of All Worlds'. This book has a section on the

'seven hurdles', the 'remedies' to some of which are what Abdullah bhai describes as the 'manazils'. And Schimmel describes the many stations on the Sufi Path to be Tauba (Repentance), Tawakkul (Trust), Faqr (Poverty), Sabr (Patience), Shukr (Gratitude), Mahabba (Love) and Marifa (Gnosis). Schimmel, 1975, pp. 109–41. But perhaps it's best not to look for scholarly exactitude or parallels, and to just appreciate Abdullah bhai's wisdom and articulation for its own beauty.

71. Though the term 'Ikhlaas' in the Sufi tradition and in a day-to-day sense means 'purity' or 'perfect sincerity', we mention it here as 'non-self' to capture the spirit of the way in which Abdullah bhai shared it with us. Abdullah bhai also tells us that Al-Ikhlas is the 112th surat/chapter of the Qur'an, which means 'sincerity', 'to become clear or pure', a purity not tainted with pride.

72. 'The reference is a legend in which the snakes that infested the jungle surrounding Junagadh were destroyed by yogis with their magical powers.' Shackle p. 642.

73. Within this beyt, Shah Latif quotes this line from a famous poem by Shah Inayat Shaheed of Jhok (see Chapter 11 for more discussion about this poem and its author).

Acknowledgements

O ur gratitude flows backwards in time across the ten years we have wandered and dwelt in the luminous landscapes of Shah Latif in Kutch . . .

To the late Abdul Hussain Abdullah Turk (d. March 2015), aka Abdullah bhai, of Dhrab village, for being an overflowing *bhandaar* (storehouse) of insights about Sufism, poetry, music, folklore, the geography and history of Kutch and Sindh . . . a bhandaar which even till his last few cancer-afflicted years remained generously open to plunder for knowledge-seekers of all kinds. For giving us a palpable *taste* of Latif and for his patient and nuanced expositions of the Sindhi language to our unschooled ears. For his unflagging joy in story-telling and *charcha* and his endearing readiness to plunge into it no matter where he was—at bus stops or tea stalls, in car journeys or rural yatras, in village squares or courtyards. For his reciprocal delight in Kabir and other mystics, and for his unflinchingly non-partisan view of the world as a true Sufi seeker.

To Umar Haji Suleiman of Asari Vaandh village of Abdasa taluka for his gentle and loving explications of stories, mythology and poems, and his wife Asibai for fuelling the narratives with chai and meals. For adding their insights to these gatherings, gratitude to Vali Mohammad, Sayid Ibrahim Shah Bawa, Anwar Lohar and especially Mazharuddin Ali Akbar Mutwa, Abdullah bhai's shagird (disciple) who became a friend over several journeys and confabulations. Gratitude to Kaladhar Mutwa, Sindhi writer and scholar, for his support in helping us get under the skin of the Sindhi language.

To Sumar Kadu Jat and Mitha Khan Jat—singers of the unparalleled waai form of song from Bhagadia village—for stirring in us a *feeling* for Shah Latif's poetry beyond anything a recitation or reading may evoke.

To Mooralala Marwada and Mavji Jagariya whose hauntingly sweet kaafis of Shah Latif were among the first to pierce our hearts, awakening in us a desire to understand Latif.

To an entire generation of singers in Kutch mentored by Abdullah bhai, whose songs brought alive the oral traditions of Latif for us—Abdullah Ismail Jat, Ismail Para, Moosa Para, Mubarak Gajjan and Ramzan Lakha Ker—and also the singer and buffalo herder Saidu Ibrahim.

To the women and men of Jhalu, Bhitara, Virani, Kunathiya, Lakhpat and Tera villages, for sharing their love of Shah Sayeen with us.

To Asif Rayama, Bharmal Sanjot, Preeti Soni, Amad and other members of Soorvani in Bhuj city for being an excellent field resource unit, assisting in multiple ways our explorations in the region.

To Sushma Iyengar and Sandeep Virmani, for consistently inviting and hosting us, and throwing open the evocative land of Kutch to us, making it place of learning, experimentation, insight and growth over many decades.

To the helpful and jovial Sahib Bijani and Lakshmi Khilnani of the Sindhology Research Centre in Adipur, who guided us to many secondary research references and books.

To Namrata Karthik, whose meticulous research and transcription support in the early years of field research in Kutch proved invaluable in the later years of work on this book.

To Smriti Chanchani, Shilo Shiv Suleiman and Namrata Karthik for being creative partners in the heady first discoveries of Latif in the villages of Kutch.

To Psalm Paul for his quiet, dependable and rock-solid presence through all the administrative, the logistical and the day to day.

To Mita Kapur of Siyahi and Swati Chopra of Penguin Random House for believing in this book and helping manifest it. To Ashok Vajpeyi and Namita Gokhale for their initial encouragement and support.

To Anju Makhija and Hari Dilgir whose wonderful translations of Shah Latif into English provided an early spark of inspiration.

To Aruna Madnani and friends from the Sindhi Culture Foundation, who partnered with us in mounting a Shah Latif festival in Bangalore in November 2010, which added great creative impetus to our research.

To Linda Hess, for her generous and detailed suggestions to the first draft of this book and for helping trace obscure research papers in overseas libraries.

To Geetha Narayanan for supporting and believing in the work of the Kabir Project with unfaltering solidarity since its inception in 2002 to this day, and providing it a nurturing ground in the community of the Srishti Institute of Art, Design & Technology in Bangalore.

Bibliography

Abbas, Shemeem Burney. *Female Voice in Sufi Ritual: Devotional Practices of India and Pakistan.* Texas: University of Texas Press, 2002.

Abram, David. *The Spell of the Sensuous: Perception and Language in a More-Than-Human World.* New York: Vintage Books, 1997.

Advani, Kalyan B. *Shah Latif.* New Delhi: Sahitya Akademi, 1970.

Agha, Muhammad Yakoob. *Shah Jo Risalo alias Ganje Latif.* Hyderabad (Pakistan): Shah Abdul Latif Bhitshah Cultural Centre Committee, 1985.

Ajwani, L. H. *History of Sindhi Literature.* New Delhi: Sahitya Akademi, New Delhi, 1970.

Albinia, Alice. *Empires of the Indus: Story of a River.* London: John Murray, 2008.

Dwivedi, Mani Shankar, trans. *Shah Latif Ka Kavya.* New Delhi: Sahitya Akademi, 1969.

Hess, Linda and Shukhdeo Singh. *The Bijak of Kabir.* New Delhi: Oxford University Press, 2002.

Makhija, Anju, and Hari Dilgir. *Shah Abdul Latif: Seeking the Beloved.* New Delhi: Katha, 2005.

Naeem, Raza. *A four-part web series on Shah Inayat Shaheed.* The Wire, 25, 26, 28, 30 October 2018.

Nicholson, Reynold A. *Mathnawi of Jalaluddin Rumi.* Warminster: Gibb Memorial Trust, 1990.

Sayed, Durreshahwar Dr. *The Poetry of Shah Abd Al-Latif.* Sindhi Adabi Board, Jamshoro/Hyderabad, 1988.

Schimmel, Annemarie. *Sufi Shah Inayat Shaheed of Jhok: A Sindhi Mystic, Liber Amicorum: Studies in Honor of Prof. C J Bleeker*. Leiden: 1969.

Schimmel, Annemarie. *Mystical Dimensions of Islam*. Chapel Hill: University of North Carolina Press, 1975.

Schimmel, Annemarie. *Pain and Grace: A Study of Two Mystical Writers of Eighteenth Century Muslim India*. Leiden: E. J. Brill, 1976.

Schwarz, Fernand. *Concentration and Inner Awakening: According to Tibetan Buddhism*. New Acropolis, France, 2007.

Shackle, Christopher. *Shah Abdul Latif: Risalo*. Cambridge, Massachusetts: Murty Classical Library of India, Harvard University Press, 2018.

Shangari, T.R. *Kamil Darvesh: Shah Latif*. Radha Soami Satsang Beas, Dera Baba Jaimal Singh, 2008.

Syed, Najm Hosain. *Recurrent Patterns in Punjabi Poetry*. Lahore: Majlis Shah Hussain, 1968.